THE SCALAWAG
IN ALABAMA POLITICS

Winner in 1974 of the Mrs. Simon Baruch
University Award, made by the United Daughters
of the Confederacy for the best unpublished
book or monograph of high merit in the field
of Southern History in or near the period of
the Confederacy or bearing upon the causes that led
to secession and the War Between the States.

BARUCH AWARDS
1927–1976

1927 Carpenter, Jesse Thomas. "The South as a Conscious Minority 1789–1861." New York University, Washington Square, New York, 1930. 315 pp.

1929 Whitfield, Theodore M. "Slavery Agitation in Virginia, 1829–1832." Out of Print.

1931 Flanders, Ralph Betts. "Plantation Slavery in Georgia." Out of Print.

1933 Thompson, Samuel Bernard. "Confederate Purchasing Agents Abroad." Out of Print.

1935 Wiley, Bell Irvin. "Southern Negroes 1861–1865." Yale University Press, New Haven, Connecticut, 1938. 366 pp.

1937 Hill, Louise Biles. "Joseph E. Brown and the Confederacy." Out of Print.

1940 Haydon, F. Stansbury. "Aeronautics of the Union and Confederate Armies." Out of Print.

1942 Stormont, John. "The Economic Stake of the North in the Preservation of the Union in 1861." Not Published.

1945 Schultz, Harold Sessel. "Nationalism and Sectionalism in South Carolina 1852–1860." Duke University Press, Durham, North Carolina, 1950. 259 pp.

1948 Tankersly, Allen P. "John Brown Gordon, Soldier and Statesman." Privately Printed.

1951 Todd, Richard Cecil. "Confederate Finance." University of Georgia Press, Athens, Georgia, 1953.

1954 Morrow, Ralph E. "Northern Methodism and Reconstruction." Michigan State University Press, 1956. 261 pp.

 Cunningham, Horace. "Doctors in Gray." Louisiana State University Press, Baton Rouge, Louisiana, 1958. 338 pp.

1957 Hall, Martin H. "The Army of New Mexico." "Sibley's Campaign of 1862." University of Texas Press, Austin, Texas, 1960. 366 pp.

1960 Robertson, James I., Jr. "Jackson's Stonewall: A History of the Stonewall Brigade." Louisiana State University Press, Baton Rouge, Louisiana, 1963. 271 pp.

1969 Wells, Tom Henderson. "The Confederate Navy: A Study in Organization." University of Alabama Press, University, Alabama, 1971. 182 pp.

1970 Delaney, Norman C. "John McIntosh Kell, of the Raider *Alabama*." The University of Alabama Press, University, Alabama, 1972. 270 pp.

1972 Dougan, Michael B. "Confederate Arkansas: The People and Policies of a Frontier State in Wartime." The University of Alabama Press, University, Alabama, 1976.

1974 Wiggins, Sarah Woolfolk. "The Scalawag in Alabama Politics, 1865–1881." The University of Alabama Press, University, Alabama, 1977.

1976 Nelson, Larry Earl. "The Confederacy and the United States Presidential Election of 1864."

The Scalawag in Alabama Politics, 1865–1881

SARAH WOOLFOLK WIGGINS

Winner of the Mrs. Simon Baruch
University Award of
the United Daughters of the Confederacy

The University of Alabama Press
University, Alabama

Library of Congress Cataloging in Publication Data

Wiggins, Sarah Woolfolk, 1934-
  The scalawag in Alabama politics, 1865-1881.

  Bibliography: p.
  Includes index.
  1. Reconstruction—Alabama. 2. Alabama—
Politics and government—1865-1950. 3. Republican
Party. Alabama. 4. Afro-Americans—Alabama.
I. Title.
F326.W53   320.9'761'06   76-56833
ISBN 0-8173-5233-3

CONTENTS

ACKNOWLEDGMENTS

I am indebted to more people than I can properly thank for their assistance with this project. Of special assistance were T. Harry Williams of Louisiana State University who advised me on the initial stages of this study and Elizabeth Tyler Coleman of the University of Alabama, Milo B. Howard, Jr., of the Alabama State Department of Archives and History, William W. Rogers of Florida State University who encouraged me to finish it. The University of Alabama Faculty Research Committee has generously provided financial support. The capable staffs of the Alabama State Department of Archives and History, Rutherford B. Hayes Library, National Archives, Library of Congress, University of Alabama Library, University of North Carolina Library, have gone out of their way to be accommodating. The Alabama State Department of Archives and History generously made available plates for all the cartoons in this book.

Annie L. Ballard and Ruth Kibbey have graciously typed and retyped the manuscript, and Claude D. Stabler and his staff have assisted me with the maps. I shall also never forget the three children who helped me pick up the manuscript one hot summer morning after it had been left on the trunk of my car while I drove off scattering three hundred pages over a mile of Loop Road. Finally, the patience and faith of my family have been essential.

In Memory of

Robert Nelson Woolfolk

THE SCALAWAG
IN ALABAMA POLITICS

A Prospective Scene in the "City of Oaks," 4th of March, 1869.

"Hang, ours, hang! * * * * * *Their* complexion is perfect gallows. Stand fast, good fate, to *their* hanging! * * * * * If they be not born to be hanged, our case is miserable."

The above cut represents the fate in store for those great pests of Southern society—the carpet-bagger and scallawag—if found in Dixie's Land after the break of day on the 4th of March next.

The genus carpet-bagger is a man with a lank head of dry hair, a lank stomach and long legs, club knees and splay feet, dried legs and lank jaws, with eyes like a fish and mouth like a shark. Add to this a habit of sneaking and dodging about in unknown places—habiting with negroes in dark dens and back streets—a look like a hound and the smell of a polecat.

Words are wanting to do full justice to the genus scallawag. He is a cur with a contracted head, downward look, slinking and uneasy gait; sleeps in the woods, like old Crossland, at the bare idea of a Ku-Klux raid.

Our scallawag is the local leper of the community. Unlike the carpet bagger, he is native, which is so much the worse. Once he was respected in his circle; his head was level, and he would look his neighbor in the face. Now, possessed of the itch of office and the salt rheum of Radicalism, he is a mangy dog, slinking through the alleys, haunting the Governor's office, defiling with tobacco juice the steps of the Capitol, stretching his lazy carcass in the sun on the Square, or the benches of the Mayor's Court.

He waiteth for the troubling of the political waters, to the end that he may step in and be healed of the itch by the ointment of office. For office he 'bums' as a toper 'bums' for the satisfying dram. For office, yet in prospective, he hath bartered respectability; hath abandoned business, and ceased to labor with his hands, but employs his feet kicking out bootheels against lamp-post and corner-curb, while discussing the question of office.

This caricature of Ohio carpetbagger A. S. Lakin and scalawag N. B. Cloud was widely copied in Alabama and in the North and reportedly cost Democrats a victory in several key states in the 1868 presidential election. The critical reaction to this cartoon was so severe that Ryland Randolph, editor of the *Independent Monitor*, later attempted to soothe matters by treating the cartoon as a joke. (Tuscaloosa *Independent Monitor*, September 1, 1868.)

INTRODUCTION

Scalawags have had a bad press in Alabama as well as elsewhere in the South. Alabamians frequently have practiced amnesia in dealing with scalawags, preferring to forget them, whether direct ancestors or not, or at least dismiss them as being guilty of a gross lapse of judgment in the turmoil of the post-Civil War years. Even historian Thomas M. Owen omitted scalawag governor William Hugh Smith from the biographical sketches in his four-volume *History of Alabama and Dictionary of Alabama Biography,* the only governor accorded such distinction. Although Willis Brewer and William Garrett bravely included prominent scalawags in their significant nineteenth-century biographical collections, someone has neatly sliced out the sketch of Alabama's other scalawag governor David P. Lewis from The University of Alabama's copy of Brewer's *Alabama.* Over the tissue-paper patch a delicate Victorian hand has inscribed, ''It seems that someone has removed the sketch of David P. Lewis which originally occupied this page; he was Alabama's second scalawag governor (1872–1874).''[1]

In the century since Reconstruction, although few kind words have fallen on the scalawags, no one has produced a more thorough or more scornful definition of a *scalawag* than did one of their contemporaries in 1868:

> Our scalawag is the local leper of the community. Unlike the carpetbagger, he is native, which is so much the worse. Once he was respected in his circle; his head was level, and he could look his neighbor in the face. Now, possessed of the itch of office and the salt rheum of Radicalism, he is a mangy dog, slinking through the alleys, haunting the Governor's office, defiling with tobacco juice the steps of the Capitol, stretching his lazy carcass in the sun on the Square, or the benches of the Mayor's Court.
>
> He waiteth for the troubling of the political waters, to the end that he may step in and be healed of his itch by the ointment of office. For office he ''bums'' as a toper ''bums'' for the satisfying dram. For office, yet in prospective, he hath bartered principle and respectability; hath abandoned business and ceased to labor with his hands, but employs his feet kicking out boot-heels against lamp post and corner curb, while discussing the question of office.
>
> The normal condition of the unofficed scalawag is seedy. Mayhap, there hang about him some remnant of gray cloth that floats him a remainder of the Confederate era, before he fell from political grace, and was changed into a scalawag. His obsequious meekness and self-abasement in the

presence of the power that confers office, causes the gorge to rise in disgust at the recreancy of human nature as developed in a full blown scalawag.

Eager to belie the past, that he may grasp office in the future, he hath curses handy for the cause he once espoused, and lauds for the loyalty of himself in season. Where half a dozen are gathered in discussion, there is to be found our scalawag in their midst, conspicuous because of his dirty linen duster and broad-brimmed hat. The vocabulary of his knowledge-box is very contracted, and he sings but few tunes, but these are loyal ones. In his estimation every feature of Reconstruction is altogether lovely; the negro eminently fit for a voter, but not to hold office. That is reserved for scalawags like himself.

The scalawag rewarded with office blooms into a new existence. He puts on good clothes, kicks his mildewed duster to the devil, shaves up, trims his straggling beard, and oils his matted shock of hair. If he is boarding, he moves into a hired house, drives a hired horse, and begins to splurge. To see the sneers of the unrewarded "bummers" his only response is the elevation of his nasal protuberance. He is an office holder, and provided he can give bond as required, he sticks; if he can not, he is officially kicked, and relapses into his original condition of a scalawag again.

The tribe of scalawags is not numerous but its members are very pestiferous, like the frogs of Egypt, that crawled into the ovens and kneading troughs of the people. We long to write the obituary of the last of the scalawags.[2]

Vilification of scalawags was not just verbal. Two Tuscaloosa newspapers, the *Independent Monitor* and the *Blade,* ran a series of pictorial attacks in the form of cartoons from 1868 to 1873. These caricatures graphically illustrate the intense social criticism Alabama scalawags regularly encountered.

The exact origin of the term *scalawag* remains obscure, but it came into frequent use in Alabama beginning in late 1867 as the designation for the Southern white Republican who had been born in the South or who had lived in the South before the Civil War.[3] It was and is understood by all to be a term of "political opprobrium."[4]

Intemperate abuse of the scalawag has been plentiful, and historians are only now moving to place him in a more accurate light. Among the rapidly growing number of revisionist histories of various aspects of Reconstruction, few biographies of individual scalawags and no full-length accounts of scalawags in a Southern state have been published.[5] The most important information on scalawags has appeared in articles.[6]

Alabama scalawags have captured little attention in state histories. If they are discussed at all, they have been dismissed as the "tory or deserter element, with a few of the obstructionists of the war time and malcontents of the present who wanted office," or as ignorant poor whites. The popular conception of Alabama scalawags has been north Alabamians of small farmer background, little education, no political experience, and Unionist sympathies in 1861, who deserted the Republicans at their first defeat.[7]

This study attempts to reevaluate the accuracy of the stereotype of Alabama scalawag leaders by investigating their backgrounds and abilities and their importance in Alabama politics during and immediately after Reconstruction. Those considered are white Southern Republicans nominated, appointed, or elected to any of these positions: state executive, judicial, or legislative office; federal executive, judicial, legislative, or diplomatic post; member of the state Republican Executive Committee; Republican presidential elector; delegate to the 1867 or 1875 constitutional conventions; delegate to the national Republican conventions; member of the national Republican Executive Committee.

Primary sources relative to a majority of Alabama scalawags do not exist nor does even a satisfactory estimate of the number of scalawags in Alabama. Simply determining the names of Republicans who held these positions, let alone identifying their origins, has been a problem. Present-day politicians would be sobered in their assumptions of immortality via officeholding if they could see the anonymity that has swallowed politicians of this unfashionable party in the last century. For example, legislative journals do not necessarily list the names of members of the legislature; if they do, they may disagree with the list of members found in the manuscript election returns, contemporary newspapers, federal documents, state documents, or standard reference books on Alabama. It is commonplace to find that no two sources list the same men for a group of offices. The utilitarian solution to the problem of conflicting names has been to use the one which research has suggested to be the most accurate. The bibliography contains the sources used for identification purposes since published biographical information on Republicans is scarce. Especially valuable were the schedules of the U.S. census for 1860, 1870, and 1880. Biographical sketches of individual identifiable Republicans have not been included as an appendix because of the space that they would require, but a list of Republican officeholders identified as scalawag, carpetbagger, or black is included.

This project does not present the entire story of the scalawag in Alabama, but at least it will refute some false ideas. At the same time it does not suggest that the native white Alabama Republican leaders mirrored in microcosm the rank and file of the Southern white Republican electorate in Alabama. Nevertheless, despite these limitations the Alabama scalawag can be placed in better perspective than that he has enjoyed in the past.

Scalawag leaders who appeared during the political, social, and economic upheavals of Alabama Reconstruction possessed a remarkable realism in their readjustment to the aftermath of civil war and in their approach to state politics. Frequently describing their times as revolutionary, these men evidenced a political realism that was pragmatic in its willingness to compromise and even retreat when the political situation so dictated in order to gain advantage later. Such perceptive men certainly merit an extensive reevaluation.

UNIONISTS HAVE THEIR DAY

Geography set the stage for nineteenth-century Alabama politics. A Black Belt of rich soil bisects the state; to the south lies the coastal plain, particularly fertile in southwest Alabama. Directly north of the Black Belt rise the foothills of the Appalachian Mountains, and behind this hilly plateau is the fertile Tennessee Valley. A plantation economy developed in the Black Belt, Tennessee Valley, and southwestern Alabama, and most of the slave population was concentrated in these areas. A white population predominated in southeastern Alabama and the mountain counties, where a small-farm economy developed.

In the antebellum period little intercourse existed between north and south Alabama, although Montgomery was the state capital after 1846. No railroads linked the country north of the mountains with the rest of the state. Commercially, the Tennessee Valley was closer to Charleston and New Orleans than to Mobile, and geographically it belonged to Tennessee. Politicians in antebellum Alabama were cognizant of this transportation deficiency and regularly proposed construction of internal improvements to connect north Alabama with the port of Mobile.

Geographic and economic differences within antebellum Alabama led to resentful sectionalism. With mounting frustration north Alabama watched the Black Belt rule the state, grasp the "lion's share of state honors, offices and benefits," and impose an "undue portion of the public burdens upon the weaker and less wealthy section, North Alabama."[1] This domination peaked in 1860–61, when south and central Alabama urged secession, while north Alabama was a Unionist stronghold. North Alabamians were unenthusiastic about slavery and feared economic strangulation should Alabama secede and Tennessee remain in the Union. The loyal whites narrowly lost Alabama to the secessionists when a state convention approved an ordinance of secession in January, 1861.

In the months between Alabama's secession and the bombardment of Fort Sumter, Alabama Unionists refused to believe that a reconciliation with the Union could not still take place. Their opinions on how to accomplish this adjustment ranged from one recommendation that the ringleaders of the rebels be hanged as pirates to another that counseled caution and patience on the part of the federal government. Joseph C. Bradley, a prominent Huntsville lawyer who made the latter suggestion, saw nothing warlike in President Abraham Lincoln's inaugural address although the Southern press teemed with denunciations of it as especially coercive. Bradley viewed these newspaper attacks as efforts to thwart any reorganization of the Union. The "precipitators" hoped that Lincoln would provoke a confrontation with the South. Southerners would then react with "warlike feeling," and civil war would follow. If such a clash could be avoided, north Alabama cooperators planned to support a gubernatorial candidate in December, 1861, to try to wrest the state from the secessionists.[2] But Fort Sumter and war intervened.

Under the Confederacy, south and central Alabama continued to control the state government. John Gill Shorter, Eufaula lawyer and ardent secessionist elected governor in 1861, supported the war effort. However, the popularity of the war quickly waned as Union troops occupied north Alabama, Mobile was blockaded, shortages and hardships increased, tax burdens and impressment of goods grew heavy, and conscription became onerous. By 1863 this disillusionment with the war caused Shorter to lose the gubernatorial election to Thomas Hill Watts, a former Whig who had opposed secession until after Lincoln's election.

In the same year, war disillusionment brought changes in the state legislature and in the representatives to the Confederate Congress. Many former cooperators went to the Alabama General Assembly; in the Confederate Senate moderate Richard W. Walker replaced fire-eater Clement C. Clay, and cooperator Robert Jemison succeeded William L. Yancey on his death. Six pacifists and enemies of Jefferson Davis' administration were sent to the Confederate House, and one of these replaced secessionist J. L. M. Curry, who had been speaker *pro tempore*.[3]

Opposition to the war effort blossomed in the white counties of north Alabama. The war was hardly under way before the small farmers of white Winston County convened a public meeting on July 4, 1861. There Charles Christopher Sheats, an opponent of secession who had voiced Winston County's opposition to secession at the 1861 constitutional convention, advocated the secession of Winston County from Alabama and the Confederacy. That same day Winston citizens created the "Free

State of Winston," thus withdrawing from Alabama, but they did not secede from the United States.[4]

By spring, 1862, when Federal troops occupied portions of the Tennessee Valley and the Confederate government resorted to conscription to bolster the Confederate army, north Alabamians began to join the Union army. Between 1862 and 1865, 2,678 white Alabamians enlisted in the First Alabama Cavalry, U.S.A.[5] Beginning in 1862, also, the old cooperator leaders organized a secret peace group known as the "Peace Society." Leaders of this movement in the white counties of the northern one-third of the state were former U.S. Senator Jeremiah Clemens, future Republican congressman C. C. Sheats, and two future Republican governors of Alabama, William H. Smith and David P. Lewis. Little concrete information exists on the "Peace Society." However, it is known that they desired peace on terms favorable to the South and communicated with federal authorities about Alabama's future. They exercised a strong voice in elections: being at home, they could and did vote, and the 1863 Alabama elections reflected their views and strength.[6]

Both Federals and Confederates attempted to control the Tennessee Valley, and their incursions devastated the more accessible areas of the Valley. Confederate raids into areas of known Union sympathy inflicted hardship and bitterness and caused many to flee through the Union lines. Many others who opposed the war and desired to evade conscription into the Confederate army took local civil and judicial positions. Thereby, they were able to stay at home and to secure some degree of safety for themselves, their families, and property.[7]

In the spring of 1865 Alabama was quiet as the state awaited news of her future. The physical scars of war were minor compared to the condition of such neighbors as Georgia and Tennessee, but everywhere the effects of the war were evident: collapsed transportation, disrupted economic life, bewildered citizens. Alabamians were relieved that the war was finally over and were ready to accept whatever peace was forthcoming from the North. Former slaves were reported as resembling "lost sheep, straying from place to place, believing no one's voice." Those whites who had heretofore "dealt humanely and truthfully" with blacks were yet able to exercise some authority with them.[8] A slight air of impatience lingered, as if Alabama had closed the door on a painful period and now was eager to get on with her future. There was no arrogance or pride in an unpopular and lost cause, and Alabamians expressed a mood of decided cooperation, if they could just be told what they were expected to do to get life functioning around them once again. By this time Alabamians, like other Southerners, had accepted the abolition of slavery, an acceptance variously described as "more or less sullen" acquiescence and as submission "with the best grace" they could muster. One Unionist admonished his contemporaries, "We must accommodate ourselves to surrounding circumstances."[9]

But although slavery was gone, prejudice was not. Unionists and ex-Confederates alike frankly regarded the blacks as "socially and intellectually inferior," and some expected the sense of inferiority to embitter the blacks and kindle resentment against the whites. One pessimist predicted that no sort of legislation would make a "good servant or citizen" out of the freedman because of his weak character and suggested that colonization offered the only solution. Despite this fundamental belief in the inferiority of the black race, white Alabamians generally faced the fact that life ahead was to be full of readjustments in race relations, and they professed willingness to assist the freedmen in fitting themselves "for their changed relations and responsibilities." However, reservations were voiced about whether whites were sufficiently flexible to cope immediately with the race question with much success. One Unionist feared that a lifetime of white rule over black slaves rendered white Southerners "incompetent" suddenly to acknowledge the rights of the former slave. He pleaded for time during which Southerners could accustom themselves to the change and to transfer the rights of the master to the individual black.[10]

The idea of black suffrage at this time was generally abhorrent in the state. The Huntsville *Advocate* observed that the black was free, and as a freedman the government would protect him in his legal rights. The *Advocate* urged its readers to accord the black man what the war had secured for him. But "legal rights and political privileges are essentially different. He has been granted the former—not the latter."[11]

One Unionist put the matter more bluntly than did the *Advocate:* "This is a white man's government, made by white men, for the benefit of white men, to be administered by white men, and nobody else, forever." Another Unionist was equally firm: "I want the negro to have his legal or civil rights and nothing more. He is not now fit for enfranchisement—as a race the Blacks are not capable of appreciating the ballot box or a free government. If they were qualified and could understandably appreciate the right of suffrage," he concluded, he would feel differently. Former non-slaveholders were reputed to be more bitterly opposed to black suffrage than even ex-secessionists. This attitude resulted from the fact that the blacks had had a "great contempt which they have not concealed for what they called poor white people of the South."[12] However, one Northerner in Alabama speculated that Alabamians might submit even to black suffrage in exchange for a "return to the prosperity of old." But even this observer who found no fault with black suffrage drew the line at putting blacks into office, saying that those who advocated such had better join those who favored female suffrage.[13]

In 1865 Unionists expected to direct the reorganization of postwar Alabama. They believed the Confederacy's collapse vindicated their earlier opposition to secession, and they considered themselves to be a better element to return the state to the civil authority of the United States than existed in any other former Confederate state. In May they acted to assume leadership in the reconstruction of Alabama. *"Original* and *unswerving* Union people" met throughout north Alabama and reported that local ex-Confederates had "suddenly faced about" and made up in "activity and shrewdness what they want in loyalty." One Unionist speculated that the ex-rebels expected "to regain by the ballot box what they have lost by the cartridge box."[14] Unionists emerged from these meetings full of plans to counter those of the ex-rebels. Assuming that a provisional governor would be selected from their ranks, they were ready with nominations. Among those suggested were Michael J. Bulger of Tallapoosa County, David C. Humphries of Madison, Daniel H. Bingham of Limestone, William H. Smith of Randolph, Lewis E. Parsons of Talladega, and Thomas M. Peters of Lawrence—all opponents of secession.[15] One Unionist succinctly expressed the views of many of his class when he asked for a governor who would "not traffic with treason in any of its ramifications" and who would accept terms based simply on the "Constitution *as it is* and the Union *as it was.*"[16]

The loyal native whites also expected to elect a large majority of the future legislature to assist the governor. This legislature could redistrict the state according to the latest census, elect representatives to Congress, and proceed as if only a brief lapse had occurred during the Civil War. Or a convention might be called to undo the work of the secessionists. Still another possibility was the appointment of a military governor to supervise the reorganization of the state.[17] Above all, time was precious—they "should not wait a day" to seize the initiative in the reconstruction of their native state, Alabama.[18]

Management of Alabama affairs remained until late June, 1865, under the direction of George H. Thomas, general of the occupation troops. The Mobile *Advertiser and Register* commended the military officers in Alabama in 1865, saying that the state was "particularly fortunate" in the character of those assigned to the state.[19] To administer civil affairs General Thomas ordered that incumbent county civil officials continue their duties with the support of Federal troops. This order outraged the loyalists who denounced these officials for having aided the rebellion. Such men, declared the Unionists, "ruled and oppressed us when treason was in the ascendant, for god's sake do not let them lord it over us now when the Union cause is triumphant. Give their offices to Union men— they had had their day—let us have ours."[20]

On May 29, 1865, President Andrew Johnson announced his program for Reconstruction, which became a reality for Alabamians on June 21 when he appointed Lewis E. Parsons as provisional governor. This appointment pleased the Unionists except the more violent Tory element who preferred Bingham.[21] Contemporaries described Parsons as portly, with a double chin but "well preserved" for a man of about fifty whose black hair and eyes contrasted with a ruddy complexion. A grandson of Jonathan Edwards, Parsons was well educated in New York before he moved to Alabama and opened a law practice in 1840. He was active in Alabama politics first as a Whig and then as a Douglas Democrat in 1860. Parsons was highly regarded as an effective public speaker. Known as a man of full and sonorous voice with clear and distinct enunciation, Parsons was termed by William L. Yancey as the ablest and most resourceful Union debater he ever encountered. During the Civil War Parsons quietly practiced law in Talladega while his sons served in the Confederate army. His appointment was a very wise choice, for as one government inspector in Alabama reported to President Johnson in September, Governor Parsons was widely esteemed as a "man of sense" who was "just and kind to all."[22]

Following Johnson's instructions from Washington, Parsons first declared in force all Alabama laws enacted before January 11, 1861, except those regarding slavery, and thus he anchored the foundations of the new civil government on what remained of antebellum local government. Those eligible were to take the amnesty oath to regain their citizenship under President Johnson's proclamation of May 29, 1865, and persons excluded were to apply for a presidential pardon. To register to vote, the restored citizen was to appear before a registration official appointed by the Provisional Governor, register, and take the amnesty oath again. Governor Parsons also ordered those men in office at the war's end to continue in their positions.[23]

Unionists quickly condemned the Governor saying that most of the officeholders were ex-rebels. They interpreted Parsons' actions as an effort to deny them their rightful opportunities of office. One disgusted loyalist wanted every secessionist removed from office in the state, and another advised that "if there are only half a dozen true men in a county, they should be appointed to office in preference to the secessionists."[24]

Governor Parsons defended his actions, saying that he did give preference to Union men in filling vacancies, trying to find one "reasonably qualified" and where necessary the "least objectionable." In no case, he insisted, had a "union man been neglected or set aside for secessionists." Although his proclamation reappointed all officers from justice of the peace down, higher county officers were specially appointed, and the Governor reserved the right to remove any appointee for disloyalty or other good cause.[25]

The reorganization of the Alabama judiciary resulted from the combined efforts of Governor Parsons and Brigadier General Wager T. Swayne, assistant commissioner of the Bureau of Refugees, Freedmen, and Abandoned Lands for Alabama. A native of Ohio educated at Yale, Swayne was the son of a U.S. Supreme Court justice and was practicing law in Columbus, Ohio, when the war erupted in 1861. He patriotically volunteered for the army and served for the duration despite the loss of his right leg in February, 1865.[26] When this thirty-year-old veteran arrived in Alabama on August 1, 1865, he found the Provisional Governor "honestly endeavoring" to carry out the views of the President and acting carefully so that his actions might not provoke the election of "bad men" to the coming constitutional convention who would cast the constitution in an "impracticable mould." Swayne determined to cooperate with the Governor's efforts to restore order and decided to see if a fair administration of justice to the freedmen could be obtained through the judicial machinery Parsons was reorganizing, rather than establish separate courts conducted by newcomers unfamiliar with state law. Too, use of existing Alabama courts would forestall criticism, as Alabamians could not impugn a judiciary that was their own.[27] Accordingly, General

Swayne designated judicial officials appointed by the Provisional Governor as agents of the bureau to administer justice to the freedmen. These officials were instructed to enforce the existing laws of the state except those which made distinctions of color, and Governor Parsons endorsed these steps of General Swayne. Subsequently, Swayne had misgivings about the functioning of the civil courts. Although there was no denial of justice, he felt blacks encountered too many opportunities to be oppressed without means or knowledge for redress of their complaints. Still, he maintained, he could see no other alternative, so the courts continued to operate as they had in the past.[28] Overall, the commissioner's conduct won respect in Alabama, and he was known as a "gentleman . . . eminently qualified for his position," a man of "integrity and brains," and a "thorough Puritan in looks and principles."[29]

A second phase in state reorganization opened on August 31, 1865, when Governor Parsons called for an election of delegates to a constitutional convention. When the ninety-nine members of this convention met in Montgomery, Carl Schurz, then a newspaper correspondent surveying the postwar South, agreed with Governor Parsons that the "most respectable persons had been chosen."[30] This Alabama convention resembled the Mississippi convention more than that of neighboring Georgia in that the Alabama convention did represent the state's loyal element. In the 1860 presidential campaign forty-five of these men had voted for John Bell, thirty for Stephen A. Douglas, and twenty-four for John C. Breckinridge.[31] However, despite the general optimism about the coming convention General Swayne expressed concern, saying that he believed the Governor to be "considerably in advance of the public sentiment, the Convention somewhat behind it."[32]

The convention opened on September 12 and followed President Johnson's plan for Reconstruction. The abolition of the institution of slavery, repeal of the ordinance of secession, and repudiation of the state war debt stirred little controversy. The most bitter fight in the convention developed over reapportionment of the legislature, a key issue if Unionists were to control Presidential Reconstruction. Ultimately, instead of apportioning representation on the whole population of the state, the Unionists based representation on the white population alone.[33] President Johnson wrote Governor Parsons of his satisfaction with the actions of the convention, saying that the proceedings met the "highest expectations of *all* who desired the restoration of the Union."[34]

In terms of dominance of Alabama politics, this reapportionment was the most significant of the convention's actions. The influence of the Black Belt, which contained large numbers of freedmen, was minimized, and north Alabama now possessed the opportunity to enjoy previously unknown political power. Had the Johnson government in Alabama survived, this legislative apportionment and the absence of black suffrage would have perpetuated this new-found political power in the hands of the north Alabama white counties.

After adopting the revised constitution of 1865 by the same method the Unionists had condemned in the secession crisis of 1861—by proclamation without referendum—the convention set an election in November for governor, members of the legislature, and representatives to Congress. The legislature would then choose other state officials. Former Governor A. B. Moore at this time wisely urged Alabama to elect men other than original secessionists. "If we elect men who have been considered ultra in their views and feelings, objections may be made to their taking their seats in Congress which could not be raised against conservative men," meaning men disassociated from secession.[35] Alabama generally heeded Governor Moore's admonition. In the governor's race all three candidates were respectable ex-Whigs from cooperator strongholds in 1860, exemplifying the persistence of Whig influence in Presidential Reconstruction in Alabama: Michael J. Bulger of Tallapoosa County, William Russell Smith of Tuscaloosa, and Robert Miller Patton of Lauderdale County.[36]

Patton was elected by a vote almost equal to the combined vote of his opponents. Described as a tall, commanding man with gray hair and beard, the latter worn "*a la* Jeff Davis," Patton was about sixty in 1865. He had lived his entire life in Alabama as a prosperous merchant who also served in the state legislature. A Douglas Democrat in 1860, he opposed secession but reluctantly cooperated with the Confederacy after its establishment. After serving briefly as president of the state senate, he resigned and retired quietly to his home in northwest Alabama for the remainder of the war.[37] General Swayne wrote General O. O. Howard, Commissioner of the Freedmen's Bureau in Washington, that he had first met Patton in 1852 and knew him to be as loyal a man as could be found in Alabama. On a later occasion Swayne described Patton to Howard as a "practical, conscientious, economical old merchant who I thought would neither deceive nor be deceived."[38]

Five of the six congressmen elected at the same time as Patton were Whigs who had opposed secession in 1861. Unfortunately, some of these men had subsequently served in the Confederate army or held some civil position that compromised their loyalty to the Union, and Unionists protested these elections. Joseph C. Bradley, Huntsville Unionist and inveterate letter writer to public officials in Montgomery and Washington, charged that such elections occurred because the amnesty oath had been laid aside and "any man and every man" had been permitted to vote, including thousands who had defiantly stated they would never take the amnesty oath. These men had elected the legislature, which would in turn elect Alabama's U.S. senators. Fearing that power was about to slip from the Unionists' hands, Bradley urged President Johnson to make a fresh start in Alabama by returning to the selection of Parsons as provisional governor and beginning Reconstruction a second time.[39]

Bradley's alarm about Alabama's choices for U.S. senators proved to be unfounded when the legislature elected two Unionists: former Governor Lewis E. Parsons and former U.S. Senator George Smith Houston. The election of Alabama moderates to lead the state paralleled a similar course in Mississippi, where moderates swept the governorship, all seven congressional seats, and the two senate chairs. However, such wisdom was not uniformly displayed in other Southern states. Georgia tactlessly elected Alexander H. Stephens to the U.S. Senate, and Texas sent former secessionists and Confederates to both the U.S. Senate and House. The publicity that followed these elections overshadowed the success of moderates elsewhere in the South and helped to convince Northerners that the South had not repented for past sins. In December, 1865, Governor Moore's fears materialized when Congress did object to these Southern congressmen and senators and refused them any recognition.[40]

The newly elected administration was inaugurated December 13, 1865. The New York *Times* commended the new legislature as being "greatly national, not sectional" and able to rise above "party spirit and political prejudice."[41] This General Assembly, estimated as being four-fifths "original Union men," had easily ratified the Thirteenth Amendment before the restoration of the state government to the elected officials of Alabama. However, the legislature, apportioned to benefit north Alabama white counties, now refused to approve the Fourteenth Amendment despite pleas for ratification by Governor Patton, who feared serious consequences if the legislature rejected the amendment.[42]

Black Belt legislators, momentarily in the minority, presented one of the most interesting proposals of Governor Patton's administration. They introduced a bill to extend suffrage based on property or education, in effect to enfranchise blacks whom the Black Belt expected to control politically. Although north Alabama easily defeated this idea, the Black Belt had now recognized manipulation of the black vote as the vehicle that could successfully undermine the power of the Unionists and restore the Black Belt to political supremacy in the state.[43]

Throughout the administrations of Governors Parsons and Patton, the Freedmen's Bureau did commendable work in alleviating the distress in Alabama that was the aftermath of war. General Swayne directed the bureau from August, 1865, to July, 1868, and was frequently praised for his "discreet, liberal, and enlightened" policies. Among blacks and whites he possessed the reputation for justice to all parties and willingness to befriend the helpless. He worked diligently to maintain good relations with Alabama civil authorities, especially the governors, so that no conflict nor embarrassment arose.[44] He also maintained a remarkable record of refusing to interfere unnecessarily in state politics, even to the point of refusing to endorse locally an Ohioan who was an old friend and who was supported by such a prominent friend as John Sherman, then U.S. senator from Ohio. Even partisan newspapers grudgingly admitted that Alabama had been "most fortunate" in the character of the military commanders in the state. Especially was there "little occasion to find fault" with General Swayne, although grounds for "grave charges" existed against some of his subordinates who were engaged in planting and were otherwise "lax in the performance of their duty."[45] Swayne perceptively understood that much of this tireless animosity directed toward the bureau was a release for men seeking to avenge themselves by "any means other than violence for being stopped in doing wrong." He was satisfied that such men did not represent the body of the community although they might appear to do so—"because one industrious and noisy person of this class is more prominent than ten men who mind their own business."[46]

The majority of the legislation during Patton's administration dealt with economic problems, and the most acute of these in 1865 was the matter of labor relations. Throughout the fall, rumors had circulated that after Christmas all the plantations and the stock provisions thereon would be divided among the freedmen. With such bounty expected, many blacks refused to make labor contracts for the following year, and the whites feared that black disappointment coupled with genuine want at Christmas time might spark an insurrection. Alarmed by the rumors, the legislature acted just before the Christmas holidays to pass discriminatory laws intended to regulate blacks. When the legislature reconvened after the holidays, the alarm had passed, and it was obvious that most Alabama laborers had made contracts for 1866. Now the legislature became "more calm," and there were no further efforts at discriminatory legislation.[47]

The other most significant economic business enacted by the legislature under Governor Patton was the decision to allow the state's credit to be used to subsidize railroad construction in Alabama. This idea was not new to the state, as the 1855–56 legislature had enacted laws to permit loans to several antebellum railroads and then repealed the laws before the bonds were issued.[48] On February 19, 1867, the General Assembly authorized the governor to endorse a railroad's first mortgage bonds for $12,000 per mile when it completed and equipped twenty miles of continuous track and to endorse its bonds at this rate for each subsequent section of twenty miles completed until the railroad was finished. Interstate as well as intrastate railroads could benefit from this act, and no endorsed bonds could be sold for less than ninety cents on the dollar. The railroad company could issue bonds whose interest was not to exceed eight percent a year to be paid semiannually. These bonds must be used to build and equip the road. At least fifteen days before the interest was due, the company was to deposit with the state comptroller the amount necessary to pay the interest. If the company proved unable to meet its interest payments, the governor was to seize the company and manage it until enough funds accumulated to pay the interest. If the company failed to pay the bonds when they fell due, the governor was to institute legal proceedings leading to the sale of the railroad and its property. Unfortunately, this blanket law, passed by the Patton administration before the Republican party was even organized in the state, made state aid available to any railroad project regardless of its merit.[49]

Governor Patton was particularly interested in encouraging railroad aid in Alabama. He was an associate of James W. Sloss, a powerful north Alabama entrepreneur, who in September, 1865, organized the merger of three small north Alabama railroads into the Nashville and Decatur Railroad. The Sloss associates were eagerly anticipating expansion to connect the rich mineral region of Alabama southward to Montgomery and northward to Nashville, but before the law to aid railroads had an opportunity to go into effect, Congress intervened with the Reconstruction Acts and suspended Governor Patton's administration.[50]

Thus far under Presidential Reconstruction until March, 1867, the Unionists had had their day in Alabama politics. Feeling vindicated by the outcome of the war, they assumed they would dominate Reconstruction, and they exhibited some flexibility in accommodating themselves to the rapidly changing political scene. They rather grudgingly acquiesced to the increased importance of the blacks, but deep-seated prejudice prevented them from doing more. They certainly did not become the champion of the freedmen. Unfortunately for the Unionists, their days of power in Alabama politics were numbered.

REVOLUTIONARY TIMES

While the Unionist-led reorganization of Alabama progressed, ominous signs in Washington suggested that Presidential Reconstruction was in trouble. In 1866 Congress daily grew stronger in its struggle for domination of the federal government as President Johnson unwittingly alienated moderate support by his vetoes of the second Freedmen's Bureau Bill and the Civil Rights Bill. After Congress overrode his vetoes in the spring of 1866, Johnson's friends urged him to organize a new conservative movement as a gamble for political survival. National Union Clubs were formed throughout the country hoping to defeat Radical candidates in the fall congressional elections, and Alabama Unionist leaders as well as ex-Confederates supported the movement. Alabama delegates to the national convention were chosen at a convention of "Constitutional Union" men meeting at Selma on August 2, 1866. After the election of thirty-two delegates (which included Unionists and ex-Confederates) the Selma convention organized itself into a new political party in Alabama to be known as the Democratic and Conservative party, recognizing the need to attract ex-Whigs as well as Democrats to their party. They created an executive committee headed by James Holt Clanton of Montgomery, an ex-Whig and a former Confederate general. Unfortunately, the momentum of the optimistic beginning to arouse support for Presidential Reconstruction soon faltered. When the National Union Convention opened in Philadelphia on August 14, 1866, there was neither unanimity of purpose among the members nor agreement on how to defeat congressional Radicals in upcoming elections.[1]

When President Johnson saw that the National Union movement was unable to generate the ground swell of support he needed, he next took his case to the people via his "swing around the circle" in late August and September, 1866. This effort dissolved into a political disaster for the President and further alienated that support he had so eagerly sought. The result was predictable. The Republican victory in the November congressional elections was so overwhelming as to provide a two-thirds majority for Johnson's opponents.[2]

As Alabamians watched these turns of national events, they did not display the flagrant arrogance prevalent elsewhere in the South in late 1866. Although the legislature had earlier passed stern black codes, Alabamians were generally reputed still to be "broken in spirit" and none so much so as the former secessionists.[3] Nevertheless, despite this lingering spirit of cooperation, some Alabamians had not come to a complete realization of what it meant to lose a war, as a favorite plea was that "all we ask is to be let alone."[4] Conservative newspapers were noticeably restrained, and although they editorialized on the potential effects of the proposed Fourteenth Amendment, there was none of the inflammatory journalism that became standard fare six months later.[5] Alabama Unionists watched national events with increasing alarm, and by early 1867 they realized that Congress' growing supremacy over President Johnson in the struggle for domination of the federal government and Southern Reconstruction endangered their control over Alabama Reconstruction. To preserve their influence enjoyed during Presidential Reconstruction these Unionists resolved to try to direct whatever new reorganization of Alabama that might lie ahead. They organized Unionist meetings to stimulate interest in the establishment of the Republican party in the state and held the first convention on January 8 and 9 at Moulton in Lawrence County, heart of the Unionist stronghold of north Alabama. The leaders present included some of the most outspoken Unionists in that area: William Bibb Figures, editor of the Huntsville *Advocate,* and Joseph C. Bradley and Nicholas Davis, prominent Huntsville lawyers. This organizational meeting in Moulton set another meeting of Unionists for March 4 in Huntsville.[6]

However, on March 2, two days before the Huntsville convention was to open, Congress overrode President Johnson's objections and passed the first of the Reconstruction Acts, which became the new framework within which the Unionists must operate. Unionists reacted with shock and dismay as they read the requirements for suffrage under the Reconstruction Acts and the requirements for officeholding under the Fourteenth Amendment, which Alabama must now ratify. While blacks were given the franchise, the disfranchisement provisions of the Reconstruction Acts caught many Unionists who had served in some minor position under the Confederacy, often a post to which they had been appointed or elected before 1860. The Fourteenth Amendment disqualified these men from officeholding because they had violated their original oath of loyalty to the Federal Constitution. Neither the Reconstruction Acts nor the Fourteenth Amendment gave any consideration to the fact that many Unionists had held such positions to avoid conscription into the Confederate army.[7]

When the Huntsville meeting opened on March 4, the delegates were eager to aid the restoration of Alabama to her proper relation to the Union. Prominent north Alabama Unionists actively participated. In addition to those who had met at Moulton, Unionists important in this convention included David C. Humphries of Madison County, William H. Smith of Randolph, Thomas M. Peters of Lawrence. The Huntsville convention also attracted representatives of two other groups who would join the north Alabama Unionists to organize the Republican party in Alabama. One such group was Northern men who had come to the state since 1865, most of them associated with the Freedmen's Bureau. Among these were Wager Swayne, John B. Callis of Wisconsin, J. W. Burke of Ohio, and John C. Keffer of Pennsylvania. Another group present was delegates from the Black Belt, some of whom had been Unionists in 1861, such as Milton J. and Benjamin F. Saffold of Selma, lawyer sons of a former chief justice of the Alabama Supreme Court, and some of whom were ex-Confederates, such as Adam C. Felder, lawyer and former legislator from Montgomery.[8]

The convention listened to many earnest Unionist speeches and then issued a statement that a large segment of the population of Alabama had politically and personally opposed the secession movement and believed the federal government was "supreme and paramount" in authority to the state government whenever the two collided. The meeting closed with the announcement of plans to hold a general convention in Montgomery at some future time to be determined by an executive committee chosen at the Huntsville convention. This committee, like the convention itself, was dominated by men from north Alabama.[9] Union men were urged to hold county meetings to select delegates to the coming convention. Beginning in March such meetings occurred throughout the state, in the Black Belt as well as north Alabama, and they endorsed a statewide meeting in Montgomery.[10]

On April 5 a convention of the Union Leagues of north Alabama met at Decatur. The league had first appeared in Alabama in 1863 as Federal troops occupied the Tennessee Valley. At first Unionists flocked to join, until by 1865 about one-third of the white population of the upland counties were members. However, no blacks then belonged. Few whites joined the league in the Black Belt or in the white counties of southeast Alabama, where any connection with the league was considered a disgrace. The largest white membership was in 1865 and 1866; thereafter, it declined steadily as the league organized the newly enfranchised blacks.[11] In the spring of 1867 all sections of the state reported to bureau headquarters in Montgomery that blacks were flocking to join the leagues. From Roanoke came "we are organizing the Darkies, to advantage," while one organizer in Talladega reported that he had taken in five hundred members at the rate of about one hundred a week, adding that he was "doing well about making voters of the Blacks."[12] The league convention at Decatur endorsed the Reconstruction Acts and recommended that a state convention meet in June in Montgomery to organize the Republican party in Alabama.[13]

Already considering the role of the blacks in the new political alignment of the state, one Unionist bluntly estimated they must "look this Negro question directly in the face" and do justice to these new and "unwelcome allies." They must make the black man the friend of the Unionist and include black delegates in the June convention, although the Negro was a "bitter pill."[14] Otherwise, the ex-rebels armed with black votes would become their masters for all time to come in Alabama. The Unionists had recognized a serious challenge to their continued leadership in Alabama politics and moved to meet it.

Another meeting to arouse interest in the formation of the Republican party in Alabama was the Freedmen's State Convention, held in Mobile on May 1, 1867, under the direction of General Swayne. Black citizens at the convention issued a series of resolutions and proclaimed themselves a part of the Republican party because this was the only party to attempt to extend the Negroes' privileges. They intended to participate in future politics in the state in a free manner, not as "political tools of their employers." If threatened with discharge from employment because of their political independence, they would appeal for troops to protect them and for Congress to punish their oppressors, even to the confiscation of the property of the guilty. In conclusion, they announced that it was their "undeniable right to hold office, sit on juries, to ride on all public conveyances, to sit at public tables, and in public places of amusement."[15] At the convention the native white Unionist received a new challenge for control of the political affairs of the state.

On June 4, 1867, the "Union Republican Convention" met in

Montgomery with the Union League Convention. About fifty whites and one hundred blacks attended. The local press classified the convention members as "Colored," "Yankee," or "Pale faced"; neither the term *carpetbagger* nor *scalawag* was yet current to designate Northern and Southern Republicans in Alabama.[16]

The New York *Herald* assessed the Union element in Alabama as "probably stronger than that in any other of the Southern states" except North Carolina, and Unionists did play an important role in the convention.[17] Francis W. Sykes, a physician from Lawrence County, became chairman *pro tempore*, and Judge William Hugh Smith, Randolph County lawyer, became permanent chairman. White Southerners predominated on the committees and made most of the important addresses. The group invited Governor Patton to speak, and he obliged briefly, assuring the members of the convention of his concern for a definite settlement of the question of Reconstruction.[18] On taking the chair Judge Smith announced the convention's purpose of reconstructing Alabama under the military laws of Congress. This reconstruction could not be done without party organization. "Let us accept the name of the Republicans," he urged, "and go to work in earnest, and without distinction of race, color or condition."[19]

Still another Unionist, David C. Humphries, led the resolutions and platform committee that made its report on the second day of the convention. Serving with Humphries were two men from each of the six congressional districts. Of the thirteen men on the committee, five are identifiable as white Southerners.[20] The convention endorsed the national Republican party and Congressional Reconstruction, political and civil equality of all men, and free education without distinction of color, and praised the Unionists who had stood "firm by the Constitution." In economic matters the convention endorsed repeal of the federal cotton tax and the state poll tax and passage of a personal tax on the value of an individual's property. These resolutions and platform reflect Republican thinking about what important voting blocs must be made Republican for their party's success. Obviously, the party intended to pitch a strong appeal to the newly enfranchised blacks and to the old conservative whites of Alabama, but given the racial prejudices of the latter, these two groups would be uncomfortable political bedfellows. For the moment at least, Republican leaders hoped to perform a miracle and weld these two blocs into a firm foundation for the Republican party. The convention went on to organize the Republican party officially in Alabama, and John C. Keffer, a bureau agent from Philadelphia, became the first chairman of the state Republican Executive Committee. Serving with Keffer were fourteen Southern whites, five Northern whites, and six blacks.[21]

Alabama Democrats were also organizing in the summer of 1867, and they were as confused about how they should cope politically with the Reconstruction Acts as were Democrats elsewhere in the former Confederate states.[22] The nucleus of an organization in Alabama had existed since August, 1866, and in the summer of 1867 the executive committee of this group met to consider their strategy. The party division on what policy to follow was reflected by the fact that one group led by James H. Clanton, committee chairman, opposed cooperation with Reconstruction, while another led by Robert Tyler, editor of the Montgomery *Advertiser,* one of the most influential newspapers in the state, decidedly favored cooperation. Throughout the summer and fall of 1867 the *Advertiser* urged Alabamians to acquiesce and cooperate with Congress, reminding them that they were at the mercy of an "angry tempest" and were "neither in the Union nor out of it." The *Advertiser* further observed that prompt Southern action meant only that Alabamians believed they were unable to secure more favorable measures and were determined to make the "best of the evils" that beset their state.[23]

When the Conservatives held a convention in Montgomery on September 5, attendance was meager: only eighty-seven delegates (including fourteen blacks) from thirteen counties out of sixty. All of the counties represented were in the Black Belt or just north of it.[24] The deliberately vague platform adopted at this meeting embodied the party's utter confusion about what political course they should take and reflected the prediction of Joseph Hodgson, editor of the Montgomery *Mail,* that the convention would adopt a platform that would "commit nobody."[25] The convention reminded Congress that the Constitution established a government of three coordinate branches, no one to be supreme over the others, and that the Constitution was the fundamental law of the land. The only specific sections of the platform recognized the coming importance of the newly enfranchised blacks and Democratic expectation to lead this bloc of voters politically. The convention urged these new voters to place their trust in men whom they knew and to "deal cautiously with strangers, who bear no evidence that they were honored where they are better known." Speakers were appointed in each county especially to instruct the "colored voters" as to the purpose of the Conservative party.[26] As much can be inferred from what was not said in the Conservative platform as by what was stated. The party obviously faced the same dilemma as Alabama Republicans: how could black and white voters be made congenial political bedfellows and how could blacks be sought for the Conservative party without alienating whites? The convention arrived at no answer to the problem, and it left the individual Conservative to decide for himself whether or not to register or to vote in the upcoming election on the question of a constitutional convention. The party's confusion and division resulted in an abdication of Conservative leadership through the fall of 1867 until outrage over the actions of the constitutional convention would galvanize Conservatives into action.

While the Republicans and Conservatives were organizing, registration of voters proceeded across the state. Alabama had been divided into forty-five registration districts with two whites and one black to compose the board of registrars in each district. Unionists eagerly sought these posts because ostracism by ex-Confederates had financially hurt many of the professional men among the native whites. One Unionist reported that former Confederates were "much more intolerant to Southern Union men" than to Northern men.[27] While seeking these positions themselves, the native whites objected to the appointment of blacks as registrars. In fact, Joseph C. Bradley predicted that such plans would "greatly impede" the growth of the Republican party in many of the counties populated by poor whites, explaining that former secessionists would convince the whites that such appointments were the method of the Republican party to humiliate the white men of Alabama. Bradley suggested that white men entirely compose those boards of registration in the mountain counties of north Alabama from Marion and Walker on the west to Cherokee and De Kalb on the east.[28]

Bradley's advice was ignored, and despite the grumbling of whites, two whites and one black composed registration boards across the state. Because registrars were required to take the "iron-clad" oath, Northern men outnumbered Southerners; yet many native whites did serve on these boards in Alabama, in contrast to the situation in other Southern states such as South Carolina, where virtually all native whites were excluded. Unionist William H. Smith became general superintendent of registration for Alabama. Voters were to be registered without distinction as to race, creed, or color, and a constitutional convention was to be held to establish a government as Congress directed.[29]

Between July 1 and August 20, 1867, the number of voters registered was 160,991: 72,748 whites and 88,243 blacks. When a supplemental Reconstruction Act provided for revisions of registration lists, registration reopened. When the lists were closed a second time, 164,800 voters had been registered: 74,450 whites and 90,350 blacks.[30] The fact that so many whites registered did not go unnoticed; the New York *Times* commented that "it would have been an easy matter to rally the whites *en masse* against reconstruction" under the Congressional plan but for the "early and bold position" assumed by a number of prominent native Alabamians. Without the "active labors" of these men the Republican party of Alabama would have been confined "almost exclusively" to black voters.[31]

On August 31, General John Pope, commander of the Third Military District, called for an election in October to determine whether a constitutional convention should be held and, simultaneously, to elect delegates to the convention.[32] This election passed quietly October 1–3, but the month between the election and the opening of the convention saw an air of uneasiness mount in the state. Alabamians well understood what the Democratic Tuscaloosa *Independent Monitor* meant when it said that politics now were "very different from what they were in old times" and that a "great revolution" was under way.[33] Alabama Unionists were especially anxious, fearful that a new constitution might rob them of their recently acquired influence in state politics.

Alabama's second constitutional convention in two years opened in Montgomery on November 5 with one hundred members. Unlike conventions meeting in South Carolina and Louisiana, white delegates outnumbered blacks, although the latter constituted a majority of the registered voters. Forty-eight of the ninety-seven Republicans in the convention can be placed in Alabama before 1860; about twenty of these had left Alabama voluntarily or had been driven out by Confederates during the war. A reporter for the New York *Herald* described these Southern Republicans as including the "moderate and rational delegates, all the men of any property or social standing in the convention," and "all the lawyers, with one or two exceptions." Most of the Southern whites were engaged in professional or agricultural pursuits, had opposed secession in 1861, and had given no more than unenthusiastic support to the Confederacy. In these qualities Alabama whites strongly resembled this group in other Southern Reconstruction conventions. Nineteen blacks, twenty-six Northern men, and three men elected by "secessionist or rebel influence'' can also be identified in the convention member-ship.[34]

The whites in the convention divided into three groups of nearly equal strength: extreme men, moderates, and men who would shift first to one side and then to the other. Control of the blacks by lavish promises of future favors strengthened the extreme men.[35] Since the white Southern-ers possessed a slight majority in the convention, they might have controlled its actions had they determined to act in a concerted fashion.

Certainly, the native whites began well enough when the convention chose E. Woolsey Peck, Tuscaloosa lawyer, as president of the conven-tion. Peck had come from Syracuse, New York, to Elyton in 1824, where he practiced law for fourteen years. In 1838 he moved to Tuscaloosa, then the state capital, where he continued his practice and served as a chancery judge in 1839 and 1840. By 1860 he was a wealthy man. As a Whig and then a Unionist, he opposed secession and subsequently ignored the Confederacy. After the war he was elected to the 1865 constitutional convention. Although he was sixty-eight, his small and fragile appearance belied his inner strength, which was capped by a logical and methodical mind.[36] Peck's opponent for convention president was John C. Keffer, chairman of the Alabama Republican Executive Committee. Known to his enemies as the ''head devil'' of the Loyal League, Keffer was no idle opponent, as he possessed considerable influence, especially with federal officials in Alabama.[37] The rules of the convention delegated wide appointive power to Peck, who gave all important offices to whites, while reserving positions as doorkeepers, messengers, and pages for blacks.[38]

The most influential man on the floor of the convention was a north Alabama Unionist, Daniel H. Bingham from Limestone County. Though born in New York, he had lived in Alabama before 1860 but had been driven out early in the war. In the convention he immediately caught the eye of a reporter for the New York *Herald,* who regarded Bingham as ''singularly repulsive'' in personal appearance and ''extremely indis-tinct'' in his speech because he had ''lost the roof of his mouth.'' Though speech impediments reduced his voice to a stage whisper, Bingham electrified the convention as he rasped scathing attacks on ex-Confederates whom he branded as ''merciless wretches,'' ''incarnate fiends,'' and ''hell-hounds of secession.'' His performance provoked Democratic newspapers to dub him ''old torch and turpentine Bingham.''[39] As leader of the extreme clique in the convention, Bingham proposed that the president of the convention appoint a committee to draft a constitution for the convention's consideration. Bingham's hope was that he would chair the committee. However, John C. Keffer countered with a resolution that Peck appoint several committees to draft different sections of the new constitution, and this resolution was eventually adopted.[40]

Whites predominated on the committees appointed to write the constitution, with only one or two blacks appointed to most committees. Peck, perhaps trying to placate the Northern men for his having defeated Keffer for the presidency of the convention, made Northern men chairmen of nine committees and Southern whites chairmen of six. No black chaired any committee. Northern and Southern whites exerted rather equal influence as committee members. For example, the committee on the legislative department included six Southern whites, no Northern men, and one black, while the committee on the executive department included five Northern men, one Southern white, and one black. The committee on the franchise, probably the most important committee, had three Northern men, three Southern whites, and one black.[41]

The work of the convention proceeded with no serious discord until the suffrage issue arose. Disagreement on this question was so violent that the Republicans decided in caucus to send a representative to Washington for instructions, saying a small minority, chiefly Southern men, threatened to bolt if the disfranchisement of the Reconstruction Acts was exceeded. Washington advised moderation, especially disapproving efforts to disfranchise all who did not participate in the upcoming referendum on the new constitution.[42]

The wrangling within the franchise committee resulted in the presentation of majority and minority reports to the convention. Disregarding warnings about the consequences of setting excessively severe qualifications, the majority report favored disfranchisement of any registered voter who did not participate in the election on the question of ratification of the new state constitution. The minority report recommended universal manhood suffrage without proscription. Two Northern men and one native white signed the majority report, while two native whites and one black endorsed the minority report.[43]

The convention modified the majority report, but the disfranchisement requirements of the constitution still exceeded those in the Reconstruction Acts. The suffrage article enfranchised the blacks, disfranchised those unable to hold office under the provisions of the proposed Fourteenth Amendment, and disfranchised those who had been convicted of treason (men who had earlier applied for presidential pardons). Such proscription was necessary, observed a reporter for the New York *Herald,* for the ''future political prosperity of the Republican party in Alabama.''[44]

Provisions of the new constitution other than suffrage qualifications further dampened Unionist hopes for future political power. The legislature was reapportioned because the constitution based representation on the whole population of the state, not just on the white population as in the 1865 constitution. The Black Belt could now regain its old power in the General Assembly, and Northern men supported by black votes could dominate the Unionists from the white counties. In another section of the constitution qualifications for officeholding barred from office those who had sworn to uphold the Federal Constitution and later aided the Confederacy.

Other than extending suffrage, the convention did little for Alabama blacks.[45] Native white delegates were obviously uncomfortable with the race issue in the convention. They had not championed Negro rights; rather, federal action forced grudging acquiescence as an inescapable political necessity. The discomfiture of the white moderates was particularly apparent when a black delegate introduced a proposal to pay freedmen for their labor as slaves from the date of the emancipation proclamation to the end of the war. White delegates, unable to vote for the bill and fearing to oppose it, hastily referred it to a committee where it conveniently died.[46]

By the closing days of the convention the native whites understood the severity of the blow dealt them by the new constitution. Strict application of the franchise section would disqualify many who had held major roles in the Johnson government in Alabama. The many who had applied for and received pardons from President Johnson were declared as having admitted commission of treason. Even more serious, there were thousands of Alabamians who had served in some minor positions under the Confederacy, often a post to which they had been first appointed or elected before 1860. These men were now disqualified from future officeholding, and no consideration was given the fact that many Unionists had held such positions to avoid conscription into the Confederate army.[47]

General Swayne had recognized this problem after the passage of the Reconstruction Acts. In June, 1867, he had advised Salmon P. Chase that before the war and up to its opening a man generally had to be a Union man to be elected to office in Alabama. Then during the war Unionists sought small offices to stay out of the army and to protect other Union men. The Reconstruction Acts disfranchised these men, and Swayne suggested that Congress modify the law in order to convert "passive well-wishers to serviceable candidates and efficient helpers."[48]

One such disfranchised Unionist questioned the justice of these disabilities:

> Is it true, that every man who held office before the rebellion, is an enemy to this nation, unless he could truthfully take the oath prescribed by the Act of Congress for office holders, as that oath is construed? And is it true, that the humble Justice of the Peace, who voted for Douglass, [sic] or Bell, and who sincerely grieved at the success of secession, and whose only crime was a fatherly sympathy for his son, who joined the rebel army to avoid the disgrace of conscription—who preferred the Union at the surrender—is it true I say, that this man is as guilty as the man who concocted, and executed the scheme of secession? . . . The humblest ante-bellum office-holder however much he preferred the Union, and hated secession, found in almost every case, that in the opinion of the Government, he was no less a rebel, than Yancey.[49]

Unfortunately for the Unionists, no amnesty provisions were made in 1867. In these closing days of the convention despair seized the native whites as they assessed their political predicament. Governor Patton's secretary, David L. Dalton, wrote the Governor that the "moderate men of the Convention have lost all heart, and are now indiffert [sic] to what is going on." Dalton expected the convention to make nominations for state officers in a few days but believed Judge William H. Smith and General Swayne were "much discouraged" because they had little influence with the extreme men. "Smith is specially disheartened. Some of the ultras are open in their opposition to Smith. They say he is too tender and moderate." Dalton believed the moderate men could go into the convention and nominate Patton. "But they are preparing to oppose the constitution, and

hence want nothing to do with nominations." The only hopeful note
seemed the feuds among the Northern men who aspired for office. "With
proper management," Dalton said, "much advantage might be derived
from these feuds. But there is here no head to direct those who might act
as a 'balance of power.' " Dalton concluded that "altogether, things
look awfully 'blue.' "[50]

The following day Dalton wrote again to Governor Patton of the
squabbles among newcomers for office. He repeated: "The moderate
men might, with proper management, control every thing in the way of a
'balance of power,' but there is no concert among them, and hence forth
they will accomplish nothing." Judge W. H. Smith was now being urged
to accept the nomination for governor. "If he would agree to do it he
might get the nomination. Otherwise, the chances favor either Peck or
Bingham. Bingham says that if he is not made either Governor or U.S.
Senator, he will burst up the whole concern."[51] The native whites had
permitted themselves a costly luxury in disunity.

Injured pride and rage soon replaced despair. One angry Alabamian
wrote Governor Patton that a protest had been prepared and signed by
about twenty of the best men in the convention "dissolving their connex-
ion with the whole concern." He reported a "universal burst of indignation at the idea of filling the State offices with the carpet bag gentry who
have squatted here for no other purpose than to fleece the people." The
author did not doubt that the men who controlled the "extreme Radicals'
hand have as little use for an Alabama union man as they have for a
violent secessionist. Alabama union men . . . stand in the way of the
pillaging adventurers and they will crush us out if they can."[52] The native
whites had finally awakened in the waning days of the constitutional
convention to the realization that they would not be given preference
simply because of their wartime loyalty to the Union. And not until it was
almost too late to salvage any political power, did the native whites turn
and begin to fight furiously for what they believed was rightfully theirs.

They recognized that the suffrage disabilities were the most damaging
blow to their future influence in Alabama politics. Consequently, at the
close of the convention one powerful Unionist took the first step toward
relaxation of these restrictions. Judge William H. Smith, who was not a
member of the convention, influenced the inclusion in the Alabama
constitution of a clause authorizing the General Assembly to remove
these suffrage disabilities, and when he became governor in 1868, Smith

would urge the legislature to exercise its authority. Later that year the legislature did amend the constitution to enfranchise men disqualified from holding office by the Fourteenth Amendment. Alabamians continued subject to the section of the Fourteenth Amendment, which required a vote of two-thirds of Congress to relieve men from the disability to hold office.[53] Many applied for and received congressional pardons, although many other Unionists proudly refused to acknowledge that they had done anything for which they should seek a pardon.[54] In the coming months scalawags would increasingly endorse universal suffrage and general amnesty now that black suffrage was a *fait accompli.*[55]

The native whites not affected by the officeholding disabilities scrambled for nominations for office as the convention organized itself into a nominating convention of the Republican party, and they did well. They gained four Republican nominations for state executive offices: governor, treasurer, attorney general, and superintendent of public instruction. The remaining four nominations, lieutenant governor, secretary of state, auditor, superintendent of industrial resources, went to men who had come to Alabama since 1865. In the nominations for the state judiciary, native white Alabamians were even more successful, capturing all three nominations for the Supreme Court, four of five nominations for chancellors, and ten of eleven nominations for circuit judges. These native whites represented all sections of the state, and most had earlier held at least some minor state political or judicial post.[56] After a period of uncertainty and disunity during the days of the convention, the native whites had now mobilized their strength and gone after the fruit of power—offices. They moved to ensure that they did not "shake the political tree and a few quasi friends . . . gather the fruit."[57] The newfound energy and determination demonstrated here would characterize the Southern white Republicans in Alabama for the remaining years of Reconstruction as they seriously battled with the Northern men in the party for control of Reconstruction in Alabama.

In its closing acts the convention petitioned Congress to amend the Reconstruction Acts so that the constitution could be adopted by a majority of those voting instead of a majority of those registered, and then adjourned on December 6 to reassemble on the call of the convention president or the commanding general. Within two weeks after the adjournment General Pope ordered an election for February 4 and 5 (later extending the election through February 7) on the ratification of the proposed constitution and the election of county, state, and federal officers.[58]

The year 1867 had been a momentous one for Alabamians. Two political parties now existed, the state government had been reorganized, and blacks had been given the franchise. The latter constituted the most revolutionary break with the past that Republicans would effect in Alabama. These rapid changes had stunned many Alabamians politically, but the campaign for ratification of the new constitution saw the reappearance of a lively two-party system in the state. As one writer has observed about Congressional Reconstruction in Florida, a Republican administration was not foisted onto a helpless native white population. It resulted from battles between groups of men of very different interests.[59]

CROSSING
THE RUBICON

The campaign for ratification of the proposed constitution began when the convention adjourned. Immediately, the suffrage article of the constitution caused a rupture in the Republican party. Thirteen members of the convention led by Virginia-born Joseph H. Speed, delegate from Perry County and member of the minority of the franchise committee, and Virginia-born Henry Churchill Semple, prominent Montgomery attorney, vigorously protested the imposition of the disabilities. They believed a government based on the new constitution would entail great evil upon the people of the state. In a subsequent address to the people of Alabama on December 10, 1867, these delegates proclaimed they had joined the Republican party because they believed that a favorable reception of the Congressional plan of Reconstruction was the only hope for the restoration of Alabama. They were now leaving the Republican party because it had broken its promise by going beyond the Reconstruction Acts. "We know not what fate may be in store for us, but it can scarcely be worse than that which we shall bring on ourselves by aiding in carrying this constitution into effect."[1]

The protesting Republican delegates later joined the Conservative or Democratic party in a crusade against the new constitution. However, Speed subsequently reconciled himself to the Republican cause and was elected state superintendent of public instruction in 1872 as a Republican.

The radical features of the constitution also disturbed Republicans who had not been members of the convention. The Montgomery council of the Union League of America denounced the constitution as "disfranchising and proscribing a large portion of the most intelligent and law abiding citizens of Alabama" and as characterized in every feature by a "fiendish motive of revenge and hatred."[2] C. C. Sheats, diehard Unionist from Winston County now editing a newspaper in Decatur, denounced the actions of the convention but pledged his continued support to the Republican party despite the "foolishness of a few unwise men." But, he added, north Alabama Unionists intended to speak out and not to "delegate away all our rights as free men, to men in Montgomery, whose greatest ambition is to secure for themselves place and power, and force

us into their support, whether we choose to do so or not."[3] Nicholas
Davis, Huntsville Unionist, criticized the constitution as "despotism"
under which he could not consent to live. As a Republican he opposed the
constitution as being "anti-Republican."[4] Another Unionist, Samuel
Dixon, reported that there was a "universal burst of indignation" in the
state "at the disfranchisement of so many of our best people and the
enfranchisement of a whole race of ignorant stupid negroes."[5]

A. W. Dillard, a Black Belt Unionist, believed the constitution was
another step in a general deterioration of affairs in the South. He predicted that an exodus of whites was imminent, and he urged upon
President Johnson a federal program to remove blacks in installments of
10,000 from each Southern state. Whites would soon fill the void, and a
temporary inconvenience from a labor shortage would be preferable to
the evils currently afflicting the South. Dillard's gloom about the South's
future stemmed from his conviction that the "immobility and idleness of
the negro are incorrigible for they were implanted by nature; and if the
South was forced to depend on *him* for labor, it might annually decline in
wealth and eventually sink into barbarism." Removal of the blacks
would benefit both races, for the blacks could work out their own destiny
beyond the Mississippi and "be entrusted with political privileges with
comparative safety to our republic." On the other hand, if they remained
in the South, Dillard predicted "they will ultimately be extirpated, as
self-preservation is above all human codes."[6] Obviously, white Republicans continued a firm belief in the racial inferiority of blacks.

On December 28, 1867, in the middle of the campaign for ratification
of the constitution, President Johnson replaced General Pope with Gen-
eral George Meade as commanding general of the Third Military District.
Two weeks later on January 11, 1868, General Swayne was relieved by
General Julius Hayden, who was to await the return of General O. L.
Shepherd from leave. General Hayden was then to turn over direction of
the District of Alabama and the Freedmen's Bureau in Alabama to
General Shepherd. Although such changes came at an inopportune time,
Alabamians were more favorably impressed with General Meade than
with General Pope, and General Hayden also was acceptable to the
people.[7] At a time of political turmoil over the approaching election,
General Hayden exercised remarkable integrity and restraint in his administration of the Freedmen's Bureau. He continued the precedent
established by General Swayne that a bureau officer could not run for

public office and retain his bureau position, and any who attempted to do both found his bureau appointment revoked.[8] Hayden believed some bureau agents had used their offices to influence the blacks to elect them to the constitutional convention over the "old resident Union citizens" to the detriment of race relations in Alabama. Henceforth, bureau agents were instructed to do their utmost to remedy this evil and, "remembering that revolutions never go backwards, to strive by every means in their power to reconcile the whites to the existing order of things."[9]

The campaign for ratification of the proposed constitution saw the Democrats and Conservatives come to life in Alabama politics. The apathy, indecision, and confusion that had characterized them months earlier were gone, and their rage over the constitution mobilized them into action. They decided against holding a convention fearing that the actions or speeches of a convention might lose them some of their new adherents or make them less earnest in opposition. Instead, Conservative leaders met several times in January, 1868, to consider how to obstruct ratification of the constitution. Their specific objections to the document were numerous, but at the root of it all were racial and economic attitudes. The Conservatives believed the constitution would make the blacks the ruling class in Alabama through disfranchisement of whites and enfranchisement of blacks. Convinced that blacks were racially inferior, white Conservatives were outraged that ignorant, propertyless, half vagabonds incompetent to comprehend politics would be allowed to tax, humiliate, and subordinate whites. Frankly, they said, "We cannot live here in Alabama under a negro government," for such black rule would quickly return some counties of the state into its "original jungle." The crux of the question of ratification was not black suffrage or black civil rights. The real issue was "shall the white man be subordinated to the negro? Shall the property classes be robbed by the no property herd?"[10]

According to James Holt Clanton, the Conservatives decided to vote against the constitution, hoping to reject it. But considering the possibility that it might be adopted, Conservatives also decided to nominate and vote for candidates under the proposed constitution. They then were persuaded to reverse their policy by Lewis E. Parsons, who returned from Washington while the Conservatives were deliberating. Urging them to "touch not, taste not, handle not, the unclean thing" (the constitution), Parsons persuaded the Conservatives to boycott the February election.

Conservatives realized the danger that a boycott could backfire into a victory by default for the Republicans as had been the case several months earlier in Georgia when Democrats boycotted the election on the convention call. Nevertheless, while Republicans made nominations for county offices in addition to the nominations made earlier for state officers, Conservatives agreed neither to run candidates for local or state offices nor to participate in the election. They hoped to defeat the constitution by staying home from the polls themselves and by intimidating others from voting. Democrats also circulated rumors about Republican mistreatment of blacks in Alabama during the Civil War, intending that such rumors would alienate black voters from the Republican party.[11] News of the proposed Conservative boycott of the election led the state Republican Executive Committee to endorse the petition of the 1867 constitutional convention that the Reconstruction Acts be amended so that the constitution could be adopted by a majority of those voting instead of a majority of those registered. The committee believed Alabama would benefit most by ratification and readmission to the Union rather than by being "tossed about not knowing where we shall land."[12]

"White man's" meetings assembled in areas politically powerful before 1860, especially in Black Belt counties. Former Governor Lewis E. Parsons and his law partner in Talladega, Alexander White, addressed many of these meetings protesting black suffrage and the 1867 constitution. They advised united action by the whites against Congressional Reconstruction and frequently equated black suffrage with black supremacy.[13]

The ratification election opened on February 4 in such a raw rainstorm that rivers and creeks became swollen. General Meade feared that the wretched weather and roads would keep many home and so added another day to the election, making five in all. Two exceedingly chilly, wet, and gloomy days were followed by three mild and sunny ones.[14] Despite the extension of the number of days for the election, only 71,817 of the 170,631 registered voters turned out. Those in favor of the constitution were 70,812, those against 1,005.[15] As Republicans had feared, though a majority of the votes cast approved the constitution, a majority of the registered voters had not participated in the election because of the successful Conservative campaign of intimidation of potential Republican voters and boycott of the election by their own members. Republicans reported that armed men kept blacks from the polls in several counties, while in others, boxes were broken open and ballots stolen. In Lowndes County one poll opened on the first day of the election with 239 votes, although an estimated 3,000 were there waiting to vote and remained all day in a cold pelting rain; some had trudged thirty or forty miles on foot through the mud. Similar problems occurred in Bullock County. Elsewhere, the election continued for two days, in some places for four days, and in still other places the polls were not opened until the last day of the election. Democrats counterclaimed the Republicans rounded up blacks threatening them with violence and a return to slavery if they did not vote.[16]

Conservative newspapers gleefully reported the rejection of the constitution. The Montgomery *Mail* proposed an epitaph for the "headboard of dead Radicalism in Alabama."

In Memory of

RADICALISM IN ALABAMA

Who died in attempting to give birth to a

BOGUS CONSTITUTION

After a painful illness of five days.

The *Mail* added that "she leaves a family of carpet-baggers and scalawags to mourn her loss."[17] This reference to the Northern and Southern whites in the Republican party as *carpetbaggers* and *scalawags* marks the beginning of frequent use of these terms both in the Alabama press and in private correspondence.

But Conservative glee at the defeat of the constitution was shortlived. Now that Republican fears of rejection of the constitution were a reality, General Meade advised that the convention reassemble, revise the constitution, and resubmit it to the people. He believed a majority of the voters would approve a revised constitution "more liberal in its terms and confined to the requirements of the reconstruction laws."[18] However, many Alabama Republicans favored immediate admission of Alabama rather than another election on the question of the constitution. Given control of the state at this time, they believed that they could build up a Republican party. Order another election and Alabama would go "irrevocably into the embrace of the Rebels."[19] Subsequently, the Fourth Reconstruction Act of March 11, 1868, provided for the adoption of the constitution by a majority of those voting. A bitter dispute arose in Congress because Alabama's ratification election had been held under the old law. Nevertheless, Alabama was readmitted to the Union on June 25, 1868, on the grounds that the people had adopted the constitution by a large majority of the votes cast.[20]

This validation of the ratification of the 1867 constitution in the February, 1868, election meant recognition of officials chosen in the same election. These men claimed their posts when the General Assembly convened on July 13, 1868, and the executive officials were sworn in on July 14. The new Governor, William Hugh Smith, was a man well known to Alabamians. Smith, a lawyer and farmer, had served as a Democrat from Randolph County in the legislature in 1857 and 1858. As a Douglas elector in 1860, Smith opposed secession and two years later went through the Union lines to remain out of Alabama until the end of the war. On his return in 1865 many mentioned him as a candidate for governor, but Lewis E. Parsons was appointed instead. Smith applied for a presidential pardon in 1865 because, although he had not voluntarily aided the rebellion, he was worth over $20,000. Governor Parsons appointed Smith judge of the tenth judicial circuit, but Smith resigned after serving only six months. Judge Smith presided at the organization of the Republican party in Alabama and worked actively for a moderate constitution in 1867. After serving as superintendent of registration of voters in Alabama, he became the state's first Republican governor.[21] Smith caught the eye of the reporter for the New York *Herald* at the Republican organizational meeting in June, 1867. This newspaperman observed Smith as a remarkably honest-looking individual about six feet tall with dark hair framing a face which "in any crowd would unmistakably point him out as a man of mark, integrity and great decision of character." Alabama Democrats, however, never saw Smith in so flattering a light.[22]

In his inaugural address Governor Smith urged the legislature to exercise the authority given it by the new state constitution to remove the extreme disabilities to vote imposed in the constitution. Because the Governor felt the registration oath would perpetually guarantee the civil and political rights of all men in Alabama, he believed any disfranchisement unwise except for crime.[23] Smith had continually advocated universal amnesty since the drafting of the constitution. At that time he had announced his belief that the enfranchisement of the blacks accomplished all that Congress designed and that he favored immediate removal of all political disabilities imposed in the 1867 constitution.[24]

Governor Smith also recommended that the legislature study Alabama's social and economic needs: encouragement of public education; development of natural and mineral resources; diversification of agriculture; improvement of waterways; attraction of immigrants and capital to the state.[25] Altogether, the address was a broad challenge for the Reconstruction legislature to attempt the social and economic dreams of generations of Alabama liberals, past and future.

As Governor, Smith made a conscientious effort to be "governor *of the State,* not *of a mere party,*" and he was rewarded with bipartisan criticism and praise.[26] However, one Democratic newspaper perceptively observed at the outset of Smith's administration that whether or not he had the power to do much good, he did have the power to "prevent much evil."[27] That assessment Smith certainly fulfilled.

In the new General Assembly scalawags were the most numerous group, as they also were in the state executive and judicial branches. Of the one hundred members of the house of representatives, three were Democrats. Among the ninety-seven Republicans were thirty-three Southerners, fourteen Northern men, and twenty-seven blacks. The remaining twenty-three Republicans are unidentified. In the senate were ten Northern men, twenty-one Southerners, one black, and one Democrat.[28] Among the first acts of this new legislature was ratification of the Fourteenth Amendment to the Federal Constitution. This action completed the last remaining requirement under the Reconstruction Acts of 1867.[29]

The next important business was the election of U.S. senators from Alabama. The legislature elected two Northern veterans to the Senate: Generals Willard Warner of Ohio and George E. Spencer of New York and Iowa. Warner had served on Sherman's staff during the war and moved to Autauga County in 1866, where he began farming.[30] Spencer had organized a regiment of Federal cavalry among north Alabama Unionists and after the war began practicing law in Decatur.[31] Governor Smith was widely discussed as a possibility for the Senate, but many Alabamians recognized his abilities as governor and wanted him to continue. Above all, he was urged not to leave the state in the hands of the Lieutenant Governor, Andrew Applegate of Ohio, more familiarly known to Alabamians as "Jack Appletoddy."[32]

Carpetbaggers also dominated Alabama's delegation to the U.S. House of Representatives. Chosen in the controversial election in February, 1868, these men were seated on July 21 and 22, 1868, and served an abbreviated term that ended March 3, 1869. The delegation included five Northern men and one white Southerner. Thus, in 1868, the carpetbaggers and scalawags satisfactorily divided the spoils of office with the scalawags predominating in the more numerous state jobs while the carpetbaggers predominated in the more prestigious federal positions.[33]

By summer 1868 the Ku Klux Klan and the Knights of the White Camellia were active in Alabama, especially in the counties of the Tennessee Valley and the western Alabama Black Belt. In hopes of carrying Alabama for the Democrats in the presidential election of 1868, they disrupted Republican meetings, lynched blacks, whipped or shot at white Republicans, blockaded roads to prevent rural blacks from registering to vote or from voting on election day. The troublemakers met little opposition from federal authorities and less from local ones when Alabama returned to civilian hands in July. Harassed Republicans regularly appealed to Governor Smith for protection, particularly after the legislature authorized the Governor to organize a militia whenever he deemed it necessary. Although Smith listened sympathetically to these pleas, his response was limited. He feared activation of a militia would alienate the native whites; a militia raised in Alabama would be predominately black because there was no large white Republican stronghold as existed in neighboring east Tennessee. At the urging of the legislature, Smith and five other Republican leaders did travel to Washington in late September to gain assurance from President Johnson that federal troops would be available if needed, but they did not ask for troops additional to the ten companies then stationed in Huntsville, Montgomery, and Mobile. Meanwhile, Republicans who lived under the Klan's reign of terror quickly lost patience with the Smith administration's apparent unwillingness to give them more than verbal support, and this situation was unfortunate for a man who faced reelection in 1870.[34]

Lewis E. Parsons had a graphic explanation of the appeal of the Klan to white Conservatives. Under slavery blacks had been controlled by the whip and lash. Emancipation without the consent of the whites or any preparation of the blacks was a shock to everyone. Whites resentfully believed that those who had formerly been their slaves were now placed over them as their superiors, and they easily "fell back into their old way of dealing with the negro with the lash. It was not safe to do it openly, but this secret organization furnished a way . . . '' Thus blacks could be made to toe the mark again, do the bidding of the employer, and be deterred from voting.[35]

While Conservatives were busy making life miserable for potential Republican voters, Conservatives also nominated an electoral ticket and registered to vote in unprecedented numbers. Although many had announced in February that they would not degrade themselves to take the registration oath even if they could, their opinion soon changed. In August the legislature removed political disabilities imposed under the 1867 constitution. Alabamians continued subject to the Fourteenth Amendment's provisions for officeholding disabilities and to the requirement of a vote of two-thirds of Congress for relief of this disability, but many Conservatives could now register to vote. In fact, a convention of Conservative leaders urged their members to do so.[36]

Some Democrats even advocated that the party solicit the black vote as Louisiana Democrats were already doing and ''thus give the southern radicals fits.'' Another was more blunt. Democrats must ''get up huge barbeques'' for the blacks and ''by all honorable means use every exertion to win their alliance in this contest.'' Democrats must prepare ''to beat the negro with the negro.'' With some effort and the judicious use of the employing power the farmers could control the entire vote of the black laborers.[37] Although the party was not united in a commitment to seek the black vote, Conservative efforts succeeded even in some strongly Republican areas. From Hale County came the reports that the Democratic club had ''many niger [sic] members'' and in Montgomery dozens of black men were reputed to have vowed that they intended to vote with their white employers.[38] Although the Conservatives had boycotted the February election, they obviously did not intend to sit this next one out.

Between the tactics of concerted registration of Conservatives and organized intimidation of Republicans, many Republicans grew anxious about the fate of their electoral ticket in a popular election. Some especially nervous Republicans promoted a bill whereby the legislature would cast the state's electoral vote. Governor Smith opposed the idea and ultimately vetoed the bill, despite the hue and cry that he was delivering the state government into the hands of his enemies. After his opponents failed to override his veto, the legislature adjourned without enacting election laws for the November election. Governor Smith then called a special session of the legislature for mid-September, and this group passed the necessary legislation. An entirely new registration of voters began, although the election was less than a month away. Registrars were appointed in each county to accept any male resident at least twenty-one years old who had lived in Alabama for six months. Those earlier disfranchised were to file an application with their probate judge for removal of their disabilities under the recent act of the legislature and then were allowed to register to vote. With this good news Democrats redoubled their campaign efforts.[39]

Conservative intimidation and violence against Republicans continued through election day, and from many parts of the state came reports that violence prevented thousands of Republicans from voting. Nevertheless, the Republican electoral ticket of seven scalawags and one carpetbagger pledged to the support of Ulysses S. Grant carried Alabama in the November election with 76,414 votes to the 72,744 cast for the Democratic ticket. Such a voter turnout represented a dramatic increase over the 71,817 who had voted in the February election. The legislature briefly considered making an investigation into election frauds and intimidations, but they did not pursue the matter.[40] Governor Smith credited the success of the ticket to the "spirit of liberality and conciliation" engendered by the legislature's relaxation of the suffrage restrictions in the 1867 constitution. Smith realistically noted that some whose disabilities had been removed supported the Democratic national ticket. "But this," he contended, "they had an undoubted right to do. Removal of political disabilities should not depend merely on party affiliations."[41]

The most ambitious project of Governor Smith's administration was the effort to stimulate railroad construction, and this was enthusiastically supported by both Republicans and Democrats. In 1868 the General Assembly broadly amended the 1867 law so that railroad bonds could now be endorsed in five-mile blocks after the completion of the first twenty miles of the road. Endorsements were increased from $12,000 to $16,000 a mile with the hope that Northern and European capital would be attracted to invest in Alabama at an unprecedented level. Counties and cities were also permitted to invest in railroad construction and to levy taxes to cover these obligations.[42]

Such financial encouragement spurred existing plans of reorganization and expansion among existing companies in Alabama. Former Governor

Robert M. Patton, now president of the Wills Valley Railroad, had been at work for months in an effort to merge this railroad with the North East and South West Railroad, hoping to build a railroad diagonally across the northern half of Alabama to connect Chattanooga, Tennessee, and Meridian, Mississippi. The Wills Valley road was now controlled by a group of Boston capitalists, which included John C. Stanton, who would soon become legendary in state railroad maneuvers.[43] Alabamians seemed much impressed with these men although they possessed little definite information about the capitalists.[44]

The ultimate plan for the consolidation of the two railroads was that the Wills Valley would buy the North East and South West at an auction held under the provisions of its mortgage to the state of Alabama. This proposal would require the cooperation of Governor Smith, who with four state senators and two state representatives, had earlier organized a railroad company of his own, the East Alabama and Cincinnati. Supposedly, Governor Smith insisted that Stanton help finance Smith's railroad in return for assistance toward consolidation of the North East and South West with the Wills Valley, and to this end Stanton's banker, Henry Clews of New York, loaned the East Alabama and Cincinnati $80,000.[45] Regardless of the degree of truth in these allegations, Governor Smith advertised the sale of the North East and South West in the fall of 1868, and one of the state senators also associated with the East Alabama and Cincinnati introduced a bill in the legislature to authorize the Wills Valley to buy the North East and South West. Early in December the board of directors of the latter company agreed to the sale.[46]

From this consolidation the Alabama and Chattanooga Railroad Company was organized with John C. Stanton as general superintendent, his brother D. N. Stanton of Boston as president, and Robert M. Patton as vice-president. Construction began a few months later on the track that was to be 295 miles long and progressed rapidly southward from Chattanooga and northeastward from Meridian aiming for completion of the line in January, 1871.[47]

J. C. Stanton is credited with persuading the 1868 legislature to raise the state endorsement of railroad bonds from $12,000 to $16,000 per mile, and this change benefited the Alabama and Chattanooga enormously. In fact, the bulk of the money to build the road came from the sale of the state endorsed bonds. Stanton fraudulently obtained the endorsed bonds first for twenty miles of track completed by the North East and

South West Railroad Company prior to the formation of the Alabama and Chattanooga. He next received bonds for fifteen miles of track constructed by the Wills Valley Company and five miles of track rented from another company.[48]

Existing laws made Governor Smith responsible to protect the state against such fraud and authorized him to investigate applications for state aid. Unfortunately, there is no evidence that the Governor exercised his responsibilities in the case of any of the railroads that requested state aid. At the close of his administration he announced that overall he had endorsed $4,000,000 in bonds for 250 miles of track for the Alabama and Chattanooga Company. Actually, he had endorsed $5,300,000, far more than legally permitted for the completed line of 295 miles.[49]

In addition to this generous financial support for the Alabama and Chattanooga Railroad, Stanton sought and received a direct loan of $2,000,000 in state bonds in February, 1870. To accomplish this goal, Stanton bribed state legislators at his hotel rooms while the bill was under consideration. The effectiveness of Stanton's tactics was not lost on Democratic railroad promoters, and bribery of legislators for railroad favors became epidemic. Three Democratic-controlled railroads, the South and North, the Montgomery and Eufaula, and the Mobile and Montgomery, also received state loans assisted by generous and well-placed bribes. Many Democratic legislators generously voted for aid to both Republican- and Democratic-controlled railroads.[50]

By May 19, 1870, the Alabama and Chattanooga Railroad had received all the bonds to which it was legally entitled. To have money to complete the road, Stanton persuaded Governor Smith to endorse an additional $580,000 in bonds, which Stanton hypothecated to a firm of Philadelphia bankers on the promise of using this loan to pay the interest due to the bondholders on January 1, 1871. Instead, he used the loan in an effort to complete the Alabama and Chattanooga Railroad.[51]

During Governor Smith's administration the Alabama and Chattanooga Railroad frequently violated the provisions of the laws whereby the state endorsed the company's railroad bonds and loaned state bonds to the company. Some of the bonds were sold for less than ninety cents on the dollar; money from the sale of bonds was used for purposes other than building the line; and the company sold some of its property received under a U.S. land grant and used the money for purposes other than payment on the $2,000,000 state loan.[52] By the end of Smith's administration the stage was set for an unpleasant day of financial reckoning.

Until the summer of 1870 the Alabama and Chattanooga and other Alabama railroads who had received state aid generally cooperated. This was especially true with the Alabama and Chattanooga and the Democratic-controlled South and North, which was building southward from Decatur toward Montgomery. The two roads anticipated mutual benefit from the founding of an industrial city at the point where the two lines would cross. Representatives of the two companies took options on almost 7,000 acres of land near Village Creek in Jones Valley (Jefferson County). Thereafter, John Milner, engineer of the South and North, discovered that J. C. Stanton had broken the agreement and instead was building toward Elyton and had acquired options on land there—options that would expire in December. When Milner found Stanton ignored his queries about the change and the Elyton options, he quietly continued work on the South and North and refused to indicate where the railroad would cross the Alabama and Chattanooga. In December, Stanton assumed the South and North could not raise the money to take up his options, and he permitted them to expire. On December 19, Josiah Morris, a Montgomery banker, bought for $100,000 the 4,150 acres on which Stanton's options had expired, and the next day the Elyton Land Company was organized to build Birmingham. The Democrats had outmaneuvered their Republican colleagues.[53]

While cooperating on economic matters, Alabama Republicans disagreed on a wide variety of political and social questions. Generally, carpetbaggers advocated creation of a state militia while scalawags opposed a militia; carpetbaggers opposed relaxation of political disabilities imposed in the 1867 constitution while scalawags favored a removal of disabilities.[54] Scalawags and carpetbaggers were about equally divided over the necessity for the electoral college bill.[55] While exhibiting no reluctance to discuss or vote on any of these issues, both scalawags and carpetbaggers dragged their feet on race relations to delay putting their views on public record. For example, on opening day of the July legislative session when a Blount County scalawag moved that black members be seated on one side of the house chamber and whites on the other, the house refused to act on the matter. Three days later John Carraway, a black representative from Mobile, introduced a common carrier bill to assure blacks equality in transportation and public accommodations. In the weeks that followed, Carraway repeatedly tried to move the bill out of the judiciary committee and before the house. Finally, near the end of the session it was considered and passed after much wrangling. It then went to the senate, only to die in the judiciary committee there. Generally, scalawags opposed the common carrier bill, and only with the support of carpetbaggers were the blacks able to push the bill through the house. With only one black and ten carpetbaggers in the senate, the bill never had a chance of passage.[56]

In addition to ideological differences, trouble was brewing within the Republican party on another front. Many old Union men were bewildered by their not being appointed to office. Chancellor A. W. Dillard of Sumter County articulated these pathetic expectations when he wrote to a friend of the Governor: "I have waited very patiently, but have not been tendered any position at all and cannot conjecture the cause of it."[57] And when they saw newcomers appointed to office, Unionists could not contain the resentment that boiled within them. David P. Lewis, a Huntsville lawyer who had served as a judge during the Civil War and had applied to Congress for removal of officeholding disabilities, exploded in a vehement expression of this sentiment to Governor Smith:

> What can a native Union man do, expect, or calculate on in the future? The Carpet-baggers have already landed everything that is Republican in Hell. The possibility of building up a national party in Alabama in affiliation with the Republican Party is utterly extinct. The political offices, the University, Schools, all carpet-bagged.
> I am sick to nausia [sic] of this damned dose—though I keep it to myself. Can the native white Union men make any movement, that will relieve themselves from the odium that stinks in the nostrils of humanity? . . .
> Party shackels [sic] are uneasy enough when everything is managed with reasonable wisdom, with decency. When both are ignored, and men are responsible for things, that they not only condemn but detest—why then a grasshopper becomes a burden.[58]

The Unionists viewed the newcomers as detrimental to the party's future in the state, especially in north Alabama. William Bibb Figures, Unionist editor of the Huntsville *Advocate,* reported that the Unionists were opposed to the Democrats and "to the *exclusive* rule and control of newcomers" and confused as to what action they should take. Many found carpetbaggers "so offensive as well as grasping" that daily many Republicans angrily took refuge in the Democratic party to manifest their repugnance to the newcomers. Figures predicted, "If the present state of things goes on much longer, only a baker's dozen of us will be left up here, aside from the colored and the carpetbaggers."[59] Joseph W. Burke, himself a newcomer to Alabama who as a Union soldier moved to Huntsville only in 1864, concurred with Figures' condemnation of the conduct of the carpetbaggers. He blamed them for the flight from the Republicans of "almost every native Union white man in North Alabama." He added that the carpetbaggers' cause was office, "their principles anything, everything, whereby they may hold on."[60]

Joseph C. Bradley was also pessimistic about the Republican party in north Alabama and estimated that the party was in a "bad fix."

> We have lost many of our native union white friends in north Alabama but they give no good reasons for doing so. Every one of them in heart are [sic] still with us but they have not the moral courage to withstand the pressure that is brought to bare [sic] on them, Social ostracism, persecution in every condition of life by the discontents are too much for their nerves. The mere fact of there being bad or worthless men in the Republican party or officeholders of that character in the state are [sic] not good reason for any man of principal [sic] to quit the national Republican party.[61]

David C. Humphries agreed that the newcomers had "heartily ruined us." He reported that men who he thought had no intention of leaving the Republicans had become so bitter that they refused to cooperate in any measure which might aid the carpetbaggers. Democratic leaders hated the native element as much as did the "carpet gentry," and the Unionists found themselves between two fires—forced to uphold the new men, because politically associated with them.[62]

These protests grossly overexaggerated the slights to the scalawags in spoils of office, and they frankly ignored the number of offices scalawags actually occupied of those positions under Republican control. In November, 1868, scalawags held four of eight state executive offices, seventeen of nineteen state judicial offices, one of eight federal legislative offices, three of five federal judicial offices, fifty-four of one hundred twenty-eight Republican seats in the state legislature, seven of eight places on the Republican electoral ticket, eleven of twenty-four places on the state Republican Executive Committee.[63] However, the injustice of the appointment of undeserving newcomers to office at the expense of a loyal native who had survived the hardships of war seemed quite real to the Unionists. They still believed, as they had in 1865, that the only sound basis for the establishment of a permanent Republican party in Alabama was the loyal white element, not the black. Having had their franchise restored by action of the 1868 legislature, many seethed at their continued exclusion from officeholding under the Fourteenth Amendment because they proudly asserted that they had not been disloyal and refused to apply for removal of disabilities by act of Congress.

Modification of these restrictions was obviously desirable, but despite numerous suggestions about the scope of amnesty to be offered, nothing was done. The most practical suggestion proposed that men who had opposed secession in 1860, then cooperated with the Confederacy only so far as honest convictions of safety demanded, and now accepted Reconstruction, be exempt from the disabilities of the Fourteenth Amendment. Such a proposal would relieve loyal men of 1860, while continuing disabilities on secessionists and active rebels.[64]

Unfortunately, Congress did not act on the amnesty question in 1868, with the result that most Douglas and Bell men of 1860 abstained from politics because they were barred from officeholding until the passage of the General Amnesty Act of 1872. The importance of the failure of the Republican party to attract the bulk of these conservative men of 1860 may be seen in the effort in December, 1868, to organize these Union men into a new political party. Alexander White of Talladega and Selma initiated the movement.

White, born in Tennessee, moved as a youth to Courtland, Alabama, in 1837. Son of an Alabama Supreme Court justice, he briefly attended the University of Tennessee and later practiced law in Talladega with Lewis E. Parsons. Combining politics and planting, White served in Congress as a Union Whig and acquired extensive holdings of land and slaves in Talladega and Dallas counties. Though he was a Douglas elector in 1860, White served in Hardee's infantry during the Civil War. In the 1865 constitutional convention he represented Talladega County.[65]

In December of 1868, White described the proposed movement to George S. Boutwell, then chairman of the Joint Select Committee on Reconstruction, as a "cordial and permanent reunion" of the old Union men of Alabama. White had already circulated an unsigned address "To the Old Union Men of Alabama," and he enclosed a copy in his letter to Boutwell. The address urged the cooperation of Union men to unite and accept the recent presidential election as settlement of the issues of

Union, Reconstruction, and suffrage, regardless of how sensitive these subjects might be. Instead of wasting energy in endless political controversy, they could then concentrate on development of Alabama's natural resources by inviting capital and labor to the state and by treating them courteously on their arrival. Bluntly, he concluded it was time Alabama took hold of the living present and advancing future to improve and mould them for the welfare and prosperity of the state.[66]

However, White realized the greatest impediment to such cooperation among Union men was the proscription of most of the old Union leaders. And therein lay the reason for White's writing to Boutwell. If Congress would remove the disabilities of the old Union men caught by the Fourteenth Amendment, the success of the movement might "fire the future political status of Alabama, and if successful in Alabama it will soon be followed in other Southern states."[67] But Congress did not act.

White's ideas also met a cool reception in Alabama. The Republican Montgomery *Alabama State Journal,* opposing the formation of such a third party, urged all Union men to cooperate with the Republican party, as did the Republican Opelika *East Alabama Monitor.*[68] At this time White confided to Governor Smith that he had few favorable responses to the movement. "Politicians," White observed, "wish time to consult and consider."[69]

A few weeks later he elaborated his theories for the movement. He expected his address to draw off the "Old Union Men" from the Democratic party and separate them from return because "it designedly builds a wall which none . . . can cross until they are washed in the political Jordan and are cleansed from the leprosy of suspicion." White astutely saw the danger inherent in Republican reliance on black votes for the party's existence. Democrats employed fully seven-tenths of the blacks, White estimated, and if there were no change from the present condition, the Republican party would soon be swept away in Alabama and in the entire South. Former owners of slaves exercised great influence over the blacks, and White believed that unless the white men of the state could be divided, all opposition to the Democrats was "idle and vain." Many who might leave the Democrats would refuse to join the Republicans, but White hoped to entice them out of the Democratic party and thus divide and weaken it. The alternative to his proposal was to watch them consolidate their strength to the detriment of the Republicans.[70]

However, when the Union men finished their consideration of the proposed movement, they refused to join. Some suspected White of intending to use them to put himself into the strongest party and to benefit personally as the leader of this group of Union men. Others denounced White as having already defected to the Republicans.[71]

White failed to create a successful third force in Alabama politics at this time, but his effort emphasized the plight of the Union men who had not swallowed their pride to apply for congressional removal of their disabilities. Since 1868 they had been barred from participation in Alabama politics. A more generous amnesty policy early in Reconstruction might have won these loyal whites as a base for a permanent Republican organization in Alabama. Instead, carpetbaggers and scalawags maintained a balance of power within the Republican party from 1867 to 1869. The strength of both factions forced each to make concessions in offices and power. Although scalawags dominated the state judiciary, they divided state executive and federal legislative offices with the carpetbaggers. The blacks were not yet sufficiently organized to demand concessions from the whites as the price for their votes.

This balance between natives and newcomers was permanently upset after the presidential election of 1868, when the scalawags received strength from an unexpected source—not from the Union men as should have been the natural consequence of the outcome of the war. A number of prominent Alabama Democrats reappraised their futures as Democrats and concluded that political survival necessitated a change in political affiliations. Accordingly, they prepared to swallow the bitter pill of ostracism and condemnation by their neighbors and in the weeks after the November election announced their defections to the Republican party. Their actions might be described by the adage, ''If you can't lick 'em, join 'em.''

In December, 1868, Samuel F. Rice signaled the beginning of these important defections to the Alabama Republican party. Rice was a South Carolina lawyer who had moved to Talladega in 1838. After representing Talladega County as a Democrat in the legislature in 1840 and 1841, he was defeated in his race for Congress in 1845, 1847, and 1851, the last time by Alexander White. Rice moved to Montgomery in 1852 and two years later was elected to the Alabama Supreme Court, where he served until January, 1859, the last three of these years as Chief Justice. He accumulated extensive holdings in land and slaves in both Montgomery and Talladega counties. A secessionist, Rice served in the Alabama senate from 1861 to 1865. In February, 1868, he campaigned vigorously against the new constitution, openly critical of black suffrage, and in November, 1868, actively opposed the Republicans. Now in the prime of his abilities at the age of fifty-two, Judge Rice was quite a "catch" for the young Republican party in Alabama. Although rather average in looks— thin, medium height, dark and restless eyes, florid complexion—he possessed the reputation for great personal charm as "one of the most fascinating of men." In an age that prized oratorical gifts he was renowned for his logic and wit on the rostrum and in the public forum.[72] Although Rice did not achieve prominence as a Republican officeholder during Reconstruction, he was highly influential behind the scenes and a close ally of L. E. Parsons, Alexander White, and W. H. Smith.

Rice announced his new political affiliations in a letter to the editor of the Camden *Wilcox News and Pacificator*. His support of the Democratic party in the November election had been, he said, the means to accomplish the "salvation of free government, . . . the revival of industry and prosperity, the lightening of debt and taxes, and the perpetuation of the right of self government." The defeat of the Democratic party ended the possibility of their achieving these goals for at least four years. "What," asked Rice, "is my duty in the mean time?" Sullen inaction and war on distasteful but uncontrollable facts were pointless. Rice concluded that what Alabama needed most was good government, and whoever secured that deserved nonpartisan support.[73] Democratic criticism of his defection prompted Rice to write two additional letters to the editor of the Camden newspaper, decrying Democratic and Republican radicalism and repeating his plea for nonpartisan support for good government.[74]

Alexander White of Talladega and Selma followed Rice into the Republican organization after his failure to organize a third force in Alabama politics late in 1868. Before White made any formal declaration of his affiliation with the Republican party, he made several statements that reflected a groping reassessment of his political position. In November, 1868, White expressed his belief that the republican form of government had not failed simply because the Democrats had been defeated in the November election. Rather, the evil to be most dreaded, South and North, was extremism. It was useless, according to White, to point out Alabama's vast undeveloped resources to Northern capitalists and then denounce them as adventurers and carpetbaggers.[75]

After White issued his address "To the Old Union Men" of Alabama in December, he confided to Governor Smith that, although he denied having joined the Republicans to make political capital for his movement, his denial was not in accord with his feelings or his judgment.[76] Shortly, White showed more precisely what was on his mind. He sent Governor Smith a labored and delicately worded inquiry about the possibilities of White's nomination as U.S. district judge should the incumbent, Richard Busteed, resign.[77] Failing to get an appointment to a judicial post himself, White then turned his efforts to obtaining one for his brother. Here again he failed.[78]

In late summer, 1869, White defected to the Republican party, defending his decision as one motivated by reason alone. To him, the Democratic party represented a bygone age and a theory exploded at the cannon's mouth, while the Republicans had received new vigor and life as the result of the war. White realistically noted that the South's wants, such as railroads, internal improvements, and the removal of disabilities, could not be obtained by sending Democrats to a Congress that was two-thirds Republican. White's views strongly resembled those of James L. Alcorn of Mississippi, another prominent antebellum Whig who would soon become a leading Republican in his state.[79]

After the November election, rumors circulated freely about the political intentions of former Governor Lewis E. Parsons, and after the passage of several months Parsons also renounced his Democratic connections. After he had served as provisional governor of Alabama in 1865, the General Assembly elected him U.S. Senator for a six-year term, but Congress refused him a seat. After remaining in Washington for a year, he returned to Alabama to campaign against the 1867 constitution. He led the Alabama delegation to the Democratic National Convention in 1868 and actively campaigned throughout Alabama for Horatio Seymour.[80]

During the spring and summer of 1869, Parsons spoke frequently at gatherings in east Alabama, delivering virtually the same speech on successive occasions. He advised the people to forget their past political differences and to unite in rebuilding their shattered fortunes. Endorsing the course of Governor Smith, he urged Alabamians to free Alabama "from the Carpetbaggers who have been misrepresenting us."[81] Democratic newspapers favorably reported Parsons' bitter denunciations of the carpetbaggers but suspiciously noted he was "painfully silent" about the Democratic party.[82] In September, Parsons ended the speculation when he spoke at Wedowee in Randolph County, home of Governor W. H. Smith. On this occasion he fully endorsed the Republican party, blaming the Democrats for all the evils resulting from the war. Parsons was reported as saying he had "crossed the 'Rubicon' and burned the bridge" after him.[83]

Parsons later candidly testified before a congressional committee about his decision after the Democratic defeat in 1868. He believed that, having voted against the Republican party "as long as it was worth while," it would be better to make terms with the Republicans, work along with them, and in that way acquire their confidence. Parsons saw no point in further opposition to Congressional Reconstruction.[84]

David P. Lewis of Madison County and Alexander McKinstry of Mobile were two other prominent Democrats who became Republicans in 1869. In 1872 Lewis would be elected Republican governor of Alabama and McKinstry, lieutenant governor. Lewis had come to Madison County as a child from Charlotte County, Virginia. A lawyer, Lewis first entered politics in 1861, when he represented Lawrence County in the 1861 constitutional convention and opposed secession. The convention elected him to the Provisional Confederate Congress, but he resigned his seat. Subsequently, he served as judge of the fourth Alabama judicial circuit before fleeing through the Union lines to Nashville in January, 1864. After the war he opened a law practice in Huntsville. Lewis, like Parsons, was a delegate to the Democratic National Convention in 1868. A forty-eight-year-old bachelor, Judge Lewis was described as tall, erect, and robust with well-chiseled features. He was known as a man of firm but not obstructive opinions, learned, and respected as a lawyer.[85] Sometime early in 1869 Lewis quietly joined the Republicans. He remained in the background of these defecting Democrats until he became the Republican gubernatorial nominee in 1872. His public statements in this period repeatedly voiced his disgust that the loyalty of the Union men of 1860 had been unrewarded.[86]

Alexander McKinstry, who was orphaned at an early age, lived with relatives in Mobile, where he found mercantile employment and later read and practiced law. His political experience began with several minor positions in the Mobile area, and he culminated his prewar career as judge of the city of Mobile from 1850 to 1860. McKinstry opposed secession but served in the Confederate army. After the war he represented Mobile in the General Assembly from 1865 to 1870.[87] Like Lewis, McKinstry did not publish his reasons for becoming a Republican, although he did summarize his political views in a statement to a Republican newspaper editor in July, 1869. He favored abandoning old issues and taking new bearings based on present conditions. Alabama had had enough of the bayonet and should rely on the ballot instead. He urged support of the Republican government in Alabama, for to do otherwise would court disaster. After all, he optimistically concluded, "Revolutions never go backwards."[88] These public statements provide anything but complete understanding of why these men became Republicans and raise as many questions as are answered about their motivations.[89]

Nevertheless, the Republican press welcomed these ex-Democrats. The Huntsville *Advocate* interpreted these defections as evidence that the people had "discarded the past; its issues are dead and can't be made alive again. . . . We are ready to strike hands with Douglas men, Bell men and with any and all who will imitate the noble example" of these defecting Democrats.[90] Another Republican paper optimistically predicted that with such prominent men as were joining the Republican party and the aid of the original native Republicans of the state, there was no doubt that "peace and quiet are going to be the order of the day in Alabama."[91]

Republican strategy with these new additions to the party was rumored to be a new effort to gain even further strength for the party. Alexander White was to attack from the "Standpoint of 'Old Line Whiggery,' " in appealing to his former political associates, while Samuel F. Rice was to attack from the "standpoint of 'Old Fashioned Democracy,' " to appeal to Democrats to quit their party.[92] Obviously, Republicans valued these additions to the party and hoped to encourage more Democrats and Conservatives to follow their examples. But the hope was too optimistic. Although one Democratic newspaper declared "bolting seems to be epidemic,"[93] men who had abstained from politics thus far in Reconstruction did not move en masse into the Republican ranks.

In their published statements discussing their political realignment, these men exhibited realistic and perceptive approaches to their own positions and to the needs of Alabama. All of these men—Rice, White, Parsons, Lewis, McKinstry—were large-property holders and wealthy men despite the postwar decline in land values and the loss of their antebellum investments in slaves. They had an important stake in Alabama's economic future. Political leaders of the past, they expected to influence the course of state government again, and to that end they had had their officeholding disabilities removed prior to their affiliation with the Republican party.[94] Perhaps they were opportunists with one eye on their financial futures, but they were also political realists.

CHAPTER 4

THE HORNS OF
A DILEMMA

Hardly had these Republicans grown comfortable with their new political affiliation when they plunged into the party's family squabbles in a determined effort to influence state politics and federal patronage. They found the seeds of dissension already flourishing within the party. The standard complaint of the natives about the division of spoils was developing into what some Democrats called a full-scale "row." Without bothering to evaluate just what portion of state offices they did control, the natives increasingly lamented that the Northern men not only did not divide fairly, but also did not divide at all.[1] A second festering sore within the party was the problem of how to retain its biracial membership.

The scalawags in their new strength directed their first assault to obtain a larger share of offices at the congressional seats to be filled in an August, 1869, election. Ku Klux Klan activity again accelerated, especially in western Alabama and in the Tennessee Valley, signifying that the Democrats intended to fight in the congressional election. Republicans nominated carpetbaggers for Congress in the first and second districts. In the third congressional district scalawag Chester Arthur Bingham of Talladega, then state treasurer, contested the renomination of the carpetbagger incumbent, Major Benjamin W. Norris of Montgomery. Bingham narrowly lost the nomination by two votes in the district convention to scalawag Robert S. Heflin of Randolph County. Norris accused Heflin of being nominated by fraud and threatened to run as an Independent Republican. Subsequently, Norris reconsidered and withdrew, urging all Republicans in the district to support Heflin.[2]

In the fourth district scalawag Charles Hays of Eutaw fought General C. W. Dustan, carpetbagger, for the congressional seat vacated by a carpetbagger. Democrats encouraged this competition between natives and newcomers rather than uniting behind one Democratic nominee. In contrast to the intra-party battle in the fourth district, the fifth district quietly nominated Judge W. J. Haralson, a prominent De Kalb County scalawag, to run against the Democratic nominee.[3]

The sixth congressional district saw even more Republican dissension. There scalawag incumbent Thomas Haughey of Morgan County ran as

Independent Republican against carpetbagger Jerome J. Hinds, the regular Republican nominee and protégé of U.S. Senator George E. Spencer. Charges of theft, bribery, corruption, and perjury flew between the two Republican candidates. On the eve of the election a friend of Hinds shot and killed Haughey as he made a political speech in Courtland.[4]

Republicans won four of the six congressional seats, losing the seats from the fifth and sixth districts. In the fifth district violence and intimidation caused the scalawag loss to a Democrat, while violence and Republican dissension resulted in the victory of a Democrat in the sixth district.[5] Of the six regular Republican nominees for Congress, three were scalawags and two carpetbaggers. Five carpetbaggers and one scalawag had represented Alabama in the preceding Congress. Scalawags had now begun inroads on carpetbagger domination of federal legislative offices.

Simultaneous with the scalawag fight to win additional congressional seats was an attempt to reelect Governor Smith for a second term and to reduce carpetbagger influence in the Republican party in Alabama. At this time the ambitions of the natives clashed with the schemes of Senator George E. Spencer, a carpetbagger elected in 1868 for a four-year term. Originally from New York, Spencer had been secretary to the Iowa Senate in 1856 at the age of twenty and had been admitted to the bar the following year. Spencer came to Alabama as a colonel in the Union army when it occupied north Alabama in 1862. After the war he again practiced law, this time in Decatur, Alabama, and in 1867 was appointed register in bankruptcy for the fourth district of Alabama. His first appearance in state politics was his election as a Republican in July, 1868, to the U.S. Senate for a four-year term.[6]

Hardly was Spencer elected before he initiated plans to manipulate the 1870 election and federal patronage in Alabama to secure his reelection in 1872. If a Democrat could replace Senator Willard Warner, his carpetbagger colleague who faced reelection in 1870, Spencer, who was an intimate of President U. S. Grant, would become the sole dispenser of federal patronage in Alabama. Spencer could use the men for whom he secured appointments and the money they controlled to eliminate any Democratic competition in 1872. The first step was to weaken Governor William H. Smith, who was certain to run for reelection in 1870, in order to elect a Democratic governor and a Democratic legislature who would elect a Democratic U.S. Senator. In this instance Spencer evidenced no scruples about loyalty to either his party or his colleagues.[7]

Smith, meanwhile, was the choice of the native white Republicans to head the state ticket, and they hoped to cement various Republican factions into a solid support for his reelection. When a vacancy occurred in the post of Chancellor of the Middle Division of Alabama, Alexander White suggested to Governor Smith that Charles Turner, a carpetbagger, be appointed to fill the vacancy, because "it would demonstrate to the party throughout the State that when a Northern man was worthy he would receive favor" from the Governor. Such appointments would encourage party unity and harmony in the Republican state convention. Smith heeded White's recommendation and appointed Turner as chancellor.[8]

But the desired unity of the party behind Governor Smith did not come. Smith, aware of Spencer's intrigues, realized Spencer might not only ruin the Governor's political future but also promote among Republicans discord that could threaten their overthrow. The Governor therefore protested to President Grant that some men regarded federal office "as so much stock in trade" to be used to return themselves to Congress. Smith complained that Alabama's representatives in Washington treated his recommendations and those of other Alabama natives with scarcely polite indifference.[9]

A month later the Governor evaluated recent federal appointments in Alabama as being what he had expected, "not likely to give a very great degree of satisfaction." Plainly, the appointments had not been made to benefit the public or the Republican party. The only conclusion possible was that the appointments had been controlled in the "interests of a few partisans, for their own selfish purposes."[10] J. J. Giers, a north Alabama Unionist, confirmed Smith's conclusions in a report of a long political discussion with several prominent Alabama carpetbaggers who believed that they had "Genl. Grant in their breeches pocket."[11] Dissension reached such a height in late 1869 that General Swayne observed privately that "only a defeat will slough off the dishonest, and if so I would rather have it now than in the national campaign."[12]

As the election year opened, violence continued in north and west Alabama. The problems of maintenance of order in Alabama, specifically the use of the militia, martial law, and Federal troops were matters on which Republicans widely differed, and this became the major issue between the Spencer and Smith wings of the Republican party in the 1870 campaign. Senator Spencer, like many other carpetbaggers, favored organization of a militia and stationing of Federal troops in Alabama, and he regularly reported to Washington on the turmoil in the state. If additional troops could be dispatched, Spencer hoped they might aid his reelection in 1872.[13] He opened his political war on Governor Smith and Senator Warner with a speech in the Senate, where he pronounced that Republicans held Alabama "by a slender thread" because they were "hampered by weak-kneed officials" in the state.[14] In another speech Spencer described the Alabama Republican party as "afflicted with a masterly inactivity" and the state in a "deplorable" condition politically and socially. To be a Republican was considered a "heinous crime" and freedom of speech or action was nonexistent except in those localities where all residents chanced to be loyal.[15] One of Spencer's associates next attacked the Governor by blaming him "for all the Ku Klux outrages" and with negligence in law enforcement. Spencer himself then denounced Smith as being "criminally derelict and flagrantly wanting in the commonest essentials of his office." These charges were intended to alienate white Unionists and blacks from Smith on the grounds that he had abandoned them to the fury of the Klan.[16]

Governor Smith denounced these accusations against him as an "organized effort on the part of Spencer and others, to strike down every native Southerner" who might oppose their schemes. He acknowledged that there had been many complaints about violence in Alabama, but he disagreed with carpetbaggers who advocated use of martial law and a militia. Frankly, he said, whites too scared to swear an affidavit against Klansmen so that the sheriff could get a warrant and make arrests would not join a militia, and a black militia could not restore peace and order against a white Klan. In the one instance where Smith proposed to organize a militia, he received numerous arguments against the idea, including letters from two men who had earlier been "most frequent in their complaints because militia had not been organized."[17] As for martial law, this could not be invoked under Alabama's constitution except in case of invasion or rebellion. Even then, such power lay with the legislature.[18]

The Governor's method to suppress violence was twofold. He urged harassed citizens to screw up their courage, swear an affidavit, and join a posse to aid the sheriff. He also urged local civil authorities to act more aggressively; get statements to obtain warrants and make arrests; raise a posse and report any who refused to join; call on Federal troops for assistance where necessary. Smith believed that as long as a community tolerated violence without punishing the offenders, so long would the violence worsen.[19]

Governor Smith consistently acted within his constitutional powers as governor and according to the letter of Alabama law as he saw it. He had no power to declare martial law, nor did he ask the legislature to do so. The legislature did authorize the Governor to organize a militia whenever he deemed it necessary, but there was no Unionist stronghold in Alabama equivalent to that in eastern Tennessee or western North Carolina from which to draw a militia, and he refused to organize a black militia for fear of alienating white Republicans. Because he lacked an element from which to recruit an effective militia, Smith was unable to suppress the Klan. In other Southern states where the governors could depend on a sizable Unionist area for a white militia, governors had more aggressive options for success. For example, in Arkansas the governor deliberately exceeded his authority, declared martial law when his state's constitution gave him no such power, organized a militia, and gambled for and won legislative support. Similarly, the governors of North Carolina and Tennessee aggressively restored peace and order after moral appeals failed; both had militia laws and dependable Unionist mountaineers behind them, and both exercised all powers at their disposal.[20] When contrasted with these men, Governor Smith seemed to harassed Alabama Republicans to be abdicating responsibility for their protection. On the other hand, from Smith's point of view, passing the responsibility for maintenance of order back to the local community was the only course open, despite its unpopularity. Unfortunately, Smith was in the middle of a tough campaign for reelection, and he needed more of a politician's touch in 1870 if he would win another term as governor.

A number of prominent scalawags quickly endorsed Smith and his conduct as governor. Samuel F. Rice dismissed the accusations as coming from men who had come to Alabama since 1865 for the sole purpose of acquiring for themselves "loaves and fishes" in the form of offices.[21] Alex White, ex-Democrat, and Thomas M. Peters of Moulton, an associate justice on the Alabama Supreme Court, also rallied to Smith's defense. They assured the Governor of their undiminished confidence in his "integrity as a Republican and in his capacity as a statesman" and expressed disbelief that they should have remained ignorant of the "fabulous and monstrous number of assassinations, had they ever occurred" in Alabama. Spencer's accusations that "union men dare not speak their sentiments in Alabama" amazed them, because as Union men themselves, the assertion did not correspond with their experience or observations.[22]

Differences between the two carpetbagger senators were also obvious, particularly on their views on amnesty and the basis for the Republican party. Senator Willard Warner urged removal of all political disabilities, because he believed that all men had the right to speak, to vote, and to use the press. Nothing was gained by continuing disabilities that more often eliminated Union men than ex-rebels. Warner firmly endorsed black suffrage, but he also believed that the Republican party must establish itself upon a permanent base of white Unionists as well as blacks in order to survive in Alabama beyond Reconstruction. The character of the party must be above reproach if it would be invulnerable to enemy attacks. Republicans were responsible for the conduct of "bad and corrupt men" within their ranks. "It is unavoidable that, in a political revolution, like the one we have had, many such men should come to the surface. Time will cure these defects."[23] In contrast, Spencer favored amnesty only for individuals who could demonstrate "upon a fair exhibit of their acts" that they had been obedient to the laws of the federal government. However, both carpetbagger senators agreed that additional troops were needed in Alabama by the time of the November election.[24]

Alabama Democrats and Conservatives were in almost as much disarray in 1870 as were Alabama Republicans. While publicly ignoring increasing Klan activities in the state, Democrats bitterly argued the question of whether the party should commit itself to solicit the black vote in the upcoming elections or to oppose black suffrage. A majority in the party favored the pragmatic approach of seeking black votes, believing that further criticism of black suffrage was futile championing of a dead issue.[25] They advocated dealing with the times as they found them. "We find negro suffrage and what shall we do with it." Use the black voter or antagonize him? The wisest course for Conservatives would be to show the black man that as a citizen and voter in Alabama his best interests were with the white people whose lands he tilled.[26]

Vocal opponents of the new movement urged instead that the race line be drawn in order that white supremacy be maintained. "Mixing up with negro suffrage" would "drive away ten white votes to every negro vote" it would gain and result in the "mongrelizing" of the Democratic party and principles.[27] Meanwhile, there was ample evidence of growing discontent among black Republicans, discontent that was very tempting to Alabama Democrats. Two black politicians campaigning in the first congressional district repeatedly complained that members of their race had been too long denied the spoils of office.[28] Blacks in Lowndes County asserted their independence from the two warring factions of local Republican politicians and announced their intention to organize and choose their own delegates to the upcoming state Republican convention.[29]

To exploit this black disaffection with the Republican party while not alienating the Conservative whites, one enterprising Democrat recommended that the party support black candidates in black districts and white men in white districts. He urged his party to "rise above prejudice and contempt for the negro, and give him credit as well as we would white men." Above all, he concluded, it was important that the "vote of the colored man should be governed by men to the 'manner born.' "[30]

When the Democratic and Conservative state convention met in Montgomery in September, they nominated for governor Robert Burns Lindsay of Tuscumbia, an advocate of a conciliatory policy toward black suffrage. Born in Scotland in 1824, he graduated from St. Andrew's University before settling in North Carolina. In 1848 he moved to Tuscumbia, where he developed a substantial law practice. He served in both the state house and senate in the 1850s, on the 1860 Douglas electoral ticket, and with Roddy's cavalry during the Civil War. In 1865 he returned again to the state senate. In contrast to the furious debates of the previous months, the convention was quiet, obviously adopting the advice of James Holt Clanton that the less said in the convention, the soonest mended. The Democratic press also moved to soothe troubled political waters by observing that the party had nominated a ticket that could be supported as the best compromise within the party. As for the platform, it was "unreasonable to assume that the platform could please everyone," although it was innocuous enough in its call for economy in government, an end to fraud and corruption, and honesty in elections.[31] Without fanfare the party embarked on a campaign to contest for the black vote with the Republican party, or as R. B. Lindsay later recalled, "to electioneer pretty strongly with the colored people."[32]

As the Republican state convention approached, the Republican press bemoaned the "sad want of unanimity" among leading Republicans.

Dissension must end, and Smith must be renominated if any old Union men were to be held with the party. Division in the Republican ranks now provided Democrats with their best chance of success since the Civil War. Democrats relished a Republican "family quarrel," hopeful that the party would be unable to reconcile differences.[33]

The Republican convention opened in Selma on August 30. The party platform commended Governor Smith's administration, particularly the recent transportation improvements, and endorsed universal amnesty, the removal of all political disabilities, and an efficient public school system. The platform omitted any reference to race or civil rights, a rather glaring omission for a party stereotyped as existing in Alabama on black votes.[34]

In the convention maneuvering, Warner and Smith cooperated against Senator Spencer. Warner proposed to aid Smith for governor in return for Smith's support to reelect Warner to the Senate. The convention, which Warner described as being controlled by his friends along with those of Governor Smith, renominated Smith for a second term as governor.[35] Smith headed a state ticket dominated by native whites but including one carpetbagger for lieutenant governor and one black for secretary of state. The Republican congressional ticket, chosen already in district conventions, included one black, two carpetbaggers, and three scalawags. On the state Republican Executive Committee, however, the scalawags lost ground. In May, 1870, the committee contained fourteen scalawags, seven carpetbaggers, one black, and one unidentified man. The August convention altered the committee so that it was composed of five scalawags, five carpetbaggers, and three blacks.[36] Reconciliation of party differences was surface deep at least; Senator Spencer termed the nominations "unfortunate" but concluded "we must do our best to succeed even with a bad ticket." He anticipated a "terrible fight" and feared the party would be "badly beaten."[37]

The two blacks who received Republican nominations to important offices reflected the contrasting backgrounds of the blacks in the Republican party. Nominated for secretary of state was James T. Rapier of Florence. The son of a wealthy free black businessman, Rapier was tutored privately in Nashville before attending school in Canada for seven years. He studied law, was admitted to the bar, but never practiced. On his return home to Florence in 1865 he became one of the most successful cotton planters in the Tennessee Valley. Benjamin S. Turner of Selma,

nominated for the U.S. House of Representatives from the first congressional district, was raised a slave but received a fair education as a young
man.[38]

Republican nominations of these two blacks were the first important
nominations for office that blacks had received in Alabama. This action
represented an awareness that in order to hold the black vote in the face of
rising Democratic pressure, the spoils of office must be shared with them,
and perhaps it was also compensation for the platform's omission of any
statement especially favorable to blacks. Such concessions were painful
to scalawags who controlled the party convention. Unionist Nicholas
Davis nominated Rapier, although a majority of the native whites vio-
lently opposed his nomination.[39]

Native white Republican reaction to the nomination of Rapier was
swift and vehement. On the floor of the convention scalawag W. J.
Haralson, judge of the fifth judicial circuit of Alabama, predicted that
Rapier's nomination, or that of any other black, would doom the Republican party in north Alabama, so fragmenting it that a tub would be
required to hold the pieces. Before the convention Haralson had said that
campaigning in his county for a black candidate on the state ticket would
require more than his life was worth.[40]

J. McCaleb Wiley, scalawag judge of the eighth judicial circuit of
Alabama, predicted that native whites in southeast Alabama would not
vote for Rapier and said that every day he remained on the ticket cost the
Republicans additional votes. Unless Rapier were taken off, it would be
impossible to stop the avalanche against the Republicans. Personally,
Wiley said, "Instead of saying my prayers every night before going to
bed—I devote about half an hour in cursing the carpetbaggers, Nick
Davis and Rapier—for they must think we are as stupid as they are
corrupt."[41]

Even more appalling than the outraged protests of the scalawags was
the flurry of defections of native white Republicans to the Democratic
party. Many old Union men who had affiliated with the Republicans
announced their defections, and among them were a number of prominent Republicans. Within a week after the Republican convention W. J.
Bibb, former postmaster of Montgomery, published cards in Alabama
newspapers and wrote letters announcing his change in politics because
of the character of the Republican nominees. Shortly, he was followed by
Robert S. Heflin, former Republican congressman from the third district;

Judge Francis Bugbee, former judge of the second judicial circuit of
Alabama; Judge Milton J. Saffold, scalawag judge of the first judicial
circuit of Alabama. All these men had opposed secession and the war.[42]

Milton J. Saffold published a lengthy explanation for his decision. In
the year since he had returned to Alabama from Washington, he had
watched unexpected evils develop from the concentration of the mass of
black voters in one party. Blacks, he pointed out, regarded their votes as
the "most valuable merchandise they possess, for which the polls and
seats in the Legislature are sure marts." Although men of integrity and
ability remained in the Republican party, the overshadowing evil of the
power of the black electorate, "like Aaron's rod, swallows every good
intent of the party." The only possible solution lay in the distribution of
the black voters into two parties where the white element would predomi-
nate in both. But because Saffold saw no prospect of such a distribution,
nor of a remedy for the situation within the party, he preferred to abandon
the Republicans rather than to give unwilling countenance to the party's
present course and nominees.[43]

Alabama Republicans in 1870 faced a crisis if they proposed to
maintain the black vote in the Black Belt and the white voters in north
Alabama. Georgia Republicans had faced a similar political crisis in
1868, and the duplicity they had employed to avoid a party split was
emulated by Governor Smith in Alabama in 1870. Just because a black
had been nominated on the same ticket with Smith did not mean that the
Governor had to canvass with Rapier or even acknowledge him in
speeches in white counties. For instance, when Smith spoke at Ashland in
white Clay County on September 7, he neglected to mention the black
candidate for secretary of state.[44] A few days later when the Governor
spoke at Gadsden in white Etowah County, his speech virtually repeated
that which he had delivered at Ashland.[45]

On the other hand, in black counties Smith demonstrated his awareness
of the important number of votes Rapier could bring to the ticket, and in
such counties as Dallas, Perry, and Marengo in the Black Belt, and
Madison in the Tennessee Valley, he endorsed the entire Republican
ticket. The ploy succeeded until he was trapped at a meeting in Columbiana in white Shelby County. Judge Robert S. Heflin, former scalawag
and now a Democrat, forced Smith to admit that he would vote for Rapier
for secretary of state.[46] Nevertheless, Smith was generally so successful
in running as an independent in north Alabama and so popular with the

white people throughout Alabama that the Democratic Montgomery *Mail* urged its readers not to split their tickets to vote for Smith while voting for the remainder of the Democratic ticket.[47]

White Republicans did not give Rapier a warm reception as he canvassed Alabama. When he spoke in Huntsville in October, 1870, no public notice had been given of the appointment, and the county executive committee was not informed of it.[48] The Attalla *Republican* (Etowah County) and the Opelika *Era* (Lee County) carried at the head of their columns the name of Smith for governor but nowhere the name of Rapier for secretary of state.[49] The Democratic *Independent Monitor* accused J. C. Stanton of offering $10,000 to Rapier if he would resign the ticket, but Rapier refused.[50] The actions of the white Republicans suggest that regardless of what happened to the rest of the ticket, they would bring about the defeat of Rapier, thinking that his fate would deter other blacks from later demanding office.

As if the campaign were not sufficiently complicated, rumors spread that Senator Spencer secretly backed Robert Burns Lindsay, the Democratic gubernatorial nominee, in some north Alabama white counties. Smith announced that Spencer's pretense of public support was "only to enable him to stab me more effectually than if he told the truth of his real opposition to me."[51] Spencer himself disclaimed any active part in the canvass except for members of the legislature. "In close counties I am trying to help my friends for I wish a colleague that will render me some assistance."[52] Stanton, indebted to Governor Smith for his financial cooperation in behalf of the Alabama and Chattanooga Railroad, contributed heavily to the Republican campaign. On election day he marched 900 of his workers to the polls to vote for Smith.[53]

In the election returns the entire Republican ticket ran close together even in the white counties, as apparently few voters split their tickets. Democrats elected their candidates to all state offices except those of governor and treasurer, which the Republican incumbents unsuccessfully disputed. The state house of representatives contained thirty-eight Republicans (including ten scalawags, nine carpetbaggers, and nineteen blacks) and fifty-seven Democrats, while the 1868 legislature had included only three Democrats. The black membership in the house dropped from twenty-seven in 1868 to nineteen in 1870. State senators did not face reelection in 1870 because the senators who had taken office in 1868 were commissioned for four years. The senate continued with one Democrat and thirty-two Republicans, one of whom was a black.[54]

Robert Burns Lindsay arrived in Montgomery on November 19 to begin his administration. Unwilling to surrender Alabama to the Democrats without a fight, Republicans encouraged Governor Smith in a desperate protest that he, not Lindsay, was the lawfully elected governor, claiming that fraudulent election returns had been reported. An injunction prevented R. N. Barr, Republican president of the senate, from opening and counting the returns for governor and treasurer. The returns for lieutenant governor, secretary of state, and attorney general were counted and Democrats declared elected to all three positions.[55]

The new Democratic lieutenant governor was sworn in, and Barr dissolved the joint convention and called the senators to follow him back to their chamber. All followed except Alfred N. Worthy, Democrat from Pike County, and Isaac Sibley, carpetbagger from Marshall County. In their chamber the senate immediately adjourned until Monday; meanwhile, in the house, Speaker John H. Hubbard called the joint convention to order. Seventy-five representatives answered roll call, among them Senators Worthy and Sibley, representing a quorum. Lieutenant Governor Edward H. Moren was escorted to the speaker's stand and sworn in. He then ordered the counting of the vote for governor and treasurer. The Lieutenant Governor announced that Robert Burns Lindsay had defeated William Hugh Smith for governor and J. F. Grant had won over Chester Arthur Bingham for treasurer. Governor-elect Lindsay was sworn into office by the Speaker, and Alabama's period of two simultaneous governors began. Smith refused to concede defeat, claiming that Lindsay had been fraudulently elected and, with Republican Treasurer Bingham, barricaded himself in his office. Smith called in U.S. troops, who took possession of the capitol.[56]

In a series of letters exchanged between Lindsay and Smith on November 28 and 29, Lindsay requested Smith to surrender; Smith refused, saying that he could not because of the court injunction against counting the votes. Lindsay declared there could be no election contest until after the votes had been counted, and Smith agreed to submit if the legality of Lindsay's election could be certified. Lindsay established his offices in the capitol, while Smith asked the legislature to formulate rules for contested elections.[57]

After Smith and Bingham had been barricaded in the Governor's office about two weeks, sustained by food handed in through the windows, the scalawag judge of the second judicial circuit in Alabama, James Q. Smith, an old enemy of Governor Smith, arrived in Montgomery, and a number of Democratic lawyers brought proceedings before Judge Smith to oust Governor Smith. Judge Smith ordered the Governor to appear before him within thirty minutes, and the Governor complied. On the advice of his friends Smith yielded, and Bingham shortly followed him. On December 10, 1870, Lindsay became the twenty-second governor of Alabama.[58]

Representatives to the Forty-second Congress chosen in the 1870 election also reflected the revived Democratic strength in Alabama. Elected were three Democrats and three Republicans, the latter including one scalawag, one carpetbagger, and one black. The preceding Congress had had four Republicans of the six representatives from Alabama. Republican dissension in the third congressional district led to a Democratic victory there, while the Democrats continued their control of the fifth and sixth districts. The Democratic General Assembly chose Democratic Judge George T. Goldthwaite of Montgomery as Alabama's new U.S. Senator. Despite a discreet last-minute endorsement of Senator Warner by no less than President U. S. Grant, Republican legislators split their votes between carpetbagger Senator Warner and scalawag Judge W. J. Haralson, although they did not divide on a strictly carpetbagger versus scalawag line.[59]

The official returns for the 1870 election demonstrate how close the election was. The Democratic Lindsay received 79,670 votes while the Republican Smith received 77,760; the margin of victory was less than 2,000 votes. Particularly illuminating is a consideration of the location of each party's strongest support in terms of black and white counties.[60] From the black counties Lindsay received 34,721, an increase from 30,145 in the 1868 presidential election; Smith received 55,379, an increase from 54,632 in 1868. From the white counties Lindsay received 18,315 votes, an increase from 14,443 in 1868, while Smith received 7,215, an increase from 6,343 in 1868. The increase in the white-county vote for the Democrats can be attributed to white Republican annoyance that the Republican state ticket included a black candidate for secretary of state and to increased registration of Democrats since the relaxation of suffrage regulations. Yet, despite the increase in the white vote for the Democrats, the white counties represented less than one-sixth of the total vote in contrast to the importance of the black counties that contributed over one-half of the total vote in 1870. If the Democratic victory could not be explained in terms of significant support from the white counties, what could explain it?

Republicans were ready with numerous explanations. Senator Spencer blamed Lewis Parsons, Alexander White, and Samuel Rice for having badly advised Governor Smith and Senator Warner, while Horace Greeley of the New York *Tribune* accused Spencer of having schemed the downfall of his colleague and the Republican ticket. The Republican *Alabama State Journal* blamed the defeat of a Republican for U.S. Senator on two Republican legislators representing Republican constituencies who openly voted for Goldthwaite.[61] All of these reasons somewhat explain the Republican disaster in 1870, but U.S. Attorney John A. Minnis hit closer to the mark when he complained that the party was not beaten in a fair count at the ballot box. Rather, violence, intimidation, fraud, and strength of the Ku Klux Klan caused the Republican defeat.[62]

Events in four black counties support these allegations. The Klan had maintained a systematic campaign of terror against Republicans in Greene and Sumter counties for over a year, and ten days before the election Democrats capped the violence with a riot at a Republican rally at Eutaw, the county seat of Greene. The blacks were driven from the courthouse square, and when they rallied and returned, they were stopped by Federal troops who had been stationed in Eutaw months earlier. With violence and intimidation commonplace in west Alabama, it was no surprise that the Democrats carried Greene County in the 1870 gubernatorial election with 1,825 to 1,790 Republican votes, and neighboring Sumter by a vote of 2,055 to 1,438. (See map on page 70.) This vote was a sharp reversal of voting patterns from the 1868 presidential election when Republicans had carried both counties: Greene had cast 2,927 Republican votes to 869 Democratic votes; Sumter had cast 2,516 Republican votes to 1,469 Democratic votes. In eastern Alabama where violence and intimidation was only slightly less prevalent than in west Alabama, Republicans carried Macon and Russell counties by a substantially smaller vote than Republicans had cast in the 1868 presidential election. Russell County went Republican in 1868 by 1,746 votes and in 1870 by 1,428; Macon County went Republican in 1868 by 2,327 and in 1870 by 1,711. Had Republicans won the same vote in 1870 in these four black counties that they had received

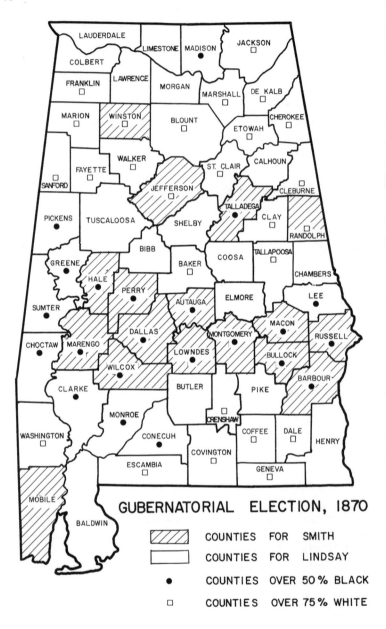

GUBERNATORIAL ELECTION, 1870

	COUNTIES FOR SMITH
	COUNTIES FOR LINDSAY
•	COUNTIES OVER 50% BLACK
□	COUNTIES OVER 75% WHITE

in 1868, they would have had more than the 2,000 votes necessary to win the election.[63]

The Republican disaster in 1870 is best understood as the product of many causes: Spencer's maneuvers to defeat his Republican senatorial colleague; white Republican defections to the Democrats because a black was on the state Republican ticket and because they believed the state government had no concern for their physical protection; Democratic violence and intimidation of white and black voters; fraud in the handling of the election; increased number of Democrats now eligible to vote; and Democratic economic pressures on potential black voters. All of these undoubtedly contributed to the Republican defeat in 1870. But on one explanation Republicans harped with increasing frequency between the elections of 1870 and 1872: defeat resulted from the alienation of the white voters who were repulsed by the nomination of Rapier on the state ticket or by the internal condition of the Republican party. This issue grew into something close to an obsession with Alabama Republicans that overshadowed all plans for future Republican campaigns. And yet the 1870 election returns do not support this belief that the key to the Democratic victory was white county support.

Meanwhile, regardless of the precise reason for the Republican failure in 1870, the meaning of the election for the immediate future of the Republican party and Alabama politics was quite clear: Senator Spencer now exercised sole control over federal patronage for Alabama despite the continued power of the scalawags in the state judiciary and their increased strength in the nominations for state offices. President Grant would need Alabama's electoral vote in 1872 to secure his reelection, and Spencer's reelection would be by the legislature elected in 1872. Grant and Spencer had a common interest in the political management of Alabama. By Smith's defeat Spencer and the national Republican party severed their scalawag obligations. For the immediate future only carpetbaggers would be appointed to federal positions in Alabama. The scalawags had lost this battle in the political war to control state politics and federal patronage for the native white element. But the war was far from concluded.

ECONOMIC AND POLITICAL LABYRINTH

The furor over the gubernatorial race had hardly ended when a new political and economic crisis beset the state. On January 1, 1871, the Alabama and Chattanooga Railroad failed to meet the interest due on its bonds. Republicans explained this default as the result of the railroad's inability to sell its state bonds as required by law at more than ninety cents on the dollar at a time when foreign wars had caused a contraction in the world market.[1] When Governor Lindsay asked the legislature for advice in coping with this emergency, the Republican senate urged him to pay the interest while the Democratic house was unable to decide what to advise.[2] While the house wrangled over the railroad question, some Northern businessmen interpreted this delay as a forecast of Democratic repudiation of the acts of its Republican predecessors.[3]

The General Assembly eventually passed the Steele Act, written by the Governor's brother-in-law. Governor Lindsay was authorized to investigate the Alabama and Chattanooga Railroad, to pay interest only on valid bonds possessed by innocent bona fide holders before January 1, 1871, and to recover the money from the Alabama and Chattanooga Railroad.[4] By early April, Governor Lindsay decided that bona fide owners held all the state bonds and the first four thousand endorsed bonds, and, accordingly, he paid the January interest on these bonds with a loan obtained from Duncan, Sherman, and Company of New York. Subsequently, he paid the interest due in July, 1871, and January, 1872.[5]

Governor Lindsay evidently believed that paying the Alabama and Chattanooga obligations strengthened the state's claim on the company. This idea received a brief setback in June, 1871, when the U.S. district court declared the Alabama and Chattanooga Railroad to be bankrupt. By this time the Republican-controlled railroad had astutely hired former Confederate general and now prominent Democrat John Tyler Morgan to represent the company in Alabama. While appeal of the district court decision was pending, Morgan and Governor Lindsay conferred about railroad matters, and the Governor attempted to persuade the Alabama and Chattanooga to convey its property to the state of Alabama. When these efforts through Morgan failed, Governor Lindsay traveled to New

York with the state's attorney, General James H. Clanton, to try to persuade the company leadership himself but without success. At this point the U.S. circuit court reversed the district court and ruled that the creditor who had sued the Alabama and Chattanooga possessed insufficient claim against the company. However, the trial made clear that anyone with a valid claim could sue the company, and obviously the state of Alabama had a substantial one.[6]

While the Republican-controlled Alabama and Chattanooga Railroad struggled with its financial difficulties, the Democratic-controlled South and North Railroad also floundered. During the Smith administration the South and North had received $2,200,000 in state endorsed bonds.[7] Unfortunately for the South and North, two associates of J. C. Stanton in Chattanooga, V. K. Stevenson and Russell Sage, acquired a majority of these bonds. In 1871 they demanded immediate settlement of the bonds and interest to date or complete transfer of the South and North to the Nashville and Chattanooga Railroad, whose controlling stockholder was V. K. Stevenson. The South and North was rescued from this impending financial disaster by Albert Fink, vice-president and general manager of the L. and N. He put forward a proposition, originated by James W. Sloss, whose Nashville and Decatur Railroad had completed 119 miles of track between the two cities. Both the Nashville and Decatur and the South and North faced ruin if Sage and Stevenson foreclosed on the South and North. To save both roads, Sloss urged that the L. and N. lease the Nashville and Decatur for thirty years, assume the bonds of the South and North, and complete the sixty-six-mile gap remaining from Blount Springs northward to twenty-seven miles below Decatur. The merger of the three roads (the L. and N., the Nashville and Decatur, and the South and North) would create a rail line running from Louisville, Kentucky, to Montgomery, Alabama, where the railroad connections already existed to the Gulf Coast. This proposition coincided with existing interests of L. and N. leaders to develop through traffic, and the directors agreed to this proposal, dating the agreement May 19, 1871.[8] The South and North was financially stabilized. (See map on page 74.)

The Alabama and Chattanooga, however, was not so lucky as the South and North. A few weeks after the L. and N. absorbed the South and North, the Alabama and Chattanooga defaulted on payment of the July interest due its bondholders. Hurrying home from New York when he heard that the circuit court had reversed the district court's decision,

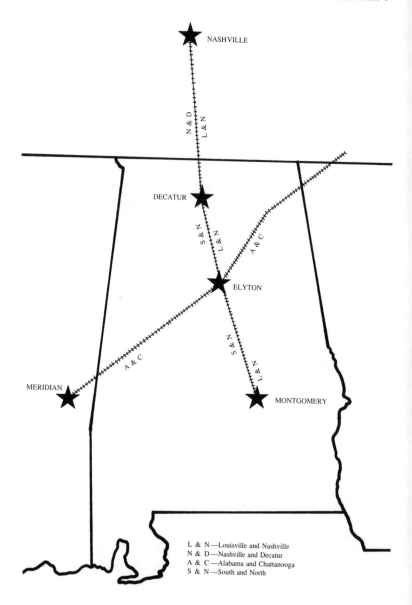

Alabama Railroads, 1871

Governor Lindsay authorized his personal secretary Colonel John H. Gindrat to seize the Alabama and Chattanooga property in Alabama.[9] With the Democratic-controlled South and North secure, Governor Lindsay's move represented a major blow to the rapidly sinking fortunes of the South and North's major competitor in Alabama, and it was not accidental that this declining competitor was controlled by Republicans who had actively aided Lindsay's opponent in the 1870 election.

During the next several months state attorneys successfully won possession of Alabama and Chattanooga property in Mississippi, Georgia, and Tennessee. In September while General Clanton was in Knoxville attending to some of the litigation against the Alabama and Chattanooga company, he became involved in a quarrel with a drunk that ended with the fatal shooting of Clanton.[10] With his death Alabama Democrats lost their most able organizer, one whose talents would be sorely missed in the 1872 elections.

In January, 1872, a house committee earlier created to investigate all railroads that had received state aid made its report. Although Democrats predominated on the committee, the report leveled bipartisan criticism at legislators and governors. The committee found that Republican and Democratic legislators had responded to bribery to enact laws to stimulate railroad construction, while Governor Lindsay had been almost as careless in endorsement of bonds for the Democratic-controlled South and North as former Governor Smith had been in his dealings with the Republican-controlled Alabama and Chattanooga. Both governors were criticized for their negligence in adequate record keeping. Governor Lindsay immediately sent the legislature an elaborate but rather feeble rebuttal to the committee's report, but this effort did nothing to salvage his sagging reputation among his own party.[11]

Two months later federal district Judge Richard Busteed ordered the bankruptcy sale of the Alabama and Chattanooga Railroad at public auction, and on April 21 the state of Alabama bought the company for $312,000. The Governor believed legal title to the company was "indispensible" if the state were to be protected against loss of investments made in the railroad. Thereafter, Governor Lindsay tried to find a suitable purchaser for the railroad, but he encountered considerable difficulty because of two lawsuits against the Alabama and Chattanooga pending in U.S. circuit court, and in May, 1872, the U.S. circuit court turned the railroad over to receivers for the first mortgage bondholders.[12]

The debate over the state's involvement with railroad construction paralyzed the General Assembly during much of Lindsay's administration. Alabama Democrats were torn between the desire to repudiate bonds that aided the Republican-controlled Alabama and Chattanooga and the necessity to protect the state's credit reputation. In the end Governor Lindsay's compromise decision to stand behind some of the questionable bonds and to make three of the interest payments satisfied no one.

Democratic denunciation of the Governor and his legislature mounted steadily through 1871 and 1872. The Governor was attacked as a man who lacked "nerve," "backbone," and the "great mainspring of common sense." Democrats even went so far as to accuse Lindsay of selling out to Stanton and his associates, but there is no evidence to support this accusation. Some Democrats argued that if the Governor could not provide the proper leadership, the General Assembly should have filled the vacuum, but both had proven "unequal to the emergency." The legislature had demonstrated a "hesitancy, a timidity, wholly unworthy of the . . . occasion. They really did *nothing*."[13]

While the Lindsay administration was demonstrating its inability to cope with Reconstruction problems any more efficiently than Republicans, the opposition party began plans for recapturing the state government in 1872. Seemingly, neither Republicans nor Democrats carefully analyzed the 1870 election returns on a county basis, and increasingly both parties focused on the white counties as the balance of power in state politics. The native whites actively encouraged the belief in their importance as a voting bloc, while they continued their complaints that they were denied offices. The issue of removal of political disabilities was more widely discussed than ever. Although able to vote, many Unionists were still denied the right to hold office by the Fourteenth Amendment, and they interpreted the situation as one in which the Republican party sought their votes but was not willing to share offices with them. Meanwhile, "bad men" were "thrust forward to place and power." The *Alabama State Journal* predicted that if the "trash and adventurers were kicked out of the Republican ranks," many old Unionists would leave the Democrats. These discussions overlooked the significant number of nominations and offices the scalawags had already gained.[14]

However, having agreed that the party needed the support of north Alabama Unionists to ensure future victory, Republicans then indulged in two bitter squabbles over distribution of federal patronage where scalawag officeholders were ousted for carpetbaggers. Trouble erupted first in the Mobile post office in May, 1871, when Senator Spencer maneuvered the replacement of Frederick G. Bromberg with George L. Putnam as postmaster, despite numerous protests to President Grant about Putnam's appointment. Earlier, a committee appointed by the state senate had found Putnam guilty of misappropriating Mobile County school money while he was county school superintendent.[15]

Critical reaction was swift. One Montgomery resident feared such an appointment would ruin the Republicans in 1872. The party had just begun to recruit Unionists who had remained Democrats because of their disgust with Republican officeholders. This appointment would drive away these men as well as others who had heretofore voted Republican.[16] The U.S. Attorney for the Northern District of Alabama assessed this appointment as doing the Republicans "incalculable damage" and predicted that a few more such appointments and the party would be "prostrate" in Alabama.[17] Eventually, the protests led to Putnam's replacement in March, 1872, by Mobile scalawag John J. Moulton.[18]

In June, 1871, a second patronage battle, which had been brewing for two months, erupted in the Mobile customhouse. In April, Senator Spencer had written to Benjamin F. Butler, influential member of the U.S. House of Representatives, that unless a change was made in the collector of customs at Mobile, there would be no Republican party in Alabama. Spencer denounced the present management of the collectorship under Unionist William Miller as a "source of great weakness to the Republican party" and urged the appointment of Timothy Pearson, a carpetbagger who had resided in Alabama for only five years. Butler subsequently recommended Pearson to Secretary of the Treasury George Boutwell.[19] While rumors circulated of the impending replacement of Miller as collector, Miller complained to Boutwell that Senator Spencer was insisting upon a number of changes in the employees of the customhouse because several men had not acted or voted with the Republican party. Miller wished no personnel changes because his employees were efficient and well qualified.[20]

However, when a change was made in the collectorship in July, ex-Senator Willard Warner was nominated to replace Miller, and the patronage fight blazed anew. Warner's nomination came through his influence with certain Northern senators and over the protests of Spencer, who, Warner charged, opposed him from "personal malice."[21] Congress was between sessions at this time, and during this recess Warner actively campaigned for his confirmation, while Spencer worked frantically to prevent it. Spencer wrote to President Grant that all but one of the Republican congressional delegation from Alabama opposed Warner's appointment and suggested that Grant "reconcile all conflicts" by appointing Robert S. Heflin, a former Republican congressman and scalawag, to the post instead. Then Warner could be offered a mission to Venezuela or the governorship of New Mexico, and either post should "suffice a moderate ambition."[22] Because the Mobile *Republican* gave Warner much favorable publicity, Spencer's supporters established a new Republican paper in Mobile called the *Herald*. This publication was devoted almost entirely to attacks on Warner and former Governor W. H. Smith, whom the *Herald* described as men who had "shaped the coffin" of the Republican party in Alabama.[23]

Because Congress was in adjournment from May 27, 1871, to December 4, 1871, no immediate action was taken on Warner's nomination. Meanwhile, Warner performed the duties of collector without official Senate confirmation. Confident by November that he could prevent confirmation, Spencer boasted that now he had "everything his own way" in Alabama and that he would "run the machine with an iron rule." Finally, when Congress convened in January, 1872, Spencer successfully pressured President Grant to withdraw the nomination and to offer Warner the position of governor of New Mexico, which Warner indignantly refused. Meanwhile, rumors circulated that the former collector, William Miller, would be reinstated.[24] The *Alabama State Journal* lamented the turmoil surrounding Warner's nomination and the "great dissatisfaction" caused by the neglect of Alabama Unionists. The *Journal* endorsed the idea of Miller's reinstatement or the appointment of some other Unionist.[25]

The Republicans were not the only party in which the Unionists felt neglected. Conservative Democrats complained that they were weary of the "yoke" the Bourbon Democracy placed upon their necks, and although the party was officially the "Democratic and Conservative Party," the Democrats always managed to keep their "conservatism under" and allowed them no influence in party politics.[26] Many conservatives voted with the Democrats only out of disapproval of the Republican party's punitive legislation in Congress. In short, they were tired of being the "conservative tail on the Democratic kite."[27]

The frustration and discontent within the two political parties in Alabama provided an excellent opportunity for a political realignment in the spring of 1872, when a revulsion against the corruption of the Grant administration provoked interest in a new national political organization called the Liberal Republican Movement. The movement was initiated in Alabama in the spring of 1872 by the nephew of the late Confederate General Sterling Price of Missouri, Thomas H. Price, who had come to Mobile in 1865. Now a prominent Mobile lawyer, Price approached scalawag Frederick G. Bromberg, Republican state senator and a known liberal Republican, to organize support in Alabama for Horace Greeley, and Bromberg agreed to Price's request. Price gave Bromberg two or three hundred dollars with which to travel and interview some prominent Republicans sympathetic with the liberal movement. Meanwhile, Price himself toured the state contacting prominent Alabamians and soliciting the support of the editors of influential Democratic papers such as Robert Tyler of the Montgomery *Advertiser* and John Forsyth of the Mobile *Register*.[28] Other Liberal Republicans in Alabama endorsed the actions of Price and Bromberg, because they agreed that bipartisan support of the best men of all old political parties was essential for the success of the new movement. Otherwise, commented one north Alabamian, they might "as well hang out the banner of the lost cause."[29]

Regular Republicans at first dismissed the liberal movement as unimportant in Alabama. Robert W. Healy, chairman of the state Republican Executive Committee, admitted that there had been complaints recently about "unfortunate" removals from and appointments to federal offices, but Healy saw no general disposition to desert the party. However, a month later Healy expressed the belief that he had underestimated the strength of the Liberal Republican Movement among north Alabama native whites. The one comfort that remained was the coolness toward Greeley exhibited in south Alabama.[30]

Meanwhile, Alabama Democrats now considered the record of Governor Robert B. Lindsay to be a political liability, and the party decided that its "best policy" was "to let him depart in peace."[31] In Lindsay's place the Democrats nominated for governor Thomas Hord Herndon of Mobile, an outspoken secessionist in 1861. Born at Erie, site in Hale County, Herndon graduated from the University of Alabama and received his law degree from Harvard. After practicing briefly in the western Alabama Black Belt he moved in 1853 to Mobile. He served in the state house of representatives, the 1861 constitutional convention, and the Confederate army.[32] The other Democratic nominees were also ex-secessionists, much to the dismay of conservative Democrats, some of whom regarded the nominations as evidence that moderates who had voted Democratic since 1865 were being cast aside and extreme men promoted. Others feared the ticket would alienate black voters.[33] This latter concern reflected the silent assumption that Democrats intended to solicit the black vote in 1872, and conspicuously missing at this time was the customary party quarrel about the wisdom of this course.

The convention endorsed law and order in Alabama and urged citizens to obey even objectionable laws until repealed or declared unconstitutional. The party denounced the stationing of troops in the state under the "pretense of protecting the freedom of elections."[34]

The month after the state Democratic party made its nominations the Democratic National Convention endorsed Horace Greeley, nominated by the Liberal Republicans in May. Among Liberal Republicans, men such as Samuel F. Rice campaigned vigorously for Greeley but refused to endorse the spirit of "ultraism" exhibited in the state Democratic nominations.[35] Willard Warner, another Liberal Republican, denounced the Democratic state nominations as a "great hindrance to the progress of liberalism in this state" and as a "straight Ku-Klux" ticket. Warner warned that unless some change was made, Greeley was in danger of losing Alabama because the state and presidential elections were on one ballot.[36]

In contrast to the divisiveness of Liberal Republicans and Democrats, exceptional unity prevailed at the Republican convention in Montgomery in August, 1872. Before the convention opened, the party leaders agreed that for the sake of Republican success and to "take the wind out of the sails" of the opposition, the state ticket would be composed entirely of native Unionists. The "lion's share" of offices—governor, secretary of state, treasurer—would go to north Alabamians, whom the Democratic state convention had ignored.[37] Therefore, the 1872 Republican convention found the scalawags at their zenith in influence in the Republican party in Alabama. Leading the ticket as Republican gubernatorial nominee was Unionist David P. Lewis of Huntsville, an ex-Democrat who had joined the Republicans after the 1868 presidential election. In the intervening years Lewis had not been actively embroiled in Republican party quarrels and had publicly said little except for occasional but vitriolic outbursts of rage at Republican neglect of the Unionists. As a man who had few enemies among Republicans or Democrats in 1872, he was the most desirable candidate among the scalawags in the Republican party.

Scalawag power in the Republican party was also reflected in the other nominations for elected offices, in the revised membership of the state Executive Committee, and in the nominations for presidential electors. All of Lewis' colleagues on the 1872 ticket were native white Southerners except for one man who had lived in Alabama for over thirty years. Of the six regular Republican congressional nominees, two scalawags were nominated by the state at large, while district conventions nominated two blacks and two scalawags. No Republican nominees were chosen in the fifth and sixth congressional districts. The convention revised the state Executive Committee to consist of six scalawags, four carpetbaggers, and three unidentified men. They also chose as presidential electors seven scalawags and three carpetbaggers.[38]

The convention endorsed support for internal improvements and public education and urged that Congress enforce with appropriate legislation the rights guaranteed by the Fourteenth and Fifteenth Amendments. Such deliberately vague statements were calculated not to offend the party's scalawags or blacks.[39]

Thus, by August, 1872, Alabama Republicans had made important strides toward the two objectives believed essential for the party's success: the support of the conservatives of 1860 and an end to party factionalism. Republicans praised the ticket as one that gave unusual satisfaction and united Alabama Republicans for the first time in three years. The Republican press commended Senator Spencer for "nobly lending his influence" to end party dissension. Spencer had come to terms with some of his former enemies among the scalawags and expected their aid in his bid for reelection to the Senate in return for his support for the scalawag-dominated state ticket.[40] This bargain did not escape criticism. One scalawag lamented that the Republicans could not use the best material they had, because to run for the legislature, a man must favor certain interests for Senator.[41] Despite this surface unity, Republican harmony had not suddenly become total and utopian, for, as the chairman of the state Executive Committee wrote to the secretary of the National Republican Committee, complaints were still being made against every member of the party except the individual complaining.[42]

Alabama Republicans believed that this ticket would attract the Douglas and Bell men of 1860, many of whom were recently relieved by the Amnesty Act of 1872.[43] Reportedly, thousands of such men were "on the fence" politically. Lewis praised the ticket as an effort to make the party foundations "wider and deeper" because the men who supported the Union in 1860 were the natural allies of the Republicans.[44]

The native whites were confused when faced with two Republican movements, as the actions of several prominent scalawags illustrated. For example, William H. Smith, Alexander White, B. F. Saffold, Lewis E. Parsons, and C. C. Sheats supported Grant and the regular Republicans. In contrast, Joseph C. Bradley and Samuel F. Rice endorsed Greeley and the Republican state ticket, while William Bibb Figures and Frederick G. Bromberg endorsed Greeley and the Democratic state ticket. Thomas Lambert, who had been a delegate to the Liberal Republican convention, rejoined the regular Republicans, who then nominated him for an office on the state ticket.[45]

The 1872 Republican campaign was quiet by comparison with that in 1870, as the party emphasized the necessity of party unity and the attraction of the north Alabama whites. The one dark spot was the shortage of campaign funds. Clearly pressed for money since they had been out of state office for two years, Republicans constantly appealed to the national Republican Committee for financial assistance, and the national secretary finally answered the appeal in the last weeks before the election, although not with as much money as Alabama Republicans desired.[46] Despite pleas for unity, Senator Spencer secretly aided opposition to two scalawag candidates for the legislature, Lewis E. Parsons and Alexander White, because Spencer feared Parsons was a rival for the Senate. Meanwhile, unaware of Spencer's activities, White and Parsons campaigned vigorously for the entire Republican ticket. Especially, they campaigned in north Alabama in an appeal to the old Douglas and Bell men.[47]

The regular Republicans carried Alabama in November, 1872, and the portents of trouble because of the Liberal Republican Movement did not materialize. Certainly, Republicans benefited from Democratic dissatisfaction with the Lindsay administration. The Grant electoral ticket and the entire state ticket were successful. For Congress, Republicans elected their two nominees for representatives at large (both scalawags) and their nominees in the second, third, and fourth districts (two scalawags and one black).[48] Despite their early promise of extensive support in Alabama, the Liberal Republicans carried only the first congressional district, where they elected Frederick G. Bromberg to Congress. As Liberal Republicans had hoped, the nomination of two blacks in the first district (one regular Republican and one bolter) divided the Republican vote and resulted in Bromberg's victory.[49]

Unlike 1870, the Republicans carried Alabama in the 1872 gubernatorial election by a decisive majority. Lewis received 89,020 against Herndon's 78,524, a total of 167,544 voters participating. From the black counties Lewis received 59,409 votes, while Herndon received 33,905. From the white counties Lewis received 9,546 votes while Herndon received 18,402. Although the Republicans increased their vote above the 1870 total by over 10,000 votes, the Democratic vote declined by only 1,100 votes. The Democratic vote in both black and white counties varied little from the 1870 total, while the Republicans added 4,000 votes from black counties and 2,000 votes from white counties to their 1870 totals. In 1872 the Republicans carried six of twenty-five white counties; in 1870 they had won only three.[50] (See map on page 84.)

A number of conclusions may be drawn from these returns. Although the Republicans increased their votes in the white counties and carried more counties in 1872 than in 1870, this area again represented only a small part of the total vote, about 10 percent. Probably, the new Republican voters in the white counties were the much-discussed conservatives of 1860 who had abstained from politics since 1865. Far more significant was the vote of the black counties, which represented 55 percent of the total vote. Again in 1872 as in 1870, the white counties should not be credited as the margin of victory in the Alabama gubernatorial campaign. If any one voting area should be noted as responsible for the Republican victory, the black counties are it. The Republicans did not win a majority of the votes in the white counties in either 1870 or 1872. In 1872, a tendency only suggested in 1870 became pronounced: the Republican party in Alabama was one dominated by whites, especially Southern whites, and sustained by black voters.

Republican success was not so clear in the General Assembly because the representation of two Black Belt counties, Barbour and Marengo, comprising two senators and six representatives, was in dispute.[51] Rather than participate in a legislature that would be Democratic, a carpetbagger

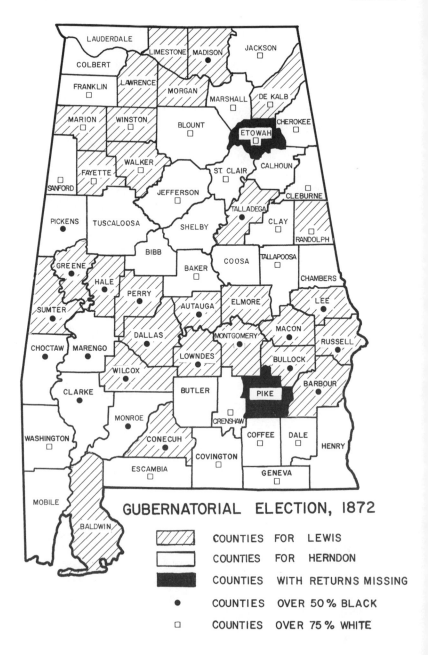

GUBERNATORIAL ELECTION, 1872

▨ COUNTIES FOR LEWIS

☐ COUNTIES FOR HERNDON

■ COUNTIES WITH RETURNS MISSING

● COUNTIES OVER 50% BLACK

☐ COUNTIES OVER 75% WHITE

suggested that the Republican legislators organize separately from the Democrats, request Federal troops, and await recognition of this legislature by the new governor whose election was unquestioned. The law on this matter required only that the legislature meet ''at'' the capitol, not ''in'' it. Accordingly, on November 18, 1872, Republicans organized at the federal courthouse, while Democrats met at the state capitol, each body claiming a working majority.[52]

Governor Lewis recognized the ''courthouse'' legislature on November 29 and requested that Federal troops be dispatched to Montgomery. That same day a caucus of the Republican legislators nominated Spencer for the Senate, and on December 3 the ''courthouse'' legislature officially elected him to office. Meanwhile, Democrats continued in possession of the legislative chambers at the state capitol.[53]

The Governor eventually sent three prominent Alabama Republicans to Washington to explain the legislative situation to President Grant and to ask for his aid in settlement of the dispute.[54] Grant referred the problem to Attorney General George H. Williams, who conferred with the Alabama delegation. This committee urged federal support to sustain the Republican governor and legislature in Alabama. Williams immediately instructed Governor Lewis to allow both bodies of the General Assembly to remain as they were until he could devise a plan of compromise. Later that day he dispatched elaborate directions for a solution, and the General Assembly was organized on these terms on December 17, 1872.[55] These efforts of the Attorney General evoked a poignant response from one scalawag, Lieutenant Governor Alexander McKinstry of Mobile.

> We who are natives of the south have been subjected to an ordeal that persons living among civilized people can form no idea of or even believe. It required rare nerve, bravery, resolution, and self abnegation to be a Republican. We have been & are considered ''Pariah.'' . . . We are about to realize the fruits of suffering & labor. Please let us hold it. We do not ask any interference, but let us be sustained.[56]

As Lieutenant Governor, McKinstry had an opportunity to assist in sustaining the Republicans in Alabama. Through his maneuvers in the reorganization of the two legislatures, the Republicans gained a majority of two in the house, and the Democrats held a majority of one in the senate after the death of a Republican senator in 1873. Republican membership in the house ultimately included fifteen scalawags, six carpetbaggers, twenty-one blacks, and three unidentified men, and in the senate ten scalawags, two carpetbaggers, and five blacks. This fusion legislature then reelected Spencer. His election was aided by scalawag cooperation, particularly that of David P. Lewis, Alexander McKinstry, and William H. Smith. This cooperation was explained in testimony in 1875 before an investigative committee of the Alabama legislature. These scalawags supported Spencer as a political necessity to secure Republican control of the legislature, although he was not their choice for the Senate. If they had not supported Spencer, they feared he would collaborate with the Democrats to secure his election. Therefore, they acted to place party ahead of personal feelings.[57]

After the reorganization of the legislature, the actions of the "courthouse" legislature were legalized on February 28, 1873. Thereafter, Governor Lewis' administration was uneventful in comparison with the turmoil of the administration of the previous Republican governor, W. H. Smith. The almost equal division of the General Assembly between Republicans and Democrats paralyzed legislative action, while the state government hovered near bankruptcy as a result of tremendous expenditures since 1868 and the effects of the Panic of 1873. During this economic depression Governor Lewis had no more luck than his predecessor in his efforts to sell the Alabama and Chattanooga Railroad, and in August, 1874, the U.S. circuit court transferred the company from the receivers to the trustees of the first mortgage bondholders.[58]

The most significant legislative activity during Governor Lewis' administration was one from which he remained entirely aloof: an effort to enact a civil rights bill. On February 2, 1873, L. J. Williams, a black representative from Barbour County, introduced a civil rights bill in the Republican-controlled house, and the bill was referred to the house judiciary committee. The bill forbade racial discrimination on common carriers, in hotels, schools, theaters, and "other places of amusement." Alexander White, scalawag chairman of the judiciary committee, sat on the bill until black legislators moved on the house floor to force committee action. When the committee finally did act, it reported adversely on the original bill and favored a substitute that provided for separate first-class accommodations on common carriers and integrated second-class accommodations. It omitted references to hotels, schools, and places of amusement.[59] After a stormy debate off and on for three weeks, the original bill was defeated on March 10 when the house concurred in the adverse report of the judiciary committee.[60]

Meanwhile in the Democratic-controlled senate on February 19, Jeremiah Haralson, black senator from Dallas County, introduced a civil rights bill similar to that first introduced in the house. After the bill was referred to the senate judiciary committee, the committee quickly reported a substitute which stated that all citizens were entitled to equal accommodations on common carriers and in hotels. This bill passed on April 4, but the legislature adjourned on April 23 without the house acting on the senate bill.[61]

These house and senate debates on the civil rights bills poignantly exposed to the public the private agony of white Republicans over the race issue. They were damned if they endorsed any of these bills and damned if they didn't, and some of the most acrimonious exchanges among Republicans during Reconstruction took place in these debates. When the delaying tactics of Alexander White in the house judiciary committee failed to rid white Republicans of the first civil rights bill introduced, carpetbaggers and scalawags were forced to hedge on the issue in public. Scalawags were more vocal than carpetbaggers with excuses for refusing to endorse the bills, saying that they dared not for fear of alienating north Alabama or that public opinion was not yet "ripe" for such a step and that laws conflicting with public opinion would not be enforced.[62]

Such pussyfooting infuriated black legislators who charged that opposition to civil rights legislation had come from an unexpected quarter—leaders of their own party—while Democrats had remained neutral.[63] The blacks accused those who opposed these bills of being "tender-footed proselytes" who pretended to be Republican only for office or personal profit.[64] Unfortunately for the blacks and their efforts to secure civil rights legislation, they did not utilize the full possibilities of their numbers in the legislature. Although they were not sufficiently strong to ram through legislation, they did possess enough strength to block passage of bills until they won passage of a civil rights bill.

While enjoying Republican discomfiture over the civil rights issue, Democrats were not exercising as much of a "hands off" policy as black Republicans thought. Some influential Democratic legislators, who no more favored these bills than did white Republicans, wanted to cut off amendments and "meet the thing in its most odious form" hoping to defeat the issue on the final vote. They believed that such strategy would

compel Republican Speaker Lewis E. Parsons and Judiciary Committee
Chairman Alexander White ''to take the bill pure et simple which will kill
[them] in the Northern counties or vote against it which will throttle them
in the nigger counties.''[65] Democrats had hit on the unpleasant truth that
Republican political success in Alabama hinged on how well Republicans could play both white ends of the state against the black middle, and
Democrats kept this fact in mind when they planned the 1874 campaign.
Meanwhile Republicans emerged from this battle with the impossible
task of explaining to their constituents the fact that a Republican house
defeated civil rights bills while a Democratic senate passed such a bill.

During Lewis' administration, with no state or national elections
immediately ahead, Republicans made some minor political adjustments
in Alabama, hoping to entrench themselves before the 1874 general
election. Like other Republicans, the Governor was still convinced the
key to victory was support of the north Alabama white conservatives.
Therefore, he attempted to reinforce Republican strength among the
group by appointing a north Alabama Democrat, Robert C. Brickell, to
fill a vacancy on the Alabama Supreme Court. Scalawag E. Woolsey
Peck had resigned as Chief Justice and Associate Justice Thomas M.
Peters, also a scalawag, succeeded Peck. Lewis tendered the appointment to fill the court vacancy to Brickell, if, Lewis wrote, Brickell were
willing to adhere to the late decisions of the present court and ''not play
the part of a bull in a china shop.'' Brickell accepted the appointment
assuring Lewis that he would adjust himself to the laws of the state as the
people of Alabama had already done. Although surprisingly few applications were made to fill this vacancy compared to such occasions during
Governor Smith's administration, some Republicans complained that
such an appointment of a Democrat implied that no Republicans who had
worked for Lewis' election were competent to receive the post. Nine
scalawags were suggested as possible nominees—all well qualified for
the position and all pronounced Republicans.[66]

Having carried Alabama in 1872 much as the result of an impressive
attempt at party unity, Republicans labored to repress any signs of
renewed dissension, and this effort was not entirely successful. One
troublesome matter was federal patronage in Alabama, as Senator
Spencer began fulfilling his promises of office to men who had assisted
him in his reelection to the Senate. He successfully obtained appointments for thirty-seven men who had aided him: the majority were carpet-

baggers, some were scalawags, and only a few were blacks. This disbursement of offices was not surprising, as federal patronage had not been a scalawag stronghold at any time during Reconstruction. However, one recommendation stirred ill feeling among Republicans reminiscent of the 1871 battles over the customhouse and post office in Mobile. Spencer urged the removal of the incumbent collector of internal revenue at Mobile, Unionist John T. Foster, and the appointment of Lou H. Mayer, Kentucky-born newcomer to Alabama and aide to Spencer. Republicans sharply divided on the wisdom of the change. Ultimately, Spencer acquired the appointment for Mayer over the especially vigorous protests of several prominent Alabama scalawags. One of these critics was Alexander White, who observed that the Alabama Republican party could not stand up under a federal policy that displaced natives of Foster's quality for men such as Mayer. For, he bitterly added, the heaviest weight the party had borne in Alabama had been the dissolute officials who in the "turbid convulsions of reconstruction" had crawled or been foisted into positions of power and trust.[67]

On another occasion the scalawags were more successful in securing an important bit of federal patronage for a carpetbagger who had cooperated closely with them. Robert McConnell Reynolds, formerly of Ohio and an eight-year resident of Alabama, replaced scalawag William Miller as collector of customs at Mobile. The change was so vehemently denounced that it was described as "raising the devil" in Alabama. Eventually, the difficulties were resolved when Reynolds received appointment as minister to Bolivia in 1874, and John C. Goodloe, Colbert County scalawag and a Spencer protégé, became collector of customs.[68]

Still another quarrel erupted over the distribution of another form of federal patronage in Alabama—the printing contract. The dispute arose when Alabama Republicans in Congress shifted the patronage for printing from the Montgomery *Alabama State Journal* to the Huntsville *Advocate* and the Selma *Republican*. The reason given for the change was the desire to strengthen needy Republican papers in other parts of the state, since the *Journal* already did the state printing and its editor was state treasurer. This shift of federal patronage out of Montgomery was intended to strengthen Republican appeal to the blacks in central Alabama and the native whites in north Alabama. The idea for the change originated with scalawag Congressman Alexander White of Selma, and the other congressmen received the impression that the *Journal* no longer

wished the contract. The *Journal,* however, did object, and angry complaints went to Alabama's congressmen.[69]

Controversy also swirled around Alabama's notorious carpetbagger
district judge, Richard Busteed of New York, who had frequently been
accused since 1870 of collaboration with Alabama Democrats. One
attempt at impeachment of Judge Busteed, spearheaded by native
Alabamians in 1867, had failed because the House Committee on the
Judiciary took no action. In February, 1874, scalawag Alexander White
presented in Congress new articles of impeachment against Judge Busteed, and rumors circulated that this move was part of a conspiracy of
White, Senator Spencer, ex-Governor Lewis E. Parsons, Congressmen
C. C. Sheats, and Charles Pelham to replace Busteed with Parsons. After
the Judiciary Committee reported the charges for investigation by a
committee of the House, Busteed resigned his office effective December
11, 1874.[70] Although the scalawags succeeded in driving Busteed from
office, they were unable to secure the judgeship for one of their own
number. John Bruce, a native of Scotland who had resided in Alabama
since 1865, received the appointment in 1875.[71]

Since mid-1872 the scalawags had dominated the Republican party in
Alabama. After the 1870 disaster they had steadily strengthened their
position within the leadership of the Republican party encouraging Republican belief that they represented a constituency essential for Republican victory in Alabama. In 1872 they won the state and congressional
ticket, outnumbered carpetbaggers and blacks on the state Republican
Executive Committee and on the presidential electoral ticket. The
number of offices they held was far out of proportion to the number of
votes they brought to the party. Unfortunately, when they finally predominated in Alabama politics, they found themselves powerless in the
face of the state's financial exhaustion and legislative deadlock.

Democrats ridiculed what they termed "fence-straddlers" as being "very scaly" and as developing into that "hideous creature known as a *scaly-wag*." The "fence-straddler" possessed the instincts of the bats in Aesop's fable of the war between the birds and the beasts, always having the disposition to join the party that triumphed in political battle. (Tuscaloosa *Independent Monitor,* July 14, 1868.)

Ridicule of individual scalawags was all too real for Southern white Republicans. (Tuscaloosa *Independent Monitor*, July 21, 1868.)

When the Montgomery *Advertiser* published a series of resolutions disavowing all sympathy with the cartoon of the hanging tree, the *Independent Monitor* cartooned the *Advertiser's* reaction. (Tuscaloosa *Independent Monitor*, September 22, 1868.)

The Nigger-Spangled Banner, or the United States Flag as it is!

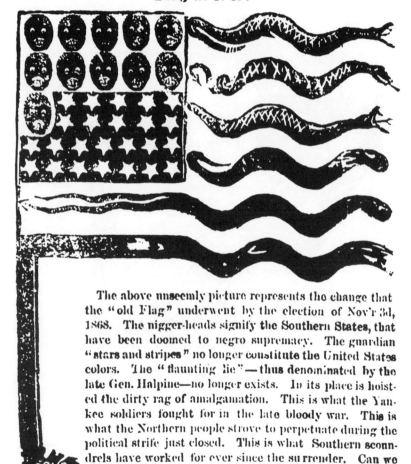

The above unseemly picture represents the change that the "old Flag" underwent by the election of Nov'r 3d, 1868. The nigger-heads signify the Southern States, that have been doomed to negro supremacy. The guardian "stars and stripes" no longer constitute the United States colors. The "flaunting lie"—thus denominated by the late Gen. Halpine—no longer exists. In its place is hoisted the dirty rag of amalgamation. This is what the Yankee soldiers fought for in the late bloody war. This is what the Northern people strove to perpetuate during the political strife just closed. This is what Southern scoundrels have worked for ever since the surrender. Can we ever love such a disgusting piece of bunting? Never.

The rage of Alabama Democrats at the outcome of the November, 1868, presidential election is here graphically depicted. (Tuscaloosa *Independent Monitor*, November 10, 1868.)

Scalawag Alexander McKinstry was ridiculed after a quarrel with General James Holt Clanton and Ryland Randolph. (Tuscaloosa *Independent Monitor*, November 30, 1869.)

This cartoon satirized Alabama's contested legislature, which came into session on November 18, 1872. Lieutenant Governor Alexander McKinstry and Speaker of the House Lewis E. Parsons played important roles in Republican activities in this legislature. (Tuscaloosa *Independent Monitor*, April 24, 1873.)

TOTAL
SHIPWRECK

On the eve of the 1874 election the Unionists' complaints of neglect by both political parties had made considerable impression on Democratic and Republican leaders. Republicans were convinced the key to victory was the support of the white counties to supplement their black voters in central Alabama. Democrats believed they needed the north Alabama whites to supplement their white planter support in central and south Alabama. Unfortunately for both parties, north Alabama white farmers were no more comfortable political bedfellows with either planters or blacks in 1874 than they had been in the late 1860s.

Alabama Democrats drew the battle lines for the coming election in the only way that could submerge the ancient economic, social, and political differences between planters and small farmers. They dropped the new departure idea of soliciting black voters and drew a strict race line as some Conservatives had advocated since 1868. The race issue had been most recently raised in December, 1873, when Charles Sumner had introduced a civil rights bill in the Senate as a supplement to the Civil Rights Act of 1866. The subsequent debate on the bill throughout the remainder of this session of Congress until its adjournment in June, 1874, provided an opportune issue for Democrats in their preparations for the fall assault on the Republicans, and they now settled upon a policy to replace the party's vacillating course since 1868. The sponsors of the bill insisted that it aimed only at ensuring equality of the races before the law. The bill eventually passed the Senate in the amended form but died in the hands of the House Committee on the Judiciary when Congress adjourned.[1]

Despite the defeat of the bill in 1874 Alabama Democrats quickly seized this emotion-charged issue, interpreted the bill as an attempt to legislate social equality of the races, and began to wave the banner of white supremacy as some Democrats had urged their party to do more than five years earlier. "Let us put the election fairly and squarely upon white or black supremacy, or in other words, whether the white man or negro shall govern Alabama," said one Democratic newspaper.[2] The Democrats accused Republicans of having so inflamed the passions and prejudices of the blacks against the whites that it was necessary for the

whites to unite "in self defense and for the preservation of white civilization."[3] The great struggle, as the Democrats saw it, was the race struggle
for political supremacy. No matter how pure the intention of the Republican voter, he was aiding and assisting the black man "to become ruler
and master of the white."[4] Accusing the blacks of voting as a Republican
bloc since their enfranchisement, Democratic whites believed their race
had no alternative but to unite politically also.[5] It was time, the Democrats believed, that it was clearly understood that Alabama was "a white
man's state" and that white men were "resolved at all hazards to rule
it."[6] Besides the emphasis on the race issue, Democrats also campaigned
for a thorough review of the state's financial condition and economy in
state government.[7]

To follow up the initial advantages gained by such racial agitation
designed to attract the north Alabama white vote, the Democrats nominated for governor George Smith Houston, Unionist from Limestone
County. Houston was born in Tennessee in 1811 and moved to Lauderdale County about 1821. After studying law in Harrodsburg, Kentucky,
he was elected to the Alabama legislature in 1832. He soon moved to
Limestone County, where he continued active in local politics until his
election to the U.S. House of Representatives in 1841, where except for
1849–1851, he served until 1861. A Douglas Democrat in 1860, he
opposed secession and retired to his home at Athens, where he "closed
his lips" and was "dead" to the general public for the duration of the
Civil War. In 1865 he was elected to the U.S. Senate but was not seated,
and the following year he was a delegate to the National Union Convention. Since 1866 he had been politically inactive. Houston brought with
him a support in the Tennessee Valley virtually unequaled by any other
Democrat. After the nomination of the rest of the state ticket, one Black
Belt Democratic editor advised that central Alabama be a "point of
assault" in the campaign because the ticket was so conciliatory to the
Northern counties that the Black Belt might seriously object.[8]

Alabama Republicans correctly predicted the coming campaign would
be a "terrible fight."[9] Not only must they withstand Democratic wooing
of white Republicans with the race issue, but also Republican leaders
encountered a growing militance among their black members. A convention of Alabama blacks which met in Montgomery in late June, 1874,
announced their intention to demand for their race first choice of nominations in black counties and a proportional share in others: "A few Federal

government crumbs won't satisfy us any longer,'' these blacks declared. They were now as militant about social equality as they had been earlier about political equality. They endorsed Sumner's civil rights bill then pending in Congress, complaining that they were denied the ''facilities of traveling'' unless they submitted to the most inconvenient and sometimes filthy accommodations while paying the same fare as those who were more favored. They were also denied accommodations in the public inns and eating houses in the country while traveling. They called for an immediate end to these practices. The convention also urged the state legislature to pass a compulsory school bill at its next session. Despite the militancy of the delegates, there was wide disagreement among them on whether or not to endorse mixed schools.[10]

The blacks also attacked the white leaders of the Republican party, especially Congressmen White and Sheats and Governor Lewis. The latter they described as a man of ''utter lack of backbone'' who had betrayed black Republicans into the hands of their enemies. The assault on White and Sheats seems to have been motivated by the desire either to defeat them for reelection and prevent their aid in the efforts to impeach federal district Judge Richard Busteed or to elect Busteed to one of these seats in Congress.[11]

The voice of restraint among the blacks was sounded, however. One black in the convention feared that excessive demands on the matter of civil rights would drive the whites from the Republican party into the arms of the Democrats. ''The idea is to hang on to what we have got [sic] and get all we can.'' A black preacher astutely summarized the situation with this analogy:

> Some men with strong stomachs [sic] would call for their whiskey or brandy straight; others with weaker stomachs, required much water in it. So it is with the members of our party. Some of them can take Civil Rights unmixed already; others with weaker stomachs must take them in a diluted form for while longer. We must wait until their stomachs grow stronger and must do nothing that will drive them off.[12]

Facing this rising militance among black Republicans, the party executive committee, dominated by scalawags, moved to blunt a confrontation in the 1874 Republican Convention. Although Alabama Republicans had grudgingly permitted blacks a larger number of minor offices, they were unwilling to make major concessions to placate blacks as Florida Republicans had done in 1872 to allow blacks a greater voice in the nominating convention. Instead, they ensured white moderate control by gerrymandering representation in the convention despite bitter black protests. Of the 208 delegates the black counties with 58,532 Republican voters received 98 delegates, while the other counties with 31,000 Republican voters received 110 delegates.[13]

The Republican state convention convened in Montgomery on August 20 with moderate whites in firm control. Their opposition coalesced around Judge Richard Busteed, who was thwarted at the convention and was reported to have been "cleaned out" completely, leaving not a "grease spot."[14] Scalawag Lewis E. Parsons presided and also served as chairman of the platform committee that drafted a platform embodying scalawag opinions. After endorsing the civil and political equality of all men, Republicans proclaimed that in the past they had never desired social equality of different individuals or races, and they did not desire it now. The platform refuted the idea that Republicans endorsed integrated schools or accommodations. However, Republicans did ask that advantages be equal. In short, the state Republican hierarchy wanted "no social equality enforced by law."[15]

Republican nominations for the state ticket also reflected scalawag power in the party. David P. Lewis and Alexander McKinstry were renominated to lead the state ticket. Of the six state executive officers nominated, five were scalawags and one was a carpetbagger. In the state judiciary all three nominees for the Alabama Supreme Court were scalawags as were four of the five nominees for chancellors. For the circuit judges the Republicans nominated ten scalawags and one carpetbagger. The convention reorganized the state Executive Committee to include six scalawags, six carpetbaggers, and one black. For congressmen-at-large the state convention renominated the two scalawag incumbents, White and Sheats, although Judge Busteed had been discussed before the convention as a candidate for one of the nominations, probably for White's place.[16]

The other congressmen were nominated in district conventions. In the first congressional district the convention nominated Jeremiah Haralson, a Dallas County ex-slave backed by Busteed, despite the efforts of White and Parsons. Also in the first district Frederick G. Bromberg, former scalawag and Liberal Republican, ran for Congress. Republicans in the second congressional district were seriously split into two factions, and the Democrats worked to encourage this division. The district convention renominated the black incumbent, James T. Rapier, who, in order to secure the nomination, signed a pledge to support one Republican faction in Montgomery County and to vote against Judge Busteed's impeachment. Once nominated, Rapier repudiated the pledge, saying that Busteed's "bullies" had taken forcible control of the district convention and demanded of him a written pledge before they would permit his nomination. Conventions in the third and fourth congressional districts quietly nominated two scalawags, W. H. Betts of Lee County and incumbent Charles Hays of Greene. In the fifth and sixth districts Republicans made no regular nominations.[17] In lieu of a national convention, since 1874 was not a presidential election year, twenty-nine Alabama Republicans joined Republicans from other Southern states in a convention at Chattanooga in October. The Alabama delegation included thirteen scalawags, seven carpetbaggers, two blacks, and five unidentified men. Lewis E. Parsons of Alabama served as president of the convention, which adopted a series of resolutions emphasizing Republican endorsement of civil and political equality of all men, carefully skirting the issue of social equality.[18]

The ensuing campaign was indeed a "life and death struggle in Alabama," and Democrats and Republicans behaved accordingly.[19] The Democrats entered the campaign determined to carry the election at any cost, and they resorted to an Alabama version of what became generally known in the South in this period as the "Mississippi plan": organized intimidation and violence that stopped short of provoking federal intervention. Their general strategy was to drive off white Republicans and destroy the influence of those who remained. Then economic pressures could be supplemented with violence against the virtually leaderless blacks. Social and economic ostracism was applied to white Republicans and extended into churches, schools, and family circles. Where business and social ostracism failed to have the desired effect, the prejudices and fears of the whites were aroused by rumors of blacks arming and drilling.[20]

Simultaneous with the attack on white Republicans, Democrats inaugurated methodical economic reprisals against blacks who were potential Republican voters. Employers fired black laborers, compiled economic "Black Lists" of men who intended to vote Republican, and organized "pledge meetings" where blacks were made to pledge to vote Democratic under threat of dismissal from employment.[21]

Economic pressures were punctuated with violence. Although the Ku Klux Klan no longer officially existed in Alabama, a reign of terror against Republicans developed in the black counties. A prominent Sumter County attorney wrote the editor of the Selma *Southern Argus* in mid-May that there were "secret plans at work" that if kept up would ensure that the Democrats would carry the county by a five-hundred-vote majority. In August local Republicans were chilled by the assassinations of two Republican county leaders, one a black and the other a carpetbagger, who were killed for their political activities.[22]

Elsewhere, armed Democrats broke up Republican political meetings and burned churches where such meetings had been held. They pelted rotten eggs at an associate justice of the Alabama Supreme Court as he made a political speech at the Butler County Courthouse, chased a Republican congressman out of Tuskegee, tried to break up the Republican convention in Barbour County, and so intimidated Republicans in Conecuh County that no Republican meetings could be held.[23] Overall, violence was so widespread that one Republican reported to the U.S. Attorney General that outside the Northern counties of the state "any man may murder a Republican, for political reasons without the slightest reason to fear that he will be punished, but with every reason to believe that he will be applauded."[24]

However, neither were Republicans the essence of integrity. In August, 1874, the U.S. Army moved 225,167 pounds of bacon to Mobile for flood relief along with the Tombigbee, Black Warrior, and Alabama rivers as authorized by Congress earlier that year. Republican Governor David P. Lewis then appointed members of his own party as the local agents to distribute the bacon; in addition, he extended provisions to counties along the Tennessee and Chattahoochee rivers, areas that had not been under water since the days of Noah's Ark. Much confusion resulted. In one area the blacks believed that the bacon had been sent for all and that people who had not been overflowed were as much entitled to government help as those who had been inundated.[25] Before bacon was distributed in one county, Republicans circulated the story that recipients must vote the straight Republican ticket. If they afterwards refused or neglected to vote, they would forfeit their rights under the law. In another county an ingenious Republican politician required applicants for bacon to swear that they had been flooded, and then he charged each man twenty-five cents for witnessing these papers. Each applicant received about two pounds of bacon by this process. Blacks could have bought nearly three pounds for the twenty-five cents they paid the agent.[26]

Race was *the* issue of the 1874 campaign and provoked the largest voter turnout in Alabama during Reconstruction. On November 3 the Democrats won a landslide victory in state executive and judicial offices as well as in the legislature, but not without considerable election-day turmoil. In Mobile and Eufaula serious violence erupted obviously intended by Conservatives to intimidate black Republican voters. In both towns armed white Democrats fired into crowds of black Republican voters, killing one black and wounding four in Mobile and killing two blacks and wounding thirty-five to forty in Eufaula. The remaining blacks fled from the polls in both towns without voting, and the Democrats carried Mobile and Barbour counties.[27]

Nonviolent but irregular methods also discouraged Republican voters. Some polls controlled by Democrats in strong Republican precincts in Russell County closed early in the day or did not open at all. In other areas polls opened briefly but closed before all who were waiting had voted.[28]

In still other counties, Republicans succeeded in voting only to have their ballots destroyed. At Spring Hill near Eufaula a group of Democrats stormed the polling place at dusk, shot out the light, and fired at a Republican manager counting the votes. While he and his sixteen-year-old son crouched behind a store counter in the darkness, the boy was fatally wounded, and the ballot box disappeared with 732 votes, predominately Republican.[29] In Opelika in Lee County the sheriff prepared two ballot boxes. Democrats voted at box one, Republicans at box two. When the Democratic board of supervisors counted the votes, they threw out box two, which one Republican manager claimed contained over 1,200 Republican votes.[30] The election supervisors in Bullock County rejected over 700 ballots, mainly Republican, because the inspectors had not certified the poll lists. The Democrats carried Lee as well as Barbour County, but they lost Bullock to the Republicans.[31]

While many Alabama Republicans faced such voting obstacles, white Georgia Democrats voted freely and sometimes repeatedly in Lee and Russell counties. Georgia involvement in the Alabama election went to the extreme of uniformed city policemen from Columbus, Georgia, guarding the polls at Girard in Russell County.[32]

These tactics of election-day fraud and violence coupled with economic and social pressures during the campaign paid handsome dividends for the Democrats in the 1874 election. In the gubernatorial race Houston won a decisive 107,118 votes against 93,934 for Lewis, a record total of 201,052 voters participating. As in earlier elections the black counties constituted the largest voting block—100,022 voters. From the black counties Houston received 38,429 votes, while Lewis received 61,593. From the white counties Houston received 32,341 votes, while Lewis received 9,895. Democrats increased their votes in every section of the state, but the sharpest increase came in the white counties. Here they gained almost 14,000 votes over their 1872 totals, while the Republican vote in the white counties remained virtually unchanged. The total vote in 1874 increased 33,000 over the total in 1872. Obviously, most of these new voters were whites, who were suddenly provoked to vote in greater numbers than at any previous time during Reconstruction.[33]

The new legislature included thirteen Republicans in the senate (four scalawags, three carpetbaggers, six blacks) and forty Republicans in the house (six scalawags, four carpetbaggers, twenty-seven blacks, and three unidentified Republicans). These thirty-three black Republicans represented the largest group of blacks elected to the legislature during Reconstruction. Earlier legislatures had included twenty-seven blacks in 1868, nineteen in 1870, and twenty-one in 1872. Obviously, in black counties white Republicans were more than ever willing to share the spoils of office in the legislative seats, and this willingness was a measure of their desperation to secure Republican voters in 1874.

Republican majorities in the black counties elected five circuit judges, two chancellors, and two congressmen. Among the circuit judges were one carpetbagger and four scalawags. The chancellors included one scalawag and one carpetbagger, and the congressmen included one scalawag and one black. Democratic success was far greater than in 1870, when Republicans had continued their domination of the state judiciary and elected three of six congressmen.

Although Republicans had repeatedly requested the stationing of Federal troops in the state, the accusation that troops sent to Alabama intimidated voters for the benefit of the Republican party is false. In fact, quite the opposite was true. In several Alabama counties Federal troops abstained from interference in local affairs to the point that Democrats carried some normally Republican counties by fraud, intimidation, and

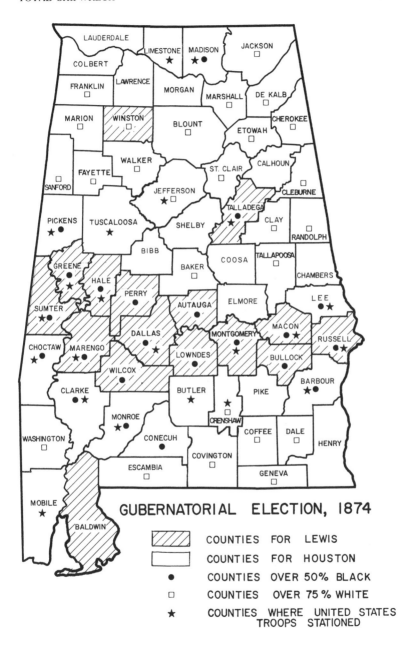

GUBERNATORIAL   ELECTION, 1874

////	COUNTIES FOR LEWIS
☐	COUNTIES FOR HOUSTON
●	COUNTIES OVER 50% BLACK
☐	COUNTIES OVER 75% WHITE
★	COUNTIES WHERE UNITED STATES TROOPS STATIONED

violence. Such conduct resulted from the confusing interpretations of the instructions under which the troops were dispatched. Army instructions stated that troops were to aid U.S. civil officers to enforce writs of the federal courts and that while enforcing one law, troops were not to be allowed to violate others.[34] Along these same lines the U.S. Attorney General instructed his marshals and attorneys that the stationing of troops in Alabama meant "no interference whatever" with "any political or party action not in violation of the law."[35]

On election day officers commanding troops carried out their instructions in different fashions. Some officers followed orders to the letter. For example, in Russell County the officer in charge refused a request from a deputy federal marshal for soldiers to be sent to the courthouse to supervise a crowd at the ballot boxes with the reply that troops were not there "for the purpose of taking part in the election or of regulating the manner in which it shall be conducted." When the rumors circulated that a riot was imminent, he repeated that he could not act except "for and in the execution of the 'Writs of the U.S. Courts.' "[36]

A similar literal interpretation of military orders was followed by officers at Mobile and in Barbour County, where disturbances occurred while troops sat on alert awaiting the appropriate summons from the federal marshal. In Mobile the federal commander dismissed the election-day disturbance in the downtown area as no more than a "drunken brawl" which the local authorities could handle. While he remained ready to comply with all legitimate calls for assistance, he saw nothing to warrant interference in the light of his orders. Only when it was too late did he learn how serious the disturbance in Mobile had been.[37]

In Barbour County the commanding officer anticipated trouble, and the day before the election nervously telegraphed for reassurance from headquarters in Louisville, Kentucky: "owing to the delicate situation here, I have instructed detachment commanders that in case of urgent necessity they may assist Sheriffs as a *posse comitatus.* Am I right?"[38] "No!" stormed the Assistant Adjutant General in reply. "You are not right. . . . You are stationed at Eufaula to aid the U.S. Civil officials to execute processes of the U.S. Courts."[39] On receipt of this telegram on the afternoon of election day the commander in Eufaula wired the lieutenant in charge of a detachment at nearby Spring Hill, where trouble was already brewing, to keep his troops away from the crowd and have nothing whatever to do with local officials. The lieutenant was handed the message in an unsealed envelope. He immediately feared that the message had been read by many before it reached him and that knowledge of its contents would encourage the Democrats, knowing the troops would not interfere.[40] And at nightfall his worse fears materialized in the storming of the polls at Spring Hill. In Eufaula itself there was sporadic shooting sufficient to deter four or five hundred voters, according to one witness. Nevertheless, the federal commander told a deputy U.S. marshal that "if the whole town was burned up, and everybody killed," he could not render any assistance under his orders.[41] In Barbour County at least, Republican observers could justifiably complain that the restraint of the troops represented a "license to the armed mob present to murder at will."[42]

In contrast to the strict reading of orders in some counties, a loose interpretation of military instructions was followed in Opelika. There the commanding officer honored the request of the deputy federal marshals and the Democratic sheriff of Lee County to place troops in the county courthouse to aid civil authorities in preserving the peace. Troops guarded the polls all day and organized voters into lines to facilitate balloting. The federal officer believed a "bloody riot" would have occurred had he and his men not interfered.[43] This effort to preserve order provoked a stinging rebuke from the department commander who admonished the officer that he should have had "nothing to do with the State officers" nor should he have quartered troops in the county courthouse.[44]

A thorough investigation of the election by a congressional committee later concluded that there had been little direct military interference. They found that the troops had studiously avoided mingling with the people and kept away from the polls except in Opelika.[45] These troops about whom such a furor was raised numbered 679; they were scattered at thirty stations in twenty-two Alabama counties on election day.[46] The fact that Republicans carried only nine of these counties reflects how exaggerated the accusations have been of their interference. In general, Republicans, not Democrats, complained about the role the Federal troops assumed during the election in Alabama.

In the postmorten of the election outcome the Republican disaster appeared to be the result of a combination of many causes. The successful agitation of the race issue increased the Democratic vote in the white counties. Intimidation deterred many blacks from voting, and the presence of Federal troops played into the hands of the Democrats, not the Republicans. Outright fraud in counting the ballots and in handling other election mechanics carried many counties for the Democrats, as one participant later confessed.[47] There was also concern that the Republican gubernatorial candidate, David P. Lewis, might resign after the election to become federal district judge after Judge Busteed's resignation became effective. This move would leave as governor Alexander McKinstry, who had opposed secession but also served in the Confederate army and was not overly popular in north Alabama.[48] Bitter dissension within the party and incessant changes of federal appointments had further weakened the party. Also, some Republicans frankly admitted that the party had not been sufficiently careful in the selection of good men for office, and dishonest and incompetent men had "weighed" the party down.[49]

In an effort to salvage something of the Republican party from the wreckage of the 1874 election, one newspaper cheerfully declared the Democratic victory to be a Republican "blessing in disguise" in ridding the party of many who had thrust themselves into leadership for purposes of plunder.[50] Chancellor A. W. Dillard, Sumter County scalawag, echoed this desire to see the party's dead wood "unloaded," and he urged the oftenheard Unionist idea that native white Republicans now be appointed to office. "The time has passed for mealey-mouthedness. When gangrene becomes apparent, prompt remedies are necessary and God knows there has been gangrene here." Native Republicans alone could lay the foundation for a revived party, and it was time to aid the natives in organizing a self-supporting Republican party able to survive without Federal troops and "like appliances." This aid must come by bestowing federal positions on able and honest Republicans and by consulting them—not Northern congressmen—about federal appointments in Alabama. Until native Republicans could control local affairs and influence federal appointments, Southern white men would continue aloof from the Republican party. In short, concluded Dillard, "We must have a new shuffle, a new cut, and a new deal in Alabama, or we must suffer total shipwreck."[51]

While Republicans agonized over their defeat, Democrats did not relax their attacks on the opposition. They renewed economic pressures on the black population and in some areas made good earlier threats to discharge those who voted Republican.[52] Some angry Alabama blacks reacted by meeting in Montgomery on November 11, 1874, to organize an exodus from Alabama to a place where there would be more tolerance of equal rights for all men. They arranged to call a general "Convention of the Colored People of Alabama" to meet in Montgomery on December 1. This convention adopted an address recapitulating the grievances of Alabama blacks, created an "Emigration Society" to plan a colony of black families in the far West, and appointed commissioners to visit Northern cities to lecture on the Alabama situation and to seek financial support.[53]

The few Republicans remaining in office despite the Democratic landslide soon found themselves harassed, too. Democrats undertook a campaign to make it difficult for Republicans to make bond for their offices, expecting the Republicans to resign and leave their positions to Democrats. One particularly absurd bond problem was the case of a scalawag who was elected treasurer of Montgomery County. Because he owned $38,000 in real estate, he expected no trouble about his bond. Once elected, however, he found that men who had promised to be his bondsmen reneged, saying that Democrats had threatened them with economic and social ruin if they went on his bond. Similar instances of Democratic harassment occurred across the state from Barbour, Talladega, and Macon counties west to Hale County.[54]

Republicans in offices that required no bonds also found themselves under attack. While Democrats failed to oust George E. Spencer from his seat in the U.S. Senate, the Democratic legislature successfully challenged the election of some Republican legislators and abolished courts presided over by Republican judges who refused to resign.[55]

Some Republicans wistfully dreamed of rescue via federal intervention to overturn the new Democratic government in Alabama and restore Republicans to power. At the urging of scalawag Representative Charles Hays a congressional investigating committee reviewed the recent election, but as much damaging evidence emerged about the tactics of Republicans as about that of Democrats, and Congress adjourned in March, 1875, without acting on the Alabama question.[56]

Simultaneous with the congressional investigation of the 1874 election, scalawag Representative Alex White introduced in Congress a bill to enforce guarantees contained in earlier civil rights acts. Included in this proposal was an authorization for the President at his discretion to declare four states (including Alabama) in rebellion, to impose martial law, and to suspend *habeas corpus*. White's bill failed to pass, but the import of the proposal was clear: if enacted, the bill could have provided the machinery to overturn the Democratic government in Alabama.[57]

When Congress had not intervened by February, 1875, the Democrats turned to redraw Alabama's congressional districts in order to minimize Republican strength in future congressional elections. Since 1872 the state's eight congressmen had been elected from six districts plus two elected from the state-at-large. Under this arrangement Republicans had won two congressional seats from the Black Belt in 1874 despite the general Democratic landslide. In February, 1875, the Democratic legislature gerrymandered five of the most populous counties into the fourth district so that it was composed entirely of the black counties of Dallas, Hale, Lowndes, Wilcox, Perry. The other black counties of central Alabama were distributed into districts where white voters outnumbered blacks.[58]

The financial problems that had blighted the administrations of Governor Houston's two predecessors remained unsolved in 1874. While the state hovered near bankruptcy, Democrats continued their intra-party quarrel over whether or not to repudiate the Reconstruction debt, especially the Alabama and Chattanooga Railroad bonds. In December, 1874, the legislature authorized the Governor to appoint two commissioners to assist him to investigate the state debt and to suggest a possible compromise. As commissioners Governor Houston appointed T. B. Bethea of Mobile and Levi W. Lawler of Talladega. Although Bethea did not appear as a director or stockholder of any companies affected by the debt question, such was not the case for the other two commissioners. Lawler had been a director of the Selma, Rome, and Dalton Railroad, a competitor of the Alabama and Chattanooga. Governor Houston had been a director of the Nashville and Decatur, an affiliate of the L. and N., and his law partner Luke Pryor had been a director of the South and North, another L. and N. affiliate. After a year of work the commission made its report recommending a complicated adjustment of the debt, which the legislature enacted although the plan completely satisfied no one. Overall, the commission recognized $18,000,000 of the $30,000,000 they cited as the direct state debt and adjusted this $18,000,000 to $12,500,000. Not surprisingly, the bonds of the Republican-controlled Alabama and Chattanooga Railroad, of all of the endorsed railroad bonds, were the most drastically adjusted: $9,000,000 in bonds were exchanged for new bonds totaling $1,000,000 and a half million acres of Alabama mineral lands.[59]

By mid-1875 Democrats felt more secure in office and began agitation for revision of the 1868 Republican-drafted constitution. Privately, one Democrat observed that there was "little to quarrel about in the present constitution" and that the mass of people were not "quarreling about it at all." Such agreement with the opposition was of no benefit to the Democrats, so they clamored that a convention was necessary to implement reforms that had been widely discussed for the last six months, including tax revision, elimination of unnecessary state and county offices, legislative reapportionment, and general economy in the operation of the state government. The legislature shrewdly apportioned delegates to the convention on the basis of the recently gerrymandered congressional districts and called for an election on the question of a constitutional convention for August 3.[60]

Failing to stifle the move for constitutional revision in the legislature, Republican leaders disagreed on what course they should next follow. The state Republican Executive Committee urged Republicans to oppose the proposed convention and make no nominations for delegates. However, the committee encouraged support for any anti-convention independent candidates that entered the race.[61]

The official party stand provoked considerable criticism among Republicans. The most organized protest came from a group of Republicans in the state house of representatives. Led by carpetbagger Datus E. Coon of Iowa, they condemned the recommendations of the party committee as a course that would lead to the complete disintegration of the Republican party. In a bid for Republican control of the convention, they urged nomination and support of Republican delegates to the convention.[62]

One articulate black Republican urged Republican support for a convention of delegates representing "all the people" which would write a new constitution giving his race precisely the same rights and guarantees as in the current constitution. If such a new constitution were written, Alabama blacks would gain the "consent, actual support, good-will and hearty protection of the white men of the State in the free enjoyment of these rights, which to a great extent we now have not."[63]

The strongest Republican newspaper in the state, the Montgomery *Alabama State Journal,* took no side in the argument, saying there had already been too much "bickering" and too much struggling for leadership. As long as this condition continued, predicted the *Journal,* defeat was inevitable.[64]

On August 3, 1875, Alabamians voted to call a constitutional convention. Elected as delegates were eighty Democrats, twelve Republicans, and seven Independents. Most of the Republicans and Independents were elected from the Black Belt, and four of the nineteen were blacks. Seven of the twelve Republicans were scalawags. Despite Democratic control over the convention, the new constitution reflected the mark of Republican Reconstruction because the convention dared not tamper with universal manhood suffrage.[65]

Most of the new features of the 1875 constitution reflected Democratic concern for economic retrenchment. Of particular interest to Republicans seeking a future political comeback in Alabama were the actions of the convention on legislative reapportionment and on election procedures, and on these two areas Republican members of the convention were unable to stifle legislation unfavorable to their party. The convention reapportioned the legislature to increase the representation of the Democratic counties at the expense of the Republican counties of the Black Belt and drafted a clause to require individuals to vote in the beat in which they resided.[66] This latter measure, although seemingly innocuous enough, would prove a great grief to Republican hopes for a revival of their political fortunes in Alabama.

The brief six-week canvass for ratification of the revised constitution further demonstrated the confusion and disorganization of the leadership of the Alabama Republican party. Divided earlier on the question of the call for the convention, Republicans now so disagreed on ratification of the new constitution that the issue had no one official party stand. The opposition to ratification included former Chief Justice of the Alabama Supreme Court Samuel F. Rice who had been a delegate to the convention, former Governor William H. Smith, former Associate Justice of the Alabama Supreme Court Benjamin F. Saffold, U.S. Senator George E. Spencer, former Chancellor Adam Felder, and the Montgomery *Alabama State Journal.* Their general estimate of the constitution was that its many undesirable provisions outweighed the satisfactory features. Nevertheless, some equally prominent Republicans endorsed ratification including former Governors David P. Lewis and Lewis E. Parsons, former Auditor Robert T. Smith, and former U.S. Attorney John A. Minnis.[67] They endorsed the document because it guaranteed equality before the law to all citizens, prohibited the loan of the state's credit for private enterprises, limited the rate of taxation, and its economy measures could save the state $264,550 a year.[68]

In the midst of the campaign for ratification a group of twelve Montgomery County Republicans circulated a demand for the reorganization of the party in the state, especially attacking the state Republican Executive Committee. The Washington, D.C., *National Republican* assessed these men as malcontents who were threatening to disorganize the party and hand the state over to the Democrats.[69] The *Alabama State Journal* urged Alabama Republicans ''to look at things as they actually are, and not as we would have them to be.'' This dissension, if continued, could jeopardize the party in the 1876 elections, for, admonished the *Journal,* ''we have not one single vote to lose, that we are able to quarrel and fight among ourselves.'' If the party genuinely required reform, Republicans could best reform it in a state convention. In the face of such Republican divisions, the Democrats easily ratified the new constitution on November 16.[70] Only four counties voted against it; all were Republican counties in the Black Belt. The Democratic party was now more entrenched in Alabama than at any time since the Civil War.

AT SEA
WITHOUT A RUDDER

Once the election for ratification of the new constitution was over, Republican dissension worsened as the battle for control of the party accelerated, and old political wounds reopened. At this time late in 1875 former Governor W. H. Smith and Senator George E. Spencer ended their period of cooperation with each other. Smith had aided in the effort to return Spencer to the Senate in 1872, and Spencer, once safely reelected, had spent much time in New York and Washington. Smith resented Spencer's leaving to other Republicans the struggle to keep Alabama in the Republican column and accused Spencer of using his official position most often to oppress those who worked hardest for party victories. For the upcoming campaigns in 1876 Spencer proposed that if he were allowed to name the delegates to the Republican National Convention, he would permit Smith to name the state candidates. Smith was indignant at Spencer's presumptuousness, and the battle between the two was again joined.[1]

Late in November another circular addressed to the state Republican Executive Committee appeared. This petition called upon the committee to meet in Montgomery on December 7 with all Republicans who would come to organize for the 1876 campaign. Seven of the twelve signers of the earlier petition supported this request, and they were joined by twenty-three other prominent Republicans, including Samuel F. Rice, William H. Smith, James Q. Smith, B. F. Saffold, J. J. Martin, Benjamin Gardner, John A. Minnis. The group met as announced at noon December 7, in Montgomery. Rice again presided and reiterated that the purpose of the meeting was preparation for the coming campaign and added that the group also intended to equalize the representation of the congressional districts (drawn February 13, 1875) on the state committee. Although not publicly discussed at the time, probably the most important reason for the interest in reorganizing the membership of the state committee was the belief that Senator Spencer controlled a majority of the existing committee because several members were indebted to Spencer for federal jobs. The meeting adopted a motion to enlarge the number of representatives on the committee so that all congressional districts had representation equal to that of the eighth district, which then had three members. Such additions would increase the committee from twelve members to twenty-four. A committee was appointed to present this recommendation to the state Executive Committee, which replied that since a majority of the committee were not present, they could not act. However, the three members of the Executive Committee who were present, carpetbagger J. W. Burke, scalawag N. S. McAfee, and black B. S. Turner, endorsed as individuals a reorganization of the committee according to this recommendation or by some other plan. The meeting then adjourned to convene again on December 29, this time hopefully with the entire state Executive Committee to reorganize the composition of the committee.[2]

On December 21 still another circular appeared, datelined Washington, D.C., and written by Charles E. Mayer, titular chairman of the state Executive Committee who had sold his law books and moved to New York in August, 1875, and Senator George E. Spencer, committee member. In discussing the proposed December 7 meeting, the circular asserted that the committee lacked the authority to reorganize itself. Only a state convention could alter the committee, and the circular recommended the calling of a convention to determine the apportionment of the various counties on the committee.[3]

The reform Republicans reconvened in Montgomery on December 29 with Judge Rice again presiding. Twelve new members were elected to the Republican Executive Committee according to the plan formulated at the December 7 meeting, which reflected the redistricting of Alabama into eight instead of six congressional districts. The Democratic Livingston *Journal* described this action as an attempt to "unload" the federal officeholders from the committee. The Republican Montgomery *Alabama State Journal* replied that all Republicans agreed that the committee needed reorganization. The question was whether the committee could enlarge itself.[4]

The reorganized committee met at noon February 2, 1876, in Montgomery. Roll call showed five of the twelve members of the old committee present along with ten of the twelve new members elected on December 29. Three scalawags were elected as officers: former Governor William H. Smith chairman, N. S. McAfee secretary, Benjamin F.

Saffold treasurer. The other major business conducted was agreement to call a Republican state convention to meet in Montgomery at noon on May 16.[5]

Meanwhile, Charles E. Mayer ran a notice in the Montgomery papers requesting members of the Executive Committee to meet him at a private room in Montgomery's Exchange Hotel. One member of the old committee, scalawag Isaac Heyman, and four other persons claiming to represent absent members by proxies joined Mayer. This group called for a state convention to meet on May 24, 1876, to select candidates for the upcoming elections.[6]

Also in February, a delegation from the Rice-Smith faction of Republicans, as the group had begun to be called, traveled to Washington and called on President Grant, heads of departments, and prominent Republican senators. Their purpose was to protest further exercise of Spencer's authority in controlling appointments in Alabama because he possessed only a small following in the state and that only among those of poor reputation. They also assured federal officials that Alabama public opinion was not hostile to the administration. The delegation returned to Alabama satisfied that Washington officials would not interfere with the controversy within the Alabama Republican party.[7]

The delegation had hardly returned home before it was obvious that Spencer's influence in dispensing federal patronage in the state was undiminished. Spencer obtained the rejection of General R. W. Healy as Marshal for the District of South and Middle Alabama and had George Turner appointed and confirmed in his stead. Although both Healy and Turner had come to Alabama since 1865, Healy supported the Rice-Smith faction while Turner supported Spencer. There were ominous warnings that Spencer, with the U.S. marshal at his back, would prevent any approaching convention from falling into the hands of his opposition.[8]

Through the spring of 1876 while individual Republicans and the Republican press urged compromise of party differences, the two factions vigorously attacked each other instead of the Democrats. Newly confirmed U.S. Marshal George Turner accused Rice of attacking Mayer, Spencer, and the regular committee simply to get control of the committee and then the state convention. The Montgomery *Alabama State Journal* continued to support the Spencer faction.[9] Speaking for the other group, Rice accused the old Executive Committee of waging an "earnest war" against the reorganization, which involved only equalizing committee representation. The eighth district had three representatives; the fifth had none.[10] Former Governor W. H. Smith followed Rice's statement with a form letter dispatched to prominent Republicans in Alabama enlisting their aid in securing county delegations to the May 16 convention. Smith accused his old enemy Spencer of attempting to destroy the "regular organization of the Republican party," meaning that reorganized on December 29, 1875. Also, Smith accused Spencer of efforts to make himself the master, not the servant, of Alabama Republicans. To publicize their views still further, the Rice-Smith faction brought out a weekly newspaper in Montgomery, the *Alabama Republican*.[11]

The anti-Spencer men grew more confident as they sought to capitalize on general public dissatisfaction with the Houston administration in the actions of both the legislature and the governor and the opposition to the pressure tactics of some Democrats determined to renominate Houston for a second term.[12] Former Senator Willard Warner described the movement to Carl Schurz as "well organized" and designed to "clear the deck of the Spencer crowd as preliminary to our progress in putting the ship on the right course."[13]

On March 21, Simon Cameron, chairman of the Republican Congressional Committee, and William E. Chandler, secretary of the Republican National Committee, proposed a compromise to resolve Republican differences in Alabama. They suggested that both existing calls for state conventions be withdrawn and opposing factions set a new date for a joint convention and pledge to abide by its action. On behalf of the Spencer faction Charles E. Mayer announced acceptance of the plan, but former Governor W. H. Smith, speaking for the other faction, dismissed the proposal as a "Spencer trap" to subdue his opposition.[14]

The Rice-Smith faction then met as announced on May 16, 1876, in Montgomery. Former Governor W. H. Smith called the meeting to order, and the convention elected scalawag B. F. Saffold, former associate justice of the Alabama Supreme Court, as chairman. The question of nomination of candidates provoked an angry debate among the delegates. One group led by black Congressman Jeremiah Haralson favored no nominations and adjournment of the convention until after the Spencer faction met on May 24. Republicans could then negotiate their differences, fully aware that they could not carry the state with two tickets in the field. Another group headed by Samuel F. Rice and B. F. Saffold opposed Haralson's suggestions and led the convention in the nomination of a state ticket. Most of the men on the ticket were not well known in Republican circles in Alabama except for the nominee for governor, Thomas M. Peters, Lawrence County Unionist and former associate justice on the Alabama Supreme Court. This state ticket also included five scalawags and one carpetbagger.[15]

The convention also chose delegates to the Republican National Convention to meet June 14 at Cincinnati. Delegates for the state-at-large were carpetbagger Willard Warner, scalawags Samuel F. Rice and W. H. Smith, and black Jeremiah Haralson. The delegates elected by districts included six scalawags, five carpetbaggers, four blacks, and one unidentified man.[16]

On May 24 the Spencer wing of the Republican party convened in Montgomery in the chambers of the state house of representatives, and chose Judge Robert S. Heflin, Randolph County scalawag and former congressman, as chairman. Scalawag Alexander White of Dallas County led the platform committee that drafted an endorsement of civil and political equality of all men, free public schools, and stimulation of labor and industry. The platform also deplored party division in Alabama as endangering the party's existence in the state. As the May 16 convention had done, this group nominated a ticket of men little known in Alabama politics. Leading the ticket was Judge James S. Clarke, Morgan County scalawag, as the nominee for governor. The only well-known figure on the ticket was the nominee for attorney general, Judge R. S. Heflin, then presiding officer of the convention. All six of the men on the ticket were scalawags.[17]

The convention also elected delegates to the Republican National Convention. Delegates from the state-at-large were carpetbagger George E. Spencer, scalawags Alexander White and Charles Hays, and black A. H. Curtis. The delegates elected by district included seven scalawags, five carpetbaggers, three blacks, and four unidentified men.[18]

After both conventions had met and nominated candidates, one former Alabama Republican, now residing in Kansas, referred to the Rice-Smith convention as that of the ''native wing'' of the Alabama Republican party.[19] This assessment was inaccurate as prominent scalawags were active in each convention. One of the most intriguing sidelights of the two conventions was the participation of Lewis E. Parsons in the May 16 convention while his former law partner and close friend Alexander

White attended the May 24 convention. Contemporary correspondence and newspapers shed no light on this unexplained split in the usual cooperation of two friends of long standing.

The Republican National Convention meeting in Cincinnati seated the delegates from the Rice-Smith faction in Alabama.[20] Alexander White charged that this recognition of the delegates from the May 16 convention was the result of a bargain with the supporters of James G. Blaine.[21] In the face of such continued recriminations among Alabama Republicans, the Montgomery *Alabama State Journal* warned that Republicans had not a "ghost of a chance" to carry the state under the party's present condition.[22]

George Spencer was not in the least daunted by this setback at Cincinnati. One newspaper compared the situation to the Civil War campaigns around Chattanooga. It appeared that while the Rice-Smith wing had won a Chickamauga victory at Cincinnati, Spencer had struck back with a Missionary Ridge. Knowing that the sinews of war in the Republican party were money and official patronage, Spencer promoted Zachariah Chandler for chairman of the National Republican Committee and the replacement of Marshall Jewell as Postmaster General with James N. Tyner, brother-in-law of Spencer's protégé Jerome J. Hinds. Spencer expected money from Chandler to oil the Republican machinery in Alabama and free use of official patronage in the post office in the state.[23]

Having secured these strategic points, Spencer had Charles E. Mayer address a conciliatory note to W. H. Smith proposing that the two committees meet and arrange a merger into a single body that would be acceptable to the entire party. Then the fusion committee should prepare state and electoral tickets to be substituted for the two nominated in May. The Rice-Smith wing, enjoying the recent recognition of the Cincinnati Convention and unaware of Spencer's flanking maneuvers, indignantly rejected the overture for compromise. The rejection noted that the 1874 Republican state convention had not chosen Mayer as chairman of the state Executive Committee or even as a member of the committee. Mayer had become chairman only after D. C. Whiting resigned because of ill health. The Rice-Smith faction contended that if the committee had the power to add Mayer as chairman, the committee had the power to add twelve new members.[24]

On July 10 the executive committee of the Spencer faction met in Montgomery. James S. Clarke withdrew from the gubernatorial race, and the committee replaced Clarke with another north Alabama scalawag,

C. C. Sheats. Since the Rice-Smith faction had refused all compromise efforts, the committee resolved to make a thorough canvass for the ticket nominated at the May 24 convention with Sheats leading the ticket.[25]

A few weeks later when members of the Rice-Smith faction approached Zachariah Chandler for campaign funds, Chandler flatly replied that unless Alabama Republicans united behind one ticket, he would not give them one cent. The Rice-Smith faction then quietly accepted Mayer's proposal for the withdrawal of both tickets and the substitution of a compromise "independent" ticket.[26] This ticket consisted entirely of men little known in Alabama politics; five were old residents of Alabama and one was a newcomer. Heading the ticket was Noadiah Woodruff, prosperous cotton factor and planter who was mayor of Selma.[27] One Democrat, evaluating the Republican nominations, described Woodruff as a "small potato" who was "hardly worth the powder" to destroy. However, illustrating that Republican defeat was not inevitable in 1876, this same Democrat added that if the Republicans had nominated another man, "say a man like Patton," Governor Houston's reelection would have been "extremely doubtful." Republicans also produced a fusion electoral ticket of eight scalawags, one carpetbagger, and one black.[28] The party endorsed support for public schools, encouragement to capital and labor to migrate to Alabama, and civil and political equality of all men.[29]

While Alabama Republicans were in a turmoil, Alabama Democrats calmly nominated Governor Houston for a second term. Their platform attacked the Republicans as being unworthy of public confidence while portraying themselves as the party of law and progress. They noted with pleasure that the "more intelligent and better class" of blacks were "awakening to the fact that their best friends were the white people of Alabama."[30]

During the campaign Republicans did not exert themselves on behalf of the compromise ticket. Among prominent Republicans only Samuel F. Rice stumped the state, spending his own money in behalf of the Republican ticket. To no one's surprise, Woodruff and the Independent ticket were beaten, as he received only 55,586 votes to Houston's 95,837. The total vote declined from a high of 201,052 in 1874 to 151,423 in 1876, and this decrease was evident in all areas of the state. The Black Belt, heavily Republican in 1874, divided its votes rather evenly between the two parties in 1876, giving the Democrats 36,544 votes and the Republicans 34,295. The white counties in 1876 gave 29,011 votes to the Democrats and 6,522 votes to the Republicans.[31] Republican strength in the legislature also dramatically declined from fifty-three members in 1874 to twenty-two in 1876. This included eighteen Republicans (five scalawags, one carpetbagger, seven blacks, and five unidentified men) in the house and four Republicans (three scalawags and one carpetbagger) in the senate.[32]

In the weeks after the August election the district conventions met to nominate candidates for Congress. In the first district the Republican convention endorsed scalawag Frederick G. Bromberg of Mobile. Bromberg had represented the district in Congress from 1873 to 1875 and had unsuccessfully contested the election of black Jeremiah Haralson of Selma in 1874. After the district convention adjourned, a dissident faction of the party reconvened and nominated Mobile carpetbagger W. W. D. Turner as the Republican Independent candidate.[33] The convention of the second congressional district nominated scalawag Gerald B. Hall of Baldwin County; the third district nominated scalawag W. H. Betts of Opelika, unsuccessful candidate from that district in 1874.[34] The convention of the fourth district saw two blacks battle for the nomination: Congressman Jeremiah Haralson of Selma, the incumbent from the old first district, versus James T. Rapier of Montgomery, former congressman from the old second district. Rapier won the nomination after a bitter fight in the convention, although neither contestant resided in the fourth district.[35] This fight reopened old party wounds, as Senator Spencer sponsored Rapier and the Rice-Smith faction supported Haralson. In the fifth district the convention nominated Daniel B. Booth of Autauga County, while Republicans in the sixth, seventh, and eighth districts made no nominations.[36] Bromberg and Rapier were the only prominent Republicans among these nominees.

The November, 1876, election was another overwhelming defeat for the Republicans; they were swept from the few offices they had retained in 1874, and the Republican fusion electoral ticket was also defeated. The only remaining Republican influence in the state was in the judiciary among those judges elected in 1874 whose terms extended until 1880.[37]

As in earlier elections, Republicans accused the Democrats of carrying the state by fraud, and Senator Spencer vainly called for a congressional investigation.[38] There was considerable substance to Republican complaints. In the black counties Republicans won 61,593 votes in 1874 but dropped to only 34,295 in 1876. Meanwhile, the Democratic vote in the black counties in these two elections changed little: 38,429 in 1874 and 36,544 in 1876. Part of the explanation for the dramatic decline in Republican votes in 1876, while the Democrats showed only a small loss, lay in Democratic manipulation of the seemingly innocuous provision of the 1875 constitution requiring individuals to vote in the beat in which they resided. Since Democrats controlled the state government, they were able to appoint their strongest partisans as election managers. In the August and November elections many election officials simply failed to open the polls, and others announced that they were not going to sit at these places all day to allow blacks to make "radical majorities." The refusal of election officials to open polls in Republican precincts in Hale, Perry, Marengo, Bullock, Barbour, Greene, Pickens, Wilcox, and Sumter counties was deemed as effective in destroying Republican strength as the earlier actions of the Ku Klux Klan, and it involved no bloodshed. Elsewhere, polls opened briefly and closed at the whim of election officials, while other polling places were moved several times during election day.[39] By these methods the Democrats successfully minimized the black Republican vote, and the elections of 1876 ratified the Republican defeat of 1874.

In future elections, when Republicans did run for office they usually allied with the Greenback movement under the "Independent" label. This course caused Democrats to fear that their opposition was only playing "possum" or "playing dead."[40] Democrats really need not have worried, for the Republican party was no longer a viable political alternative to the Democrats in Alabama.

After their defeat in 1876, Alabama Republicans seemed bewildered as to where they should turn as a party and as individuals, and in their efforts to gain some sense of direction they held repeated postmortems to determine why they had lost the last two state elections. Republicans themselves most often explained their political collapse as the result of intra-party quarrels and the poor quality of party personnel. There is ample evidence that Republicans wasted considerable energy fighting among themselves, and the dissension thus encouraged made cooperation in state campaigns virtually impossible.[41] A scalawag reported that one group in the Republican party had decided that the most effective way to neutralize their opponents in the party was to kill the party so dead it "could never kick." Then, when discordant elements among the Democrats produced a rupture, take over the most conservative wing of that party.[42] Another Republican observed that it was no wonder Republicans lost elections in Alabama when they held two conventions and "republicans fought republicans," shirking much of the labor of a state campaign.[43]

The dissatisfaction over the distribution of federal patronage led to incessant appointments and removals as first one Republican faction and then another pressed for rewards for their group. Republicans out of office so attacked those who were in that often Democrats more willingly endorsed a Republican officeholder than did a member of his own party.[44] One Republican observed that "all talk of the great good of the government and the higher standards of morality to be achieved by further changes . . . is simply all bosh." Constant changes had well nigh ruined the party.[45] Another Republican candidly explained that one "good" appointee was removed and another less desirable one left because "one would divide and the other would not." He added that the attitude of some Alabama Republicans was that with federal patronage from Washington plus the colored vote and plenty of whiskey at home, "they could palm off any one they wished upon the people."[46] Nevertheless, the overall quality of Republican candidates and officeholders in Alabama, with the exception of the outrageous George E. Spencer, does not appear generally worse than the Democrats. Seemingly, Alabama Republicans worried more about whether an officeholder was black or white, native or newcomer, than about a man's reputation for honesty and integrity.

The scalawags bitterly resented the appointment of newcomers or blacks to office. Unionists who felt vindicated by the war's outcome only now to be ignored for patronage were particularly outraged. However, they overlooked the number of places they did win on the state level and the fact that these rewards were far out of proportion to the number of votes they brought to the party. Native white Republicans were most angry about appointments to federal jobs and blamed President Grant for "almost entirely overlooking the tried and true Union men of the South and the most prominent Northern men who have settled here since the war who had the influence and the nerve to protect the colored voter in casting his vote."[47] Whether it was true or not, Unionists believed that strangers and adventurers had been forced upon Alabamians while Union men were left to bear the "brunt of the most wanton and reckless persecution."[48]

However, the truth of the matter is that the reasons for the Republican party's failure in Alabama go far beyond the problems of personnel and patronage. For example, organized, unrelieved ostracism, intimidation, and violence also discouraged many from voting Republican in 1874 and 1876. Although the Ku Klux Klan no longer officially existed in Alabama, a reign of terror against Republicans continued, especially in west Alabama counties with a heavy black population. Fear among Republicans was so widespread in the fall of 1874 that U.S. troops were again dispatched to maintain order in the most troubled areas of the state.[49] Democratic economic pressures on the blacks paid off heavily in the black counties, where the Democratic vote in 1874 jumped to 38,429 from 33,905 in 1872, an increase of 5,500, while the Republicans increased their vote only to 61,593 from 59,409 in 1872. In 1876 fraud, intimidation, and arrest, especially directed against the black population, caused a dramatic decline in the Republican vote in the black counties from 61,593 in 1874 to 34,295 in 1876, the smallest Republican vote polled in these counties during Reconstruction in Alabama. Republicans alleged that over 1,000 blacks were prevented from voting in Mobile alone.[50]

Still more significant as a reason for the Republican defeat in Alabama was the race issue. In the crucial election of 1874, Democrats leveled their greatest efforts at winning white Republicans. Where business and social ostracism failed to have the desired effect, fears of the whites were aroused by rumors of blacks arming and drilling, and in general Democrats successfully played upon the whites' deep-seated beliefs of black inferiority. Race was *the* issue of the 1874 campaign and provoked the largest voter turnout in Alabama during Reconstruction. The Democrats successfully carried all the white counties except Winston and almost doubled their vote in these counties from 18,402 in 1872 to 32,341 in 1874.[51] Democratic gains here and in the black counties plus Democratic success in discouraging many blacks from voting at all made possible their landslide in 1874.

The reactions of the scalawag leaders to what obviously was the indefinite eclipse of their party in Alabama politics were varied. Few prominent native whites did as some historians have suggested was the course for most scalawags after the Republican defeat in 1876—join the Democratic party. In the fall of 1876 former Governor David P. Lewis and former Congressman Frederick G. Bromberg endorsed the national Democratic ticket headed by Samuel Tilden. Lewis explained his decision by saying that the Republican policy of Reconstruction had been a "disgraceful failure" and that he saw nothing in the future of the party that promised hope to Southern men of national and conservative sentiments.[52] Lewis had tried unsuccessfully to be appointed as the replacement for Judge Richard Busteed when he resigned in 1874, and perhaps this disappointment influenced Lewis' decision to leave the Republican party. In May, 1882, former U.S. District Attorney John A. Minnis also joined the Democrats.[53] Others such as Alexander White and Alexander McKinstry retired from state politics to private business.[54]

Withdrawals from Republican politics were the exception, not the rule. The majority of the scalawags who had been candidates or officeholders continued active as Republicans. Although the party did not make nominations in 1878 or 1880, Republicans engaged in a spirited competition for federal positions to be appointed by Republican presidents. As one scalawag candidly put it, Republicanism was very dead in Alabama unless native Republicans who were honest, capable, and faithful received some recognition from the administration.[55]

Alabama scalawags found President Rutherford B. Hayes highly responsive to their suggestions about federal patronage for the state primarily because of their opposition to Senator George E. Spencer. Spencer's corrupt reputation, the contest over his election in 1872, and the investigation of his political activities by the Alabama legislature in 1875 disgusted the reformer instinct in Hayes. Also, President Hayes was a long-standing friend of former Senator Willard Warner, who blamed Spencer for the loss of his Senate seat in 1870 and the position of collector of customs at Mobile in 1872. But an even more significant reason for the President's dislike of Spencer was the Senator's conduct during the dispute over the results of the election of 1876. At a time when Hayes needed all the support he could get, Spencer demanded to know who would run Hayes' administration before he made up his mind. "If it is to be a [B. H.] Bristow administration, we want Tilden—he would suit us decidedly better."[56]

For advice on patronage distribution in Alabama President Hayes relied on Robert McConnell Reynolds, an Ohio carpetbagger who had come to Wilcox County, Alabama, in May, 1867, and later that year served in the constitutional convention. Elected in 1868 as state auditor on a ticket headed by W. H. Smith, Reynolds was known as a man of "high character, conspicuous ability, and efficiency." In the 1870s he held a succession of federal positions: collector of customs at Mobile, minister to Bolivia under President Grant, and first auditor in the Treasury Department under President Hayes.[57] Senator Spencer opposed the appointment of Reynolds as collector in 1873, predicting that it would ruin him if allowed to stand. When it did stand, he asked W. E. Chandler to "reconnoitre around the White House and see what the trouble is," complaining that the appointment was "raising the devil." A year later President Grant yielded to Spencer's requests by appointing Reynolds as minister to Bolivia and a scalawag protégé of Spencer as collector of customs.[58] When Hayes came into office, he appointed Reynolds to the post of first auditor early in 1878, and Reynolds' influence was so significant that he was known as the "special pet of the President" who controlled patronage for Alabama.[59]

Senator Spencer fiercely opposed scalawag efforts to enjoy more federal patronage, and although he was not reelected in 1878, he continued to wield formidable influence. Spencer was not about to fold his tents in Washington and steal silently away with his new bride to his investments in the Black Hills. Well aware of scalawag maneuvers, he moved early in the Hayes administration in an effort to discredit them. Because he felt they were unfitted for the job of "Southern regeneration," he predicted that it would be a "grave mistake" to place them in positions of power. Spencer had little patronage success during the Hayes administration, and he hoped for an improvement in 1881 with a new administration. Although out of office for over two years, he proposed a "deal" with the administration of President James A. Garfield if Spencer men in Alabama received a half dozen appointments.[60] After 1876, Spencer consistently opposed any nominations of scalawags for federal positions in Alabama and on occasion endorsed Democratic candidates, instead of Republicans, in order to gain Democratic help to defeat scalawag appointments in Alabama.[61]

Hayes at this time was implementing his so-called "Southern strategy": by judicious use of federal patronage he hoped to attract whites from the Democratic party and build a Southern Republican party capable of their continued support. Thereafter, he intended to rely on economic rather than racial issues to sustain their loyalty. Hayes' distribution of patronage in Alabama differed from the pattern he followed in other Southern states where he channeled extensive patronage to Southern

Democrats at the expense of Southern Republicans. Alabama Democrats did communicate to Hayes their preferences for Southerners to man the courts, but they usually recommended Republicans who had been Southern Unionists. Alabama scalawags benefited tremendously from the hands of Hayes, but this fact did not prevent them from complaining when any Democrat received an appointment.[62]

President Hayes' first patronage action in Alabama was the removal of two Spencer protégés in Mobile: scalawags J. C. Goodloe as collector of customs and Thomas C. Bingham as postmaster. Hayes appointed carpetbagger Morris D. Wickersham as postmaster despite some criticism, but the real uproar came over the vacancy in the customhouse.[63] Former Senator Willard Warner, still smouldering over his loss of that job in 1872, launched a campaign to regain it as vindication of President Grant's wrong to him.[64] Warner's efforts went unrewarded as the post was first offered to former Governor William H. Smith, who declined in favor of his brother Robert T. Smith, former state auditor.[65] Unlike so many other disappointed officeseekers, Warner gracefully accepted Hayes' choice, repeating that his desire to be vindicated had been the only reason he sought the office again. Warner praised Smith as a good Union man who would make a good officer.[66] Senator Spencer, however, was not so gracious. Smith's appointment so outraged him that he announced that he preferred the appointment of a Democrat.[67]

President Hayes informed representatives of the Rice-Smith group that his recent appointments for Alabama were, as he understood, men from their wing of the party and expressed the hope that they would give satisfaction in the state. Thus encouraged by Hayes' favor, they then urged the removal of three more Spencer associates: George Turner, U.S. Marshal for the Southern District; Charles E. Mayer, U.S. District Attorney for the Northern and Middle Districts; and Louis H. Mayer, Collector of Internal Revenue in the first district.[68]

A few weeks later Hayes asked Turner and Charles Mayer to resign, and when they refused, Hayes suspended them. Former Governor Lewis E. Parsons was then nominated U.S. District Attorney and Samuel G. Reid, scalawag newspaper editor in Montgomery, was appointed U.S. Marshal.[69] The nominations provoked a storm of controversy, especially that of Parsons. Former federal district Judge Richard Busteed, now practicing law in New York, was one of several who dispatched critical letters to the Senate Judiciary Committee urging rejection of Parsons' nomination.[70]

Meanwhile, endorsements of Parsons poured in. Willard Warner expressed the belief that it would be a "great political blunder" for the Senate to fail to confirm Parsons.[71] Former Postmaster General Marshall Jewell sent Attorney General Charles Devans an unsolicited testimonial for Parsons. Jewell had found "honest, sound, and reliable" Republicans so scarce, especially in the South, that he felt moved to give testimony when one was considered for public office. He knew Parsons to be a man of "good sense" who had been "shamefully abused for years by his political opponents"—some of them Republicans. Parsons, and men like him, ought to be sustained by the administration.[72] Alabama Senator John Tyler Morgan, a Democrat, also endorsed Parsons, adding a private comment that he had "no desire to have appointments in Alabama made from the Democratic party."[73] The Democratic Montgomery *Advertiser* endorsed the nominations of Parsons and Reid as changes made "decidedly for the good" of the federal government and the people of Alabama. The Tuskegee *News* urged confirmation of these appointees "until we can do better."[74]

Weeks, then months, passed, and Congress did not act. The reason was George E. Spencer, who was busy maneuvering to aid New York Senator Roscoe Conkling in defeating Hayes' New York appointments in return for Conkling's support to protect Spencer's friends in Alabama. When Spencer made a strenuous effort to discredit Parsons before the Senate Judiciary Committee, Parsons ably defended himself. The Senate finally discussed Parsons' nomination at the end of March, 1878, and Senator John Tyler Morgan gave a lengthy defense against the questions raised about Parsons' integrity but made no comment about his political record. But the effort was to no avail. The Senate rejected Parsons' nomination by a vote of 22 to 16.[75]

Hayes' nomination of Reid fared no better. Reid might have been confirmed in the early part of the regular session of Congress had not papers containing damaging evidence against Turner been stolen from the Senate desk of John Tyler Morgan. Reid's nomination was held in committee until a few hours before the final adjournment of Congress, and he was not confirmed. Shortly thereafter, Reid returned the office to George Turner.[76]

The collectors of internal revenue in the first and second districts of

Alabama were two more patronage battlegrounds. In the first district carpetbagger Louis H. Mayer, whom Grant had appointed in 1871 at Spencer's request, was an anathema to the Rice-Smith faction. After years of efforts Spencer's opponents finally forced Mayer's resignation in August, 1880, and A. L. Morgan, a New York carpetbagger, replaced him.[77]

The scalawags saw the collectorship in the second revenue district as a device to recapture a congressional seat from the fourth congressional district. Judge Charles Pelham, former congressman, expressed the belief that the "colored men in that district could be induced to nominate some reliable white Republican who can be elected if the Collector, etc. is given to a colored man." He suggested former Congressman James T. Rapier for the collectorship because he had served as a revenue assessor before he was elected to Congress. Then, too, Senator Spencer would not oppose Rapier's confirmation because many of Spencer's strongest friends were "more friendly to Rapier than to Spencer."[78]

Accordingly, Hayes removed scalawag Daniel B. Booth, earlier recommended by Spencer, and nominated Rapier as collector in the second district. Protests flooded President Hayes. Booth was described as having been Spencer's man in the past, but he had been an honest, efficient, and acceptable officer. Rapier was accused of having weighed down the Republican state ticket in 1870 and as being one who would aid President Hayes' opposition in Alabama.[79] These protests caused Hayes to have second thoughts about the nomination, and he relayed these to John Sherman. "These dispatches tend strongly to show that the nomination of Rapier is a mistake. Can't you ask to have no action upon it until we can look into it?"[80] Look into it they did, and Hayes then went ahead with the nomination of Rapier. The Senate confirmed him in early June, 1878.[81] However, Rapier's appointment failed to have the desired results of winning the fourth congressional district for the Republicans in 1878.

Complaints about the conduct of the U.S. Marshal in the Northern District provoked President Hayes to make another removal and appointment in Alabama. Carpetbagger Robert P. Baker was replaced by Joseph Sloss, a scalawag who had at one time been a friend of George Spencer, and this change elicited only unenthusiastic approval of the Rice-Smith faction.[82]

In June, 1878, the Smith and Spencer wings of the Republican party in Alabama buried the hatchet and agreed to meet together to make plans for upcoming elections. The Republican state convention met in Montgomery on July 4 and elected former Congressman Charles Hays, Eutaw scalawag, as president, and H. V. Cashin, a black from Montgomery, as secretary. The convention decided not to nominate a state ticket for the August 5 election but instead to concentrate their efforts on election of members of the legislature and Congress in those areas of Alabama where their vote would be counted. The new state Executive Committee contained nine scalawags, two carpetbaggers, three blacks, and two unidentified men.[83]

Republicans made active campaign efforts only in the second and fourth congressional districts, both with a heavy black majority. In the second district Republicans divided over support for James P. Armstrong, obscure Greenback candidate, against the Democratic incumbent Hilary A. Herbert.[84] The Republican convention in the fourth district nominated former Congressman Jeremiah Haralson after three days of balloting. Some Republicans believed there would be less prejudice against a native white Republican than anyone else and consequently a better chance for a fair count. A large number of black delegates objected, saying no one could be elected except with black votes and that white men could not represent them. The blacks prevailed, and Haralson was nominated.[85] The Democrats easily carried all congressional districts in Alabama in November, 1878, and in the legislature only eight Republicans (seven scalawags and one black) were elected to the state house of representatives. However, the defeated black candidate in the fourth district was a member of the Rice-Smith faction, and as such President Hayes rewarded him a year later with the appointment of collector of customs at the port of Baltimore, displacing a Maryland black.[86]

During the first year of the Hayes administration R. M. Reynolds grew in influence, and the first instance in which it is clear that he determined the outcome of a patronage battle was the case of the postmaster of Montgomery. In January, 1879, President Hayes removed scalawag J. J. Martin, and nominated Paul Strobach, a controversial carpetbagger who had been Montgomery County sheriff for years. Alabama Republicans interpreted the appointment as a ''friendly act toward Senator Spencer.'' Auditor Reynolds intervened and recommended to the President the appointment of Israel W. Roberts, a little-known Unionist resident of Alabama for forty years, adding that Senator Morgan wished Strobach's name withdrawn because he did not want "to openly and bitterly oppose confirmation." He also reported that those Democrats who favored Strobach did so because they believed that this would most injure the Republican party. Reynolds' comments impressed the President, and after inquiring of Willard Warner's opinions of Strobach, Hayes withdrew the nomination of Strobach and appointed Roberts.[87]

Agitation continued for a change in the U.S. Marshal of the Middle and Southern Districts in Alabama. When it was clear that Reid would not be confirmed, the Rice-Smith faction pressed for the nomination of carpetbagger Matthias C. Osborn, a business partner of former Governor Smith, to replace George Turner. In 1872 L. H. Mayer had Osborn fired from his position as assistant assessor of internal revenue because of political differences with Osborn. Reynolds described Osborn to President Hayes as a man whose appointment would give satisfaction to "all republicans not especially interested in the appointment of some other man." Hayes complied, and Osborn was nominated and subsequently confirmed.[88]

While engaged in these contests for federal patronage Alabama Republicans did not attempt to regain control of the state government. In 1880 they again did not nominate candidates for state offices when the state convention met at Selma on May 21. Instead, they agreed to support the Independent ticket when that group made nominations in late June. The enemies of the Rice-Smith faction dominated the convention with George Turner elected as chairman. The most exciting business of the convention was selection of delegates to the Republican National Convention. Strong feeling existed for Grant and Sherman as possible candidates, although the political liabilities of both men bewildered many Republicans. One Alabama carpetbagger remarked, "When I look the field over, it only leaves me in the greatest doubt what course to pursue," and his general reaction to Republican politics was "I am 'at sea' without a rudder." So were many other Republicans in Alabama. The state convention chose four delegates-at-large, while each of the eight congressional districts had earlier chosen two delegates; all were pledged to Grant.[89]

At the state convention Willard Warner and W. H. Smith unsuccessfully contested the delegates to the national convention chosen in the seventh district, but this setback was only temporary for the Rice-Smith group. The Republican National Convention admitted Warner and Smith as anti-Grant delegates at the Chicago meeting in June. Two weeks later the Rice-Smith faction received more encouragement from a new nomination for U.S. District Attorney for the Northern and Middle Districts of Alabama. President Hayes appointed former Governor Smith to replace Charles Mayer, who had resumed the post after the Senate failed to confirm Lewis E. Parsons in 1878.[90] This nomination provoked one frustrated officeseeker to howl to President Hayes that "*4/5* of the federal officers" in Alabama were members of the "Warner-Smith-Reynolds-Pelham ring, who are proclaiming it all over Alabama that they will control the patronage!" In contrast to these complaints, R. M. Reynolds wrote President Hayes his "*sincere* thanks" for this nomination, while Willard Warner expressed the belief that Alabama Republicans were about to rid the party of "Spencerism" and to get the party on a footing of honesty and good repute.[91] When W. H. Smith received his commission as U.S. District Attorney in July, he called on Mayer for possession of the office, books, etc. A tug of war briefly ensued as Mayer refused to yield, saying Smith was not yet confirmed. In March, 1881, despite an adverse report from the Senate Judiciary Committee, the Senate confirmed Smith as U.S. District Attorney for the Northern and Middle Districts of Alabama.[92]

In July, 1880, when Robert T. Smith resigned as collector of customs at Mobile, a carpetbagger member of the Rice-Smith faction, Joseph W. Burke, was appointed in his place. With this appointment the controversy over the collectorship ceased, and Burke held the position into the administration of President Grover Cleveland.[93]

The Democrats easily carried Alabama in the November, 1880, election. Congressional candidates who had been nominated in district conventions were carpetbagger James Gillette and black Frank Threatt in the first district; carpetbagger Paul Strobach in the second; black William J. Stevens and scalawag James Q. Smith in the fourth; and scalawag Arthur Bingham in the seventh. These nominees and the electoral ticket of five carpetbaggers, four scalawags, and one black were soundly defeated. One Walker County scalawag survived in the Alabama legislature in the house.[94]

Also in 1880, Justice William Strong resigned from the U.S. Supreme Court, and there was much feeling that this vacancy should be filled by a jurist from the South. President Hayes responded in December by appointing Judge William B. Woods, a former Alabama Chancellor in 1868 and now a judge of the U.S. Fifth Circuit. Woods had been strongly recommended for a court position in 1877. This nomination again pleased the Rice-Smith faction, especially Willard Warner, whose sister was the wife of Judge Woods.[95]

By the end of Hayes' administration in March, 1881, the scalawags who predominated in the Rice-Smith faction or men who had the group's blessings had superseded the most objectionable Spencer men in the important and lucrative federal positions available in Alabama by presidential appointment. Although R. M. Reynolds continued as first auditor in the Treasury Department until mid-1885, he was no longer the influential patronage broker that he had been under President Hayes.

Encouraged by the change of administrations, Spencer men launched a new campaign for control of federal patronage in Alabama. They believed they were not extravagant in their demands, and they did not ask "indiscriminate slaughter. We want those places only which it is absolutely necessary should be controlled in harmony with the party machinery" to produce beneficial results. However, they made little headway, as there were few changes in officeholders, and Spencer grumbled, "I am awfully disgusted."[96]

Clearly, Alabama scalawags did not retire from the political arena after the disastrous Republican defeats in 1874 and 1876. They simply changed battlefields. Although "at sea" about how to regain control of the state government, they eagerly seized proffered federal patronage, which was more available to native Southern whites under President Hayes than it had ever been under President Grant. Alabama scalawags seemingly were never really aware (or would never really admit) how much they did receive in important and lucrative offices. They controlled the Republican party and offices in Alabama during Reconstruction, and when that benefit evaporated at the end of Reconstruction, they enjoyed the best of federal patronage or influenced who did enjoy it—not a bad record for men generally dismissed as political novices and incompetents.

CONCLUSION

The traditional stereotype of the scalawag as the north Alabama small farmer of little education, no political experience, and Unionist sympathies does not hold true for Southern white Republican leaders in Alabama. Despite impressive evidence that most scalawag voters in Alabama lived in the Northern half of the state,[1] scalawags from black counties were highly influential in the Alabama Republican party and included organizers of the party in the state as well as latecomers who joined only after the 1868 presidential election. Prominent scalawags from black counties included jurists Benjamin F. and Milton J. Saffold, Adam C. Felder, Anthony W. Dillard, Samuel F. Rice, George H. Craig, Benjamin L. Whelan, Littleberry Strange, George W. Gunn; Provisional Governor Lewis E. Parsons; Superintendents of Public Instruction Noah B. Cloud and Joseph H. Speed and Republican nominee for this post in 1874, John T. Foster; Attorney Generals Joshua Morse and Benjamin Gardner; Congressmen Charles Hays, Alexander White, and Charles Pelham, and Republican nominees for Congress Daniel B. Booth and William H. Betts; Republican electors Thomas O. Glascock, Charles C. Crowe, William J. Gilmore, John L. Pennington, S. S. Booth, William B. Jones, Winfield S. Bird; U.S. Sixth Auditor John J. Martin.

Instead of being small farmers with little education, a significant number of these men read law or attended college (including the Universities of Alabama, Georgia, Virginia, Tennessee, North Carolina; Jefferson Medical College at Philadelphia, South Carolina College, New Orleans Medical College, Hampden-Sydney College, Harvard University, Yale University, Davidson College, Centenary College in Louisiana, Centre College and Transylvania University in Kentucky, Erskine College in South Carolina) or received some other type of formal education. Of the seventy-one identifiable scalawags nominated, elected, or appointed to the most lucrative and important positions between 1868 and 1881 (state executive and judicial offices and federal legislative and judicial offices) forty-six were lawyers. Others developed successful careers as newspaper editors, businessmen, physicians, teachers, manufacturers, merchants, planters, and clergymen. One listed his occupation in the 1860 census as "gentleman."[2] Few were small farmers.

Many leading scalawags represented prominent families. For example, the father of Benjamin F. and Milton J. Saffold was chief justice of the Alabama Supreme Court and a member of the 1819 constitutional convention, while Alexander White's father was an associate justice on the Alabama Supreme Court. Adam C. Felder's father was a judge in South Carolina, while the father of J. McCaleb Wiley was secretary of the Mecklenburg Convention. Charles Hays' father served in the legislatures of South Carolina and Alabama, while Henry Churchill Semple was nephew of President John Tyler. Lewis E. Parsons was grandson of Jonathan Edwards of Massachusetts, and Charles Pelham was son of a prominent North Carolina physician and brother of Major John Pelham, Confederate military hero. Joseph H. Speed was a cousin of James S. Speed, U.S. Attorney General in 1865. The uncle of Thomas O. Glascock represented Georgia in the U.S. Congress, while the father of Robert S. Heflin was a planter who served in the legislatures of both Georgia and Alabama. The father of James S. Clarke was a prominent physician in Lawrence County, while Clarke's brother, another physician, represented Lawrence County in the Alabama legislature. Francis W. Sykes' father was president of the branch bank of Decatur. The father of C. S. G. Doster represented Autauga County in the Alabama house of representatives, and the father of N. S. McAfee was probate judge of Talladega County and also represented that county in the Alabama house of representatives. L. V. B. Martin's father served Alabama as attorney general, circuit judge, and legislator. The father of B. M. Long was clerk of the superior court of Carrollton, Georgia, for forty years, while one grandfather of N. W. Trimble was a Tennessee circuit judge and another grandfather was a judge of the Tennessee superior court. The father of A. W. Dillard was a prominent physician in Amherst County, Virginia, while the father of William Bibb Figures served as a major under the command of General John Coffee. One grandfather of Robert A. Moseley was a physician at Montevallo and another was a judge. The ancestors of Samuel G. Reid included the Lord High Admiral of Scotland in the days of Bruce. Albert Elmore's father was the senior partner of a prominent Montgomery law firm which included William L. Yancey. The father of Nicholas Davis represented Limestone County in the 1819 constitutional convention and in the Alabama legislature, twice ran for governor, and twice was a presidential elector.

Scalawag leaders were men of considerable property. For example, in 1865 and 1866 President Andrew Johnson granted pardons from disabilities of ownership of property worth $20,000 to a number of Alabamians who were later prominent scalawags: Adam C. Felder, Charles Hays, William B. Jones, William Miller, George W. Malone, Thomas M. Peters, Joseph H. Speed, William H. Smith, Henry C. Semple, L. V. B. Martin, Nodiah Woodruff.[3] A study of the 1860 property holdings of men who later became scalawags and held the most important offices in Alabama shockingly contradicts the notion of their poverty. Twenty-three of the twenty-seven scalawags nominated for state executive offices during Reconstruction owned a total of $187,750 in real property and $331,102 in personal property in 1860; seventeen of the twenty-four scalawags nominated for state judicial office owned a total of $203,615 in real property and $539,650 in personal property in 1860 (the four scalawags who served on the Supreme Court alone accounted for real property valued at $100,900 and personal property valued at $273,255); eleven of the fifteen scalawags nominated for federal legislative offices owned a total of $187,100 in real property and $223,050 in personal property; five of the ten scalawags nominated for federal judicial offices owned a total of $73,000 in real property and $123,540 in personal property in 1860.[4]

Probably the most significant information about the backgrounds of these scalawag leaders is their extensive political experience prior to their affiliation with the Republican party. About evenly divided as Whigs and Democrats in the antebellum period, these men had active public careers in a wide variety of elective and appointive offices. More than half of the scalawags nominated to the most important offices possessed some form of administrative, legislative, or judicial experience: fourteen of the twenty-seven scalawags nominated for state executive offices, fifteen of the twenty-four scalawags nominated for state judicial offices, six of the fifteen scalawags nominated for federal legislative offices, and five of the ten scalawags nominated for federal judicial offices. These men had been legislators, congressmen, judges, members of the 1861 or 1865 constitutional conventions, or local civil officials. In the 1867 constitutional convention nineteen of the forty-eight identifiable scalawag members had held some office before 1866.

One group of scalawags easily identified as former officeholders was those who applied to Congress for removal of their officeholding disabilities under the Fourteenth Amendment. Included were Benjamin F. Porter, Sidney C. Posey, Thomas D. Fister, William S. Mudd, William B. Jones, George W. Malone, William J. Haralson, Joshua Morse, John T. Foster, Joseph Bradley, David C. Humphries, David P. Lewis, William Bibb Figures, Charles Pelham, Robert S. Heflin, Adam C. Felder, Thomas O. Glascock, Milton J. Saffold, C. S. G. Doster, William J. Gilmore. These applications meant that these men had at some earlier time held a position where they took an oath of loyalty to the federal government and subsequently broke the oath by aiding the Confederacy.[5]

Only on the issue of Unionism in 1860 and 1861 does the stereotype of the background of the Alabama scalawags hold true. Most of the prominent scalawags supported Douglas or Bell in 1860 and opposed secession in 1861, although many subsequently served in the Confederate army or held office under the Confederate government, often to escape conscription. Those who opposed secession and later reversed themselves by supporting the Confederacy were frequently described as giving only reluctant support.

Obviously, Alabama scalawag leaders were men superior to the unflattering concept portrayed in the traditional stereotype. Representing many old and prominent families in Alabama, these men enjoyed advantages not readily available to the less affluent whites. Education, legal training and experience, and extensive public careers prior to their affiliation with the Republican party enabled these men to be more than novices to the intricacies of politics and government. They were on at least an equal footing with the Northern men in the party and certainly ahead of the blacks in the scramble for political power.

Thus well equipped, Alabama scalawags exercised considerably more influence in the Alabama Republican party and in Alabama Reconstruction than historians have usually acknowledged. One hundred seventeen Republicans were nominated, elected, or appointed to the most lucrative and important positions (state executive and judicial offices and federal legislative and judicial offices) between 1868 and 1881, including seventy-six scalawags, thirty-five carpetbaggers, and six blacks. In state offices scalawags were even more predominant, as fifty-one native whites won nominations, compared to eleven carpetbaggers and one black. Twenty-seven scalawags won state executive nominations (75%), twenty-four won state judicial nominations (89%), and one hundred one were elected to the state legislature (39%), clearly contradicting traditional views that Alabama under the Republicans endured a "carpetbag judiciary" and suffered under general "carpetbag and Negro rule."[6] However, fewer scalawags won nominations to federal offices: fifteen were nominated or elected to Congress (48%) compared to eleven carpetbaggers and five blacks, while only ten were nominated or appointed to federal judicial offices (43%) compared to thirteen carpetbaggers. Alabama scalawags won five miscellaneous federal appointments outside the state (38%).[7]

Among party positions that signified influence but no financial benefit, scalawags also exerted power. Fifty-seven scalawags served on the state Republican Executive Committee between 1867 and 1878 (50%); twenty-five scalawags were nominated as presidential electors between 1868 and 1880 (70%); twenty-five scalawags were delegates to Republican National Conventions between 1868 and 1880 (38%); one scalawag was a member of the national Republican Executive Committee between 1868 and 1880 (25%); forty-eight scalawags were members of the 1867 constitutional convention (49.5% of the Republican membership); and seven scalawags were members of the 1875 constitutional convention (58% of the Republican membership).[8]

Yet despite this impressive showing, scalawags continually complained that they were excluded from office. Either they were unaware or they refused to admit the proportion of officers who were scalawags, and the incessant complaints aided the establishment of the stereotype that carpetbaggers and blacks dominated the Alabama Republican party. The only basis for these complaints during Reconstruction was that scalawags were outnumbered in the federal judiciary and that Alabama's carpetbaggers in the U.S. Senate determined federal appointments in the customhouse, post offices, and internal revenue service.

In a valiant effort to silence these protests in 1872 the Montgomery *Alabama State Journal* published this analysis:

Native Born Republicans

1 governor	11 officers and employees state senate
1 treasurer	12 officers and employees house of representatives
1 attorney general	
1 superintendent of public instruction	

(continued on p. 133)

21 state senators
27 members lower house
 3 supreme judges
 4 chancellors (judges)
60 probate judges of counties
11 circuit judges
64 county solicitors
 2 collectors of internal revenue
 2 assessors of internal revenue
 1 surveyor of customs, port of Selma
 1 collector, port of Mobile
 1 appraiser merchandise, port of Mobile
24 employees, port of Mobile
 1 U.S. district attorney
 1 U.S. marshal
 1 judge, supreme court, District of Columbia
 1 sixth auditor, U.S. Treasury Department
 1 U.S. consul at Elsinore
 2 members of congress

Carpet-bag Republicans
 1 lieutenant governor
 1 secretary of state
 1 auditor
 1 commissioner of industrial resources
 4 officers and employees state senate
 3 officers and employees house of representatives
11 senators
 8 members lower house
 1 chancellor (judge—appointed)
 5 probate judges of counties
 1 county solicitor
 2 U.S. senators
 1 collector of internal revenue
 1 assessor of internal revenue
 4 employees customhouse, Mobile
 1 U.S. judge
 1 U.S. district attorney
 1 U.S. marshal
 1 member of Congress

According to these figures, scalawags held an overwhelming number of offices between 1868 and 1872 when compared with those held by carpetbaggers.[9] However, these figures failed to satisfy scalawags who resented the nomination, appointment, or election of *any* newcomer or *any* black to *any* office as an affront to loyal native whites who had survived the hardships of war.

The scalawags did a superb job in convincing themselves, their party, and their political opposition that they were an essential voting bloc for political victory in Alabama. The Democratic Selma *Southern Argus* accused the scalawag of taking his seat at the table of the Republican party only "when the feast was spread to his liking."[10] That the feast *was* spread to his liking and that he *was* permitted to take a seat at the table only further emphasize the superior job accomplished in convincing Republicans of the scalawags' importance to the party's success in Alabama. However, the returns for Alabama elections during Reconstruction do not support the scalawags' concept of their importance as voters. The elections of 1870 and 1872 illustrate the necessity of the black counties for a Republican victory, while only in 1874 were the white counties significant in determining the election's outcome. The number of scalawags who held office was far out of proportion to the number of votes they brought to the party, and the Republican party in Alabama is best understood as a party of white officeholders, primarily native white officeholders, sustained by black voters. One Northern traveler in Alabama in 1875 who came to similar conclusions about the power of the scalawags in Alabama Reconstruction commented that this state suffered far less from carpetbaggers than any of the other Southern states which he had visited (Arkansas, Louisiana, Mississippi). However, his contemporaries ignored his observations.[11]

At the first Republican defeat in Alabama in 1870, respectable scalawags did not immediately desert the party. Scalawag leaders remained Republican despite this setback and worked frantically for a Republican victory in 1872. After the Republican disaster in 1874 most prominent scalawags still continued active as Republicans, although many chose the safer label "independent" in the 1880s.

While scalawags exercised political power in Alabama, they differed little in attitudes or actions from their white contemporaries in both parties. On economic matters scalawags and Democrats eagerly sought aid for economic development of projects in which they had an economic stake, and they exhibited few scruples in the methods used to push beneficial financial legislation through the Alabama legislature. The quality of the bookkeeping habits of both Republicans and Democrats was equally notorious.

On the race issue carpetbaggers in Alabama were thoroughly divided; however, scalawags were as convinced of the inferiority of blacks as were Democrats, and few were any more committed to civil rights. Throughout the Reconstruction years white Republicans as well as Democrats solicited black votes but reluctantly rewarded blacks with nominations for office only when necessary, even then reserving the more choice positions for whites. The results were predictable: these half-a-loaf gestures satisfied neither black nor white Republicans. The fatal weakness of the Republican party in Alabama, as elsewhere in the South, was its inability to create a biracial political party.[12] And while in power even briefly, they failed to protect their members from Democratic terror. Alabama Republicans were forever on the defensive, verbally and physically. Many Republican voters simply saw little reason to vote after

1874, as the shrinking election returns illustrate. W. R. Brock might have had Alabama Republicans in mind when he observed that Republicans were "children of their age" who were "bound by its assumptions and inhibitions."[13]

The most intriguing question about these scalawags still remains: Why did they become Republicans? Why were they willing to bear the social ostracism and danger of physical violence for a political affiliation? Doubtless, they did not present all of their motives to public scrutiny in letters to newspaper editors or testimony before congressional committees or even in their private correspondence. Yet, with what evidence remains, some general evaluations of the motives of these leaders may be made. Many sincerely believed their political views incompatible with the Democratic party. Others possessed an acute awareness that they were living in revolutionary times and recognized the futility of further opposition to Radical Republican rule. Others frankly saw that their political alignment meant the difference between financial success or failure in the immediate future. Regardless of their precise reasons for becoming Republicans, they determined to join the party and battle for control of it in order to shape the revolution they saw before them. And it was this struggle to control and shape the revolution that is the story of the scalawags in Alabama Reconstruction.

The scalawag leaders exemplified clear-sighted political realism in assessing the political situation for what it was in Alabama, not as they might have wished it to be. These men understood the desirability of uniting the Black Belt Negro and the north Alabama white for the maintenance of a permanent Republican party in the state. Unfortunately, they misjudged the cost of such an alliance and found the party unable to make sufficient concessions to satisfy black constituents without alienating white ones. Scalawag leaders failed to weld these two uncomfortable allies into anything more than a temporary accommodation, as in the Republican victory of 1872. Faced with pressure from without by Democratic use of the race issue, intimidation of black voters, and fraudulent elections, and battered from within by jealous dissension among scalawags, carpetbaggers, and blacks, the party went into a permanent eclipse after 1874. Despite their failure to erect a permanent Republican party in Alabama, the scalawag leaders were realistic and perceptive men who hardly deserve the epithet of "local lepers," which they have borne for a century.

APPENDIX

REPUBLICAN NOMINATIONS AND APPOINTMENTS, ALABAMA, 1868–1881

REPUBLICAN STATE NOMINATIONS[1]

1868

GOVERNOR: William H. Smith (s)
LIEUTENANT GOVERNOR: Andrew J. Applegate (c)
SECRETARY OF STATE: Charles A. Miller (c)
AUDITOR: Robert McConnell Reynolds (c)
TREASURER: Chester Arthur Bingham (s)
ATTORNEY GENERAL: Joshua Morse (s)
SUPERINTENDENT OF INDUSTRIAL RESOURCES: John C. Keffer (c)
SUPERINTENDENT OF PUBLIC INSTRUCTION: Noah B. Cloud (s)
SUPREME COURT JUSTICES:
  E. Woolsey Peck (s)
  Thomas M. Peters (s)
  Benjamin F. Saffold (s)
CHANCELLORS:
  William Skinner (s)
  William B. Woods (c)
  Adam C. Felder (s)
  Anthony W. Dillard (s)
  B. B. McCraw (s)
CIRCUIT JUDGES:
  Benjamin L. Whelan (s) later replaced by
  Milton J. Saffold (s)
  James Q. Smith (s)
  William S. Mudd (s)
  James S. Clarke (s)
  William J. Haralson (s)
  John Elliott (s)
  Luther R. Smith (c)
  J. McCaleb Wiley (s)
  Littleberry Strange (s)
  Charles Pelham (s)
  Benjamin F. Porter (s) later replaced by
  Philemon O. Harper (s)

1870
GOVERNOR: William H. Smith (s)
LIEUTENANT GOVERNOR: Pierce Burton (c)
SECRETARY OF STATE: James T. Rapier (b)
TREASURER: Chester Arthur Bingham (s)
SUPERINTENDENT OF PUBLIC INSTRUCTION: Noah B. Cloud (s)
ATTORNEY GENERAL: Joshua Morse (s)

1872
GOVERNOR: David Peter Lewis (s)
LIEUTENANT GOVERNOR: Alexander McKinstry (s)
SECRETARY OF STATE: Patrick Ragland (s)
AUDITOR: Robert T. Smith (s)
TREASURER: Chester Arthur Bingham (s)
ATTORNEY GENERAL: Benjamin Gardner (s)
SUPERINTENDENT OF PUBLIC INSTRUCTION: Joseph H. Speed (s)
SUPERINTENDENT OF INDUSTRIAL RESOURCES: Thomas Lambert (s)

1874
GOVERNOR: David Peter Lewis (s)
LIEUTENANT GOVERNOR: Alexander McKinstry (s)
SECRETARY OF STATE: Neander H. Rice (s)
TREASURER: Chester Arthur Bingham (s)
ATTORNEY GENERAL: George Turner (c)
SUPERINTENDENT OF PUBLIC INSTRUCTION: John T. Foster (s)
SUPREME COURT JUSTICES:
   Thomas M. Peters (s)
   Benjamin F. Saffold (s)
   Adam C. Felder (s)
CHANCELLORS:
   Benjamin Lane Posey (s)
   Charles Turner (c)
   Anthony W. Dillard (s)
   George W. Gunn (s)
   Richard S. Watkins (s)
CIRCUIT JUDGES:
   George H. Craig (s)
   James Q. Smith (s)
   William S. Mudd (s)
   James S. Clarke (s)
   William J. Haralson (s)
   John Elliott (s)
   Luther R. Smith (c)
   J. McCaleb Wiley (s)
   Littleberry Strange (s)
   Lewis E. Parsons (s)
   Philemon O. Harper (s)

1876

Nominations of May 16, 1876, Convention
  GOVERNOR: Thomas M. Peters (s)
  SECRETARY OF STATE: J. J. McLemore (s)
  ATTORNEY GENERAL: J. S. Clarke (s)
  AUDITOR: C. Cadle, Jr. (c)
  TREASURER: W. B. Harris (s)
  SUPERINTENDENT OF EDUCATION: J. H. Houston (s)
Nominations of May 24, 1876, Convention
  GOVERNOR: James S. Clarke (s)
  SECRETARY OF STATE: Thomas T. Allington (s)
  AUDITOR: George Plowman (s)
  TREASURER: Benjamin M. Long (s)
  ATTORNEY GENERAL: Robert S. Heflin (s)
  SUPERINTENDENT OF EDUCATION: P. J. Glover (s)
Fusion Ticket
  GOVERNOR: Noadiah Woodruff (s)
  SECRETARY OF STATE: Amos Moody (s)
  SUPERINTENDENT OF EDUCATION: H. J. Livingston (s)
  ATTORNEY GENERAL: Egbert H. Grandlin (c)
  AUDITOR: Lewis Owen (s)
  TREASURER: Walton B. Harris (s)

REPUBLICAN CONGRESSIONAL NOMINATIONS[2]

1868
SENATORS:
  Willard Warner (c)
  George E. Spencer (c)
CONGRESSMEN:
  Francis W. Kellogg (c)
  Charles W. Buckley (c)
  Benjamin W. Norris (c)
  Charles W. Pierce (c)
  John B. Callis (c)
  Thomas Haughey (s)

1869
CONGRESSMEN:
  Alfred E. Buck (c)
  Charles W. Buckley (c)
  Robert S. Heflin (s)
  Charles Hays (s)
  William J. Haralson (s)
  Jerome J. Hinds (c)

1870
SENATORS:
  Willard Warner (c)
  William J. Haralson (s)
CONGRESSMEN:
  Benjamin S. Turner (b)
  Charles W. Buckley (c)
  Benjamin W. Norris (c)
  Charles Hays (s)
  Lemuel J. Standifer (s)
  B. O. Masterson (s)

1872
SENATOR:
  George E. Spencer (c)
CONGRESSMEN:
  Alexander White (s)
  C. C. Sheats (s)
  Benjamin S. Turner (b)
  James T. Rapier (b)
  Charles Pelham (s)
  Charles Hays (s)

1874
CONGRESSMEN:
  Alexander White (s)
  C. C. Sheats (s)
  Jeremiah Haralson (b)
  James T. Rapier (b)
  W. H. Betts (s)
  Charles Hays (s)

1876
CONGRESSMEN:
  Frederick G. Bromberg (s)
  Gerald B. Hall (s)
  James T. Rapier (b)
  Daniel B. Booth (s)

1878
CONGRESSMEN:
  James P. Armstrong (Greenback)
  Jeremiah Haralson (b)

1880
CONGRESSMEN:
  James Gillette (c)
  Frank Threatt (b)
  Paul Strobach (c)
  William J. Stevens (b)
  James Q. Smith (s)
  Arthur Bingham (s)

REPUBLICAN FEDERAL JUDICIAL APPOINTMENTS[3]

1867
Northern District
  JUDGE: Richard Busteed (c)
  ATTORNEY: Francis Bugbee (s)
  MARSHAL: Edward E. Douglas (s)
Southern District
  JUDGE: Richard Busteed (c)
  ATTORNEY: L. V. B. Martin (s)
  MARSHAL: Robert W. Healy (c)

1869
Northern District
  JUDGE: Richard Busteed (c)
  ATTORNEY: Francis Bugbee (s)
  MARSHAL: Edward E. Douglas (s)
Southern District
  JUDGE: Richard Busteed (c)
  ATTORNEY: John P. Southworth (c)
  MARSHAL: Robert W. Healy (c)

1871

Northern District
  JUDGE: Richard Busteed (c)
  ATTORNEY: John A. Minnis (s)
  MARSHAL: Zachariah E. Thomas (c)
Middle District
  JUDGE: Richard Busteed (c)
  ATTORNEY: John A. Minnis (s)
  MARSHAL: Robert W. Healy (c)
Southern District
  JUDGE: Richard Busteed (c)
  ATTORNEY: John P. Southworth (c)
  MARSHAL: Robert W. Healy (c)

1873

Northern District
  JUDGE: Richard Busteed (c)
  ATTORNEY: John A. Minnis (s)
  MARSHAL: Zachariah E. Thomas (c)
Middle District
  JUDGE: Richard Busteed (c)
  ATTORNEY: John A. Minnis (s)
  MARSHAL: Robert W. Healy (c)
Southern District
  JUDGE: Richard Busteed (c)
  ATTORNEY: George M. Duskin (s)
  MARSHAL: Robert W. Healy (c)

1875

Northern District, 5th Circuit
  CIRCUIT JUDGE: William B. Woods (c)
  DISTRICT JUDGE: John Bruce (c)
  DISTRICT ATTORNEY: Nicholas S. McAfee (s)
  MARSHAL: Robert P. Baker (c)
Middle District, 5th Circuit
  CIRCUIT JUDGE: William B. Woods (c)
  DISTRICT JUDGE: John Bruce (c)
  DISTRICT ATTORNEY: Nicholas S. McAfee (s)
  ASSISTANT DISTRICT ATTORNEY: Vacant
  MARSHAL: Robert W. Healy (c)

Southern District, 5th Circuit
CIRCUIT JUDGE: William B. Woods (c)
DISTRICT JUDGE: John Bruce (c)
DISTRICT ATTORNEY: George M. Duskin (s)
ASSISTANT DISTRICT ATTORNEY: John H. Wallace (c)
MARSHAL: Robert W. Healy (c)

1877
Northern District, 5th Circuit
CIRCUIT JUDGE: William B. Woods (c)
DISTRICT JUDGE: John Bruce (c)
DISTRICT ATTORNEY: Lewis E. Parsons (s)
ASSISTANT DISTRICT ATTORNEY: Lionel W. Day (c)
MARSHAL: Robert P. Baker (c)
Middle District, 5th Circuit
CIRCUIT JUDGE: William B. Woods (c)
DISTRICT JUDGE: John Bruce (c)
DISTRICT ATTORNEY: Lewis E. Parsons (s)
MARSHAL: Samuel G. Reid (s)
Southern District, 5th Circuit
CIRCUIT JUDGE: William B. Woods (c)
DISTRICT JUDGE: John Bruce (c)
DISTRICT ATTORNEY: George M. Duskin (s)
MARSHAL: Samuel G. Reid (s)

1879
Northern District, 5th Circuit
CIRCUIT JUDGE: William B. Woods (c)
DISTRICT JUDGE: John Bruce (c)
DISTRICT ATTORNEY: Charles E. Mayer (c)
ASSISTANT DISTRICT ATTORNEY: Lionel W. Day (c)
MARSHAL: Joseph H. Sloss (s)
Middle District, 5th Circuit
CIRCUIT JUDGE: William B. Woods (c)
DISTRICT JUDGE: John Bruce (c)
DISTRICT ATTORNEY: Charles E. Mayer (c)
MARSHAL: George Turner (c)
Southern District, 5th Circuit
CIRCUIT JUDGE: William B. Woods (c)
DISTRICT JUDGE: John Bruce (c)
DISTRICT ATTORNEY: George M. Duskin (s)
MARSHAL: George Turner (c)

1881

Northern District, 5th Circuit
  CIRCUIT JUDGE: Don A. Pardee (c)
  DISTRICT JUDGE: John Bruce (c)
  DISTRICT ATTORNEY: William H. Smith (s)
  ASSISTANT DISTRICT ATTORNEY: Lionel W. Day (c)
  MARSHAL: Joseph H. Sloss (s)
Middle District, 5th Circuit
  CIRCUIT JUDGE: Don A. Pardee (c)
  DISTRICT JUDGE: John Bruce (c)
  DISTRICT ATTORNEY: William H. Smith (s)
  MARSHAL: M. C. Osborn (c)
Southern District, 5th Circuit
  CIRCUIT JUDGE: Don A. Pardee (c)
  DISTRICT JUDGE: John Bruce (c)
  DISTRICT ATTORNEY: George M. Duskin (s)
  MARSHAL: M. C. Osborn (c)

REPUBLICAN PRESIDENTIAL ELECTORS[4]

1868

C. C. Crowe (s)
Joshua Morse (s)
Alfred E. Buck (c)
Thomas O. Glascock (s)
Robert S. Heflin (s)
W. J. Gilmore (s)
Duncan L. Nicholson (s)
C. C. Sheats (s)

1872

Lewis E. Parsons (s)
John L. Pennington (s)
L. C. Coulson (s)
W. J. Gilmore (s)
Charles E. Mayer (c)
William H. Black (c)
J. J. McLemore (s)
William B. Jones (s)
George Malone (s)
Eli F. Jennings (c)

1876

Lewis E. Parsons (s)
Benjamin F. Saffold (s)
Gustavus Horton (s)
Robert W. Healy (c)
John R. Ard (s)
A. H. Curtis (b)
S. S. Booth (s)
A. B. Hays (s)
Henry C. Sanford (s)
Joseph B. Bates (s)

1880

George Turner (c)
Willard Warner (c)
Luther R. Smith (c)
Charles W. Buckley (c)
John J. Martin (s)
Benjamin S. Turner (b)
Daniel B. Booth (s)
Winfield S. Bird (s)
Nicholas S. McAfee (s)
James S. Clarke (s)

STATE REPUBLICAN EXECUTIVE COMMITTEE

1867[5]
CHAIRMAN: John C. Keffer (c)
SECRETARY: C. S. G. Doster (s)
TREASURER: Thomas O. Glascock (s)
Albert Griffin (c)
Moses Avery (b)
Datus E. Coon (c)
Benjamin F. Saffold (s)
Holland Thompson (b)
Peyton Finley (b)
Chester Arthur Bingham (s)
Benjamin W. Norris (c)
Littleberry B. Strange (s)
L. Reese (b)
Samuel Blandon (b)
W. T. Blackford (s)
Joshua Morse (s)
E. Woolsey Peck (s)
T. C. Fullerton (c)
Madison Hendricks (s)
David A. Self (s)
Larkin Robinson (b)
Thomas M. Peters (s)
Francis W. Sykes (s)
Daniel H. Bingham (s)
Sidney C. Posey (s)

1868[6]
Benjamin W. Norris (c)
John Silsby (c)
J. H. Burdick (c)
William W. Buckley (c)
W. H. Black (c)
Chester Arthur Bingham (s)
Pierce Burton (c)
Tobias Lane (c)
Luther R. Smith (c)
J. R. Walker (s)
Andrew J. Applegate (c)
John Morgane (s)
Thomas M. Peters (s)
William Skinner (s)
Samuel T. Fowler (s)
Charles O. Whitney (c)
Augustus W. Jones (s)
John Carraway (b)
S. S. Gardner (c)
Thomas O. Glascock (s)
John O. D. Smith (s)
Samuel Blandon (b)
Thomas Haughey (s)
W. C. Garrison (s)

1870 (May)[7]
CHAIRMAN: Thomas O. Glascock (s)
SECRETARY: J. A. Farden (c)
Benjamin F. Saffold (s)
R. N. Barr (c)
C. C. Colton (c)
Frederick G. Bromberg (s)
Phillip King (s)
Jacob Black (c)
S. S. Gardner (c)
William Bibb Figures (s)
T. D. Fister (s)
John Morgane (s)

1870 May, continued
S. P. Fowler
John J. Martin (s)
Dallas B. Smith (s)
A. W. McBrayer (s)
W. V. Turner (b)
William Miller (s)
C. L. Drake (c)
John Smith (s)
Charles Womble (s)
David Humphries (s)
Eli F. Jennings (c)

1870 (September)[8]
CHAIRMAN: Robert W. Healy (c)
SECRETARY: John C. Keffer (c)
James Bragg (b)
C. Cadle, Jr. (c)
L. S. Speed (b)
Chester Arthur Bingham (s)
Isaac Heyman (s)
Benjamin S. Williams (c)
Robert Reid (b)
William Bibb Figures (s)
P. J. Smith (s)
Neander H. Rice (s)
Eli F. Jennings (c)

1872[9]
CHAIRMAN: D. C. Whiting (c)
SECRETARY: P. G. Clarke (c)
John J. Moulton (s)
George F. Beach
J. V. McDuffie (c)
Phillip King (s)
Charles Pelham (s)
Isaac Heyman (s)
Charles Hays (s)
James M. Edgar
P. J. Smith (s)
George E. Spencer (c)
Myer Goldthwaite

1874[10]
CHAIRMAN: Charles E. Mayer (c)
SECRETARY: M. D. Brainard (c)
John Bruce (c)
B. S. Turner (b)
Phillip King (s)
Isaac Heyman (s)
Nicholas S. McAfee (s)
Charles Hays (s)
P. J. Glover (s)
Joseph W. Burke (c)
A. W. McCullough (c)
George E. Spencer (c)
John C. Goodloe (s)

December 10, 1875[11]
CHAIRMAN: Charles E. Mayer (c)
William Henderson (c)
B. S. Turner (b)
Mark D. Brainard (c)
Phillip King (s)
Isaac Heyman (s)
Nicholas S. McAfee (s)
Charles Hays (s)
P. J. Glover (s)
Joseph W. Burke (c)
A. W. McCullough (c)
George E. Spencer (c)
C. C. Sheats (s)

December 29, 1875[12]
CHAIRMAN: William H. Smith (s)
P. J. Glover (s)
M. D. Wickersham (c)
J. W. Dereen (c)
Mark D. Brainard (c)
Robert W. Healy (c)
Charles W. Buckley (c)
Phillip King (s)
Isaac Heyman (s)
Walton B. Harris (s)
Benjamin S. Turner (b)

Dec. 29, 1875, continued
William Henderson (c)
Benjamin F. Saffold (s)
W. G. M. Gholson (s)
Samuel Cain (b)
J. J. McLemore (s)
C. C. Sheats (s)
John Oliver (s)
Nicholas S. McAfee (s)
Joseph W. Burke (c)
George E. Spencer (c)
A. W. McCullough (c)
John C. Goodloe (s)

1878[13]
CHAIRMAN: J. V. McDuffie (c)
Philip Joseph (b)
Allen Alexander (b)
Nathan D. Wright (s)
William Johnson
H. C. Russell (s)
H. G. McCall
Greene S. W. Lewis (b)
Lewis E. Parsons, Jr. (s)
Samuel D. Oliver (s)
Amos Acker (s)
Alfred Collins (s)
Winfield S. Bird (s)
B. M. Long (s)
A. W. McCullough (c)
Samuel C. Stafford (s)

DELEGATES TO REPUBLICAN NATIONAL CONVENTIONS[14]

1868
DELEGATES AT LARGE:
Robert M. Reynolds (c)
David C. Humphries (s)
James P. Stow (s)
Thomas D. Fister (s)
DELEGATES BY DISTRICTS:
1. Albert Griffin (c)
   Almon M. Granger (c)
2. Willard Warner (c)
   John C. Keffer (c)
3. John J. Martin (s)
   Robert T. Smith (s)
4. Thomas L. Tullock
   Benjamin S. Williams (c)
5. William J. Haralson (s)
   Joseph W. Burke (c)
6. G. M. Tabor
   Jacob Y. Cantwell (c)

1872
DELEGATES AT LARGE:
Robert M. Reynolds (c)
Noah B. Cloud (s)
Lewis E. Parsons (s)
P. G. Clarke (c)
Joseph W. Burke (c)
George E. Spencer (c)
James P. Stow (s)
Paul Strobach (c)
DELEGATES BY DISTRICTS:
1. Datus E. Coon (c)
   Philip Joseph (b)
2. J. V. McDuffie (c)
   E. M. Keils (s)
3. Isaac Heyman (s)
   William V. Turner (b)
4. W. B. Jones (s)
   W. G. M. Gholson (s)
5. William Gaston
   P. J. Smith (s)
6. C. C. Sheats (s)
   S. Bynum (b)

1876
Nominations of May 16, 1876,
   Convention
DELEGATES AT LARGE:
Jeremiah Haralson (b)
Willard Warner (c)
Samuel F. Rice (s)
William H. Smith (s)
DELEGATES BY DISTRICTS:
1. Morris D. Wickersham (c)
   Frank H. Threatt (b)
2. Robert Knox (c)
   Hershal V. Cashin (b)
3. M. S. Patterson (b)
   Robert T. Smith (s)
4. J. V. McDuffie (c)
   Greene S. W. Lewis (b)
5. Charles A. Miller (c)
   William H. Nichols (s)
6. J. A. Cowdery
   William Miller (s)
7. Joseph W. Burke (c)
   Robert A. Moseley (s)
8. J. R. Coffey (s)
   Thomas Masterson (s)

Nominations of May 24, 1876,
   Convention
DELEGATES AT LARGE:
George E. Spencer (c)
Alexander White (s)
Charles Hays (s)
A. H. Curtis (b)

DELEGATES BY DISTRICTS:

1. C. Perez
   George Turner (c)
2. Paul Strobach (c)
3. Isaac Heyman (s)
   A. E. Williams (b)
4. P. D. Barker
   Thomas Walker (b)
5. D. B. Booth (s)
   H. C. Bryan (b)
6. C. C. Sheats (s)
   John D. Ferrell
7. Arthur Bingham (s)
   Robert S. Heflin (s)
8. J. J. Hinds (c)
   P. J. Kaufman (c)

1880
DELEGATES AT LARGE:
George Turner (c)
Benjamin S. Turner (b)
J. A. Thomasson (b)
George M. Braxdall (b)
DELEGATES BY DISTRICTS:
1. James Gillette (c)
   Allen Alexander (b)
2. Paul Strobach (c)
   George W. Washington (b)
3. Isaac Heyman (s)
   William Youngblood (s)

4. William J. Stevens (b)
   James T. Rapier (b)
5. Lewis E. Parsons, Jr. (s)
   H. C. Bryan (b)
6. W. S. Bird (s)
   N. W. Trimble (s)
7. William H. Smith (s)
   Willard Warner (c)
8. J. M. Hinds (c)
   A. W. McCullough (c)

NATIONAL REPUBLICAN COMMITTEE[15]

1868	James P. Stow (s)	1876	Jere Haralson (b)
1872	George E. Spencer (c)	1880	Paul Strobach (c)

ALABAMA SENATE

1868[16]	1870[17]
R. N. Barr (c)	R. N. Barr (c)
F. G. Bromberg (s)	F. G. Bromberg (s)
W. M. Buckley (c)	W. M. Buckley (c)
D. E. Coon (c)	D. E. Coon (c)
J. A. Farden (c)	J. A. Farden (c)
John T. Foster (s)	John T. Foster (s)
W. W. Glass (s)	W. W. Glass (s)
J. J. Hinds (c)	J. J. Hinds (c)
Burrell Johnston (s)	Burrell Johnston (s)
W. B. Jones (s)	W. B. Jones (s)
Phillip King (s)	Phillip King (s)
Thomas Lambert (s)	Thomas Lambert (s)
Benjamin Lentz (s)	Benjamin Lentz (s)
J. W. Mabry (s)	J. W. Mabry (s)
Jesse W. Mahan (s)	Jesse W. Mahan (s)
Green T. McAfee (s)	Green T. McAfee (s)
A. M. McIntosh (s)	A. M. McIntosh (s)
W. B. Martin (s)	W. B. Martin (s)
William Miller (s)	William Miller (s)
J. F. Morton (s)	J. F. Morton (s)
John Oliver (s)	John Oliver (s)
J. L. Pennington (s)	J. L. Pennington (s)
J. D. F. Richards (c)	B. F. Royal (b)
B. F. Royal (b)	Henry C. Sanford (s)
Henry C. Sanford (s)	D. V. Sevier (s)
D. V. Sevier (s)	Isaac D. Sibley (c)
Isaac D. Sibley (c)	J. P. Stow (s)
J. P. Stow (s)	C. O. Whitney (c)
C. O. Whitney (c)	H. H. Wise (s)
Hicks H. Wise (s)	F. D. Wyman (c)
F. D. Wyman (c)	J. A. Yordy (c)
J. A. Yordy (c)	

1872[18]
Jacob Black (c)
A. H. Curtis (b)
J. W. Dereen (c)
C. S. G. Doster (s)
George M. Duskin (s)
W. J. Gilmore (s)
W. W. Glass (s)
J. C. Goodloe (s)
Jere Haralson (b)
W. B. Harris (s)
J. W. Jones (b)
Lloyd Leftwich (b)
William Miller (s)
S. H. Murphy (s)
J. L. Pennington (s)
B. F. Royal (b)
A. P. Wilson (s)

1874[19]
Jacob Black (c)
A. H. Curtis (b)
J. W. Dereen (c)
J. A. Farden (c)
W. G. M. Gholson (s)
W. W. Glass (s)
J. K. Greene (b)
Jere Haralson (b)
W. B. Harris (s)
J. W. Jones (b)
Lloyd Leftwich (b)
William Miller (s)
B. F. Royal (b)

1876[20]
J. T. Harris (s)
Robert H. Knox (c)
Paschal H. Owen (s)
Benjamin F. Saffold (s)

ALABAMA HOUSE OF REPRESENTATIVES

1868[21]
Benjamin Alexander (b)
William Alley (s)
James H. Alston (b)
John Ard (s)
T. W. Armstrong (c)
C. W. Attaway
Alfred Baker
M. R. Bell (s)
Samuel Blandon (b)
J. J. Boyle
Nathan Brewster
S. Brunson (b)
Pierce Burton (c)
M. G. Candee (c)
John Carraway (b)

E. T. Childress
William R. Chisholm (s)
Churchill Corprew (s)
Wesley Cole
George Cox (b)
M. T. Crossland
James W. Daniel
A. R. Davis (s)
J. W. Dereen (c)
Thomas Diggs (b)
O. C. Doster (s)
Joseph Drawn (b)
Alden Emmons (c)
Thomas D. Fister (s)
Ovide Gregory (b)

1868, continued
James K. Greene (b)
Greene M. Haley
John Hardy (s)
John T. Harkins
George Harrington (c)
Rice E. Harris
John A. Hart
A. C. Hewling
D. H. Hill (b)
————— Holman
George Houston (b)
W. F. Hurt (s)
Benjamin Inge (b)
E. F. Jennings (c)
Columbus Jones (b)
S. W. Jones (b)
P. A. Kendrick (s)
S. F. Kennemer (s)
Horace King (b)
E. W. Laurence (s)
Thomas Lee (b)
Greene S. W. Lewis (b)
David Lore (s)
Levi Mahan (s)
E. J. Mancill (s)
Thomas Masterson (s)
George Malone (s)
B. B. McCraw (s)
Jefferson McCalley (b)
John G. Moore
D. S. Neville
Thomas W. Newsom (s)
John Nininger (c)
C. C. Page
James Quinn
H. W. W. Rice
J. D. F. Richards (c)
A. G. Richardson (b)
Justin Romayne (c)
Edward R. Rose
Thomas Sanford

James Shaw (b)
C. P. Simmons (s)
W. H. Slaughter (s)
L. S. Speed (b)
H. J. Springfield (s)
L. R. Smith (c)
William G. W. Smith (s)
Thomas C. Stewart (c)
Paul Strobach (c)
W. T. Stubblefield
John Taylor (s)
W. L. Taylor (b)
Holland Thompson (b)
Charles T. Thweatt (s)
E. E. Tiller (s)
Coke Tucker (s)
William V. Turner (b)
James Vanzandt (s)
J. M. Walker
Willard Warner (c)
Spencer Weaver (b)
George White (s)
L. J. Williams (b)
Jack R. Wilson (s)
Jack Wood (s)
John M. Yates (s)

1870[22]
William Alley (s)
Jacob Black (c)
George W. Braxdell (b)
Thomas Clark (b)
H. Cochran (b)
H. H. Craig (b)
Lewis C. Carlin (c)
A. H. Curtis (b)
Thomas H. Diggs (b)
C. S. G. Doster (s)
John Dozier (b)
George M. Drake (s)
George Duskin (s)
C. W. Dustan (c)

1870, continued
George Forrester (s)
W. G. Gaskin (b)
James H. Graham (s)
Edward Gee (b)
James K. Greene (b)
Jere Haralson (b)
William Henderson (c)
Horace King (b)
Robert Knox (c)
R. L. Johnson (b)
Thomas D. McCaskey (s)
D. A. McCall (s)
George F. Marlowe, Jr. (s)
John Nininger (c)
J. S. Perrin (c)
L. S. Speed (b)
Henry St. Clair (b)
N. D. Stanwood (c)
Paul Strobach (c)
Holland Thompson (b)
Mansfield Tyler (b)
Levi Wells (b)
L. J. Williams (b)
Ashley C. Wood (s)

1872[23]
Jonathan Barton (s)
Granville Bennett (b)
John Bruce (c)
William E. Carson (b)
P. G. Clarke (c)
N. B. Cloud (s)
Henry Cochran (b)
S. W. Cockrell (s)
C. H. Davis
John Dozier (b)
C. W. Dustan (c)
Hales Ellsworth (b)
J. H. Goldsby
J. K. Greene (b)
J. B. Hannon (s)

1872, continued
Thomas C. Hawkins (s)
W. H. Hunter (c)
R. L. Johnson (b)
Reuben Jones
John Lamb (s)
George W. Lawrence (s)
G. S. W. Lewis (b)
W. D. Lovvorn (s)
N. S. McAfee (s)
T. D. McCaskie (s)
Thomas Masterson (s)
Perry Mathews (b)
January Maull (b)
Willis Merriwether (b)
G. R. Millen (b)
J. M. Moss (c)
Lewis E. Parsons (s)
Samuel J. Patterson (s)
George Patterson (b)
Robert Reed (b)
W. G. W. Smith (s)
L. S. Speed (b)
Henry St. Clair (b)
James W. Steele (c)
Lawson Steele (b)
William Taylor (b)
J. R. Treadwell (b)
Thomas H. Walker (b)
Alexander White (s)
L. J. Williams (b)

1874[24]
G. W. Allen (b)
Elijah Baldwin (b)
Granville Bennett (b)
W. H. Blevins (b)
James Bliss (b)
M. Boyd (b)
J. E. Bozeman (s)
Warren A. Brantley (s)
John Bruce (c)

1874, continued
H. V. Cashin (b)
W. E. Cockrell (s)
Elijah Cook (b)
D. E. Coon (c)
D. J. Daniels (b)
Charles Fagan (b)
Adam Gashet (b)
Prince Gardner
William Gaskin (b)
Captain Gilmer
Charles E. Harris (b)
J. T. Harris (s)
A. W. Johnson (b)
Samuel Lee (b)
G. S. W. Lewis (b)
S. A. McDuffie
Jacob Martin (b)
Perry Mathews (b)
Willis Merriwether (b)
Edmund R. Mitchell (c)
Edward Odum (b)
George Patterson (b)
B. W. Reese (b)
R. Reid (b)
J. A. J. Sims (c)
Charles Smith (b)
A. E. Williams (b)
J. R. Witherspoon (b)
Charles S. Wood (s)
Ashley C. Wood (s)
M. Wynn (b)

1876[25]
Elijah Baldwin (b)
Francis N. Baxter (s)
W. H. Blevins (b)
Samuel S. Booth (s)
Warren A. Brantley (s)
H. V. Cashin (b)
William E. Cockrell (s)
Ben Delemos (c)
Captain Gilmer
C. O. Harris (b)
Green T. Johnson
Greene S. W. Lewis (b)
William B. Manasco
Richard J. Mayberry
Samuel F. Rice (s)
Nimrod Snoddy (b)
William J. Stevens (b)

1878[26]
Samuel Boger (s)
Eli Clarke (s)
John M. Clarke (s)
Benjamin Curtis (s)
George English (b)
John W. Foshee (s)
A. H. Owens (s)
John A. Steele (s)

1880[27]
Benjamin M. Long (s)

1867 CONSTITUTIONAL CONVENTION[28]

Thomas Adams (s)
Ben. F. Alexander (b)
J. L. Alexander (s)
Andrew J. Applegate (c)
William A. Austin (s)
J. H. Autry (s)
Arthur Bingham (s)

Daniel H. Bingham (s)
Samuel Blandon (b)
W. H. Black (c)
W. T. Blackford (s)
Mark D. Brainard (c)
Simon Brunson (b)

Alfred E. Buck (c)
Charles W. Buckley (c)
William M. Buckley (c)
J. H. Burdick (c)
Pierce Burton (c)
John Carraway (b)
Alfred Collins (s)
Datus E. Coon (c)
Joseph H. Davis (s)
Ransom Deal (s)
Thomas Diggs (b)
Charles W. Dustan (c)
George J. Dykes (s)
George Ely (c)
W. T. Ewing (s)
James Falmer
Peyton Finley (b)
Samuel S. Gardner (c)
William C. Garrison (s)
J. J. Gilder
George W. Graves (s)
Early Greathouse (s)
James K. Greene (b)
Ovide Gregory (b)
Albert Griffin (c)
Thomas Haughey (s)
Jordan Hatcher (b)
Charles Hays (s)
Gustavus Horton (s)
James F. Hurst (s)
Benjamin Inge (b)
James A. Jackson (s)
R. M. Johnson (c)
Washington Johnson (b)
John C. Jolly (s)
Augustus W. Jones (s)
Columbus Jones (b)
William R. Jones
John C. Keffer (c)
Samuel F. Kennemer (s)
L. S. Latham (b)
Thomas Lee (b)

David Lore (s)
Henry McGowan (s)
Jesse W. Mahan (s)
J. Wright McLeod (b)
J. J. Martin (s)
B. O. Masterson (s)
Charles A. Miller (c)
Stephen Moore (s)
A. L. Morgan (c)
John T. Morton (s)
Benjamin W. Norris (c)
E. Woolsey Peck (s)
Thomas M. Peters (s)
George Plowman (s)
James T. Rapier (b)
Robert M. Reynolds (c)
Lafayette Robinson (b)
Benjamin Rolfe (c)
Benjamin F. Royal (b)
H. C. Russell (s)
Timothy J. Russell (s)
Benjamin F. Saffold (s)
Henry Churchill Semple (s)
J. Silsby (c)
C. P. Simmons (s)
William S. Skinner (s)
Luther R. Smith (c)
Joseph H. Speed (s)
Henry Springfield (s)
N. D. Stanwood (c)
Charles L. Steed
James W. Stewart (s)
J. P. Stow (s)
Littleberry Strange (s)
Alfred Strother (b)
Taliaferro Towles (s)
J. R. Walker (s)
W. A. Walker (c)
Benjamin L. Whelan (s)
Charles O. Whitney (c)
John W. Wilhite (s)
J. A. Yordy (c)

1875 CONSTITUTIONAL CONVENTION[29]

Daniel B. Booth (s)

Samuel F. Rice (s)

J. V. McDuffie (c)

A. H. Curtis (b)

John T. Foster (s)

G. W. Delbridge (s)

W. C. Bulger (s)

Burrell Johnston (s)

H. A. Carson (b)

Robert H. Knox (c)

Greene S. W. Lewis (b)

A. T. Plowman (s)

DELEGATES TO CHATTANOOGA CONVENTION OF REPUBLICANS, 1874[30]

Charles E. Mayer (c)

D. J. Hayne

J. H. Speed (s)

J. D. Sibley (c)

Thomas M. Peters (s)

Benjamin F. Saffold (s)

Adam C. Felder (s)

Alexander White (s)

W. H. Council (b)

Lewis E. Parsons (s)

David P. Lewis (s)

J. K. Green (b)

Alexander McKinstry (s)

C. C. Sheats (s)

Arthur Bingham (s)

L. C. Coulson (s)

Robert T. Smith (s)

Eli F. Jennings (c)

J. A. Patterson

J. F. Bailey (c)

R. Blair

E. M. Keils (s)

George E. Spencer (c)

James Elliott

C. J. Hassett

D. R. Lindsay

P. G. Clarke (c)

D. Woodruff (c)

D. C. Rugg

MISCELLANEOUS FEDERAL APPOINTIVE POSTS, 1869–1881[31]

1869–1873 CONSUL AT ELSINORE, DENMARK: Charles C. Sheats (s)

1869–1875 U.S. SIXTH AUDITOR: John J. Martin (s)

1871–1881 ASSOCIATE JUSTICE, SUPREME COURT OF DISTRICT OF COLUMBIA: David C. Humphries (s)

1871–1873 CONSUL TO RIO DE JANEIRO, BRAZIL: Charles T. Thweatt (s)

1873–1879 CONSUL TO RIO DE JANEIRO, BRAZIL: Joseph M. Hinds (c)

1873–1877 CONSUL TO HAMILTON, CANADA: Henry Ray Myers (c)

1875–1879 GOVERNOR OF DAKOTA TERRITORY: John L. Pennington (s)

1875–1877 MINISTER TO BOLIVIA: R. M. Reynolds (c)

1877–1879 CONSUL TO HAMILTON, CANADA: Robert H. Knox (c)

1879–1883 COMMERCIAL AGENT TO SPAIN: Datus E. Coon (c)

1879–1885 U.S. FIRST AUDITOR: R. M. Reynolds (c)

1881–1885 COMMERCIAL AGENT TO DUNFERMLINE: Henry Ray Myers (c)

1881–1887 CONSUL TO LAGUAYRA, VENEZUELA: Winfield Scott Bird (s)

NOTES

INTRODUCTION

1. Thomas McAdory Owen, *History of Alabama and Dictionary of Alabama Biography* (4 vols., Chicago, 1921); Willis Brewer, *Alabama: Her History, Resources, War Record, and Public Men from 1540 to 1872* (Montgomery, 1872), 368; William Garrett, *Reminiscences of Public Men in Alabama for Thirty Years* (Atlanta, 1872).

2. Montgomery Daily *Advertiser*, August 7, 1868.

3. For discussion of origin of the term *scalawag* see Sarah Woolfolk Wiggins, "What Is A *Scalawag?*" *Alabama Review*, XXV (January, 1972), 56–61.

4. United States Senate *Reports*, No. 22, "Alabama Testimony in Ku Klux Report," 42nd Cong., 2nd Sess., vol. IX, 888, hereafter cited as Alabama Testimony.

5. For summaries of scholarly trends in the writings on Reconstruction see Richard O. Curry, "The Civil War and Reconstruction, 1861–1877: A Critical Overview of Recent Trends and Interpretations," *Civil War History*, XX (September, 1974), 215–38; Bernard A. Weisberger, "The Dark and Bloody Ground of Reconstruction Historiography," *Journal of Southern History*, XXV (November, 1959), 427–47; Robert Reid, "Changing Interpretations of the Reconstruction Period in Alabama," *Alabama Review*, XXVII (October, 1974), 263–81. Carl N. Degler, *The Other South: Southern Dissenters in the Nineteenth Century* (New York, 1974), devotes more attention to the scalawag than have historians of Reconstruction; Chapters V and VI summarize much of what has appeared in state historical journals and in unpublished dissertations about the scalawag. Kenneth M. Stampp, *The Era of Reconstruction, 1865–1877* (New York, 1965), 156–65, has the fullest discussion of the scalawag in any revisionist survey of Reconstruction. Other recent surveys which touch briefly on the scalawag are Allen W. Trelease, *Reconstruction: The Great Experiment* (New York, 1971), 107–08; John Hope Franklin, *Reconstruction: After the Civil War* (Chicago, 1961), 98–103; William R. Brock, *Conflict and Transformation: The United States, 1844–1877* (Middlesex, England, 1973), 375–76. Biographies of individual scalawags include Lillian A. Pereyra, *James Lusk Alcorn, Persistent Whig* (Baton Rouge, 1966); Donald Bridgman Sanger, *James Longstreet: Soldier, Politician, Officeholder, and Writer* (Gloucester, Mass., 1968); Lillian Adele Kibler, *Benjamin F. Perry, South Carolina Unionist* (Durham, N.C., 1946); E. Merton Coulter, *William G. Brownlow, Fighting Parson of the Southern Highlands* (Chapel Hill, 1937).

6. David Donald, "The Scalawag in Mississippi Reconstruction," *Journal of Southern History*, X (November, 1944), 447–60; Allen W. Trelease, "Who Were the Scalawags?" *Journal of Southern History*, XXIX (November, 1963),

445–68, and rejoinder by David Donald, "Communications," *Journal of Southern History,* XXX (May, 1964), 253–56; William C. Harris, "A Reconsideration of the Mississippi Scalawag," *Journal of Mississippi History,* XXXII (February, 1970), 3–42; Otto H. Olsen, "Reconsidering the Scalawags," *Civil War History,* XII (December, 1966), 304–20; Warren A. Ellem, "Who Were the Mississippi Scalawags?" *Journal of Southern History,* XXXVIII (May, 1972), 217–40, and rejoinder by Allen W. Trelease, "Communications," *Journal of Southern History,* XXXVIII (November, 1972), 703–05; Sarah Van V. Woolfolk, "Five Men Called Scalawags," *Alabama Review,* XVII (January, 1964), 45–55; Thomas B. Alexander, "Persistent Whiggery in Alabama and the Lower South, 1860–1867," *Alabama Review,* XII (January, 1959), 35–52, and "Persistent Whiggery in the Confederate South, 1860–1877," *Journal of Southern History,* XXVII (August, 1961), 305–29. The need for more information on the socioeconomic origins of Reconstruction politicians was noted in Larry Kincaid, "Victims of Circumstance: An Interpretation of Changing Attitudes Toward Republican Policy Makers and Reconstruction," *Journal of American History,* LVII (June, 1970), 48–66.

7. Walter Lynwood Fleming, *Civil War and Reconstruction in Alabama* (New York, 1905), 402; Horace Mann Bond, *Negro Education in Alabama: A Study in Cotton and Steel* (Washington, D.C., 1939), 25; A. B. Moore, *History of Alabama* (Tuscaloosa, 1951), 17. Even so recent a study as Jack B. Scroggs, "Southern Reconstruction: A Radical View," *Journal of Southern History,* XXIV (November, 1958), 407–29, refers to these Southern whites as the "heretofore politically submerged class" (p. 407).

CHAPTER 1

1. Huntsville *Advocate,* July 12, 1865. Northern and European travelers commented extensively on the geography of Alabama, its untapped economic resources, and geographic influences on politics. See John T. Trowbridge, *The South, A Tour of Its Battlefields and Ruined Cities, A Journey Through the Desolated States . . .* (Hartford, Conn., 1868), 441–51; Robert Somers, *The Southern States Since the War, 1870–71,* introduction by Malcolm C. McMillan (University, Ala., 1965), 11–125, 157–64; Edward King, *The Great South: A Record of Journeys . . .* (Hartford, Conn., 1875), 328–38.

2. John G. Winter to Andrew Johnson, March 18, 1861, Joseph C. Bradley to Andrew Johnson, March 8, 1861, in Andrew Johnson Papers, Division of Manuscripts, Library of Congress.

3. Malcolm C. McMillan, *Alabama Confederate Reader* (University, Ala., 1963), 233–35.

4. Birmingham *News,* March 21, 1962; McMillan, *Alabama Confederate Reader,* 172–73.

5. W. S. Hoole, *Alabama Tories, The First Alabama Cavalry, U.S.A., 1862–1865* (Tuscaloosa, 1960), 14.

6. McMillan, *Alabama Confederate Reader*, 233–35. Horace Mann Bond, "Social and Economic Forces in Alabama Reconstruction," *Journal of Negro History*, XXIII (July, 1938), 294, confused this William Hugh Smith of Randolph County, the future Republican governor, with William Russell Smith, Tuscaloosa County cooperator who was a gubernatorial contender in 1865. Bond mistakenly combined the two men into one as William R. Smith, member of the 1861 convention who helped Winston County's C. C. Sheats, another dissenter from the same general section of the north Alabama hill country, to organize the Republican party in Alabama.

7. David P. Lewis to J. J. Giers, November 26, 1870, in Records of the Select Committee on Reconstruction, 40 and 41 Cong., Records of the U.S. House of Representatives, Record Group 233, National Archives, hereafter cited as Records of the Select Committee.

8. R. H. Ervin to C. W. Tait, June 27, 1865, in C. W. Tait Papers, Alabama State Department of Archives and History, Montgomery. See also Alabama Testimony, VIII, 226.

9. J. L. M. Curry to E. B. Washburne, January 11, 1865, in Elihu B. Washburne Papers, Division of Manuscripts, Library of Congress; John W. Ford to Andrew Johnson, June 29, 1865, in Johnson Papers; Livingston *Journal*, August 5, 1865.

10. Benjamin F. Saffold to L. E. Parsons, August 2, 1865, in Governor Lewis E. Parsons Papers, Alabama State Department of Archives and History, Montgomery; Livingston *Journal*, August 5, 1865; David C. Humphries to Wager Swayne, November 25, 1865, in Letters Received, Records of the Bureau of Refugees, Freedmen, and Abandoned Lands, Record Group 105, National Archives.

11. August 31, 1865. See also Livingston *Journal*, August 5, 1865, and J. L. M. Curry to E. B. Washburne, January 11, 1865, in Washburne Papers.

12. Livingston *Journal*, August 5, 1865; Joseph C. Bradley to John C. Keffer, April 17, 1867, in Papers of the Bureau of Refugees, Freedmen, and Abandoned Lands, Alabama State Department of Archives and History, Montgomery, hereafter cited as BRFAL.

13. F. W. Kellogg to Zachariah Chandler, June 19, 1865, in Zachariah Chandler Papers, Division of Manuscripts, Library of Congress; Benjamin F. Saffold to L. E. Parsons, August 2, 1865, in Governor Parsons Papers; F. W. Kellogg to Elihu Washburne, December 16, 1867, in Washburne Papers.

14. John J. Seibels to Abraham Lincoln, April 14, 1865, J. J. Giers to Andrew Johnson, May 30, 1865, in Johnson Papers. For comment on the general temper of Alabamians toward their old leaders see Whitelaw Reid, *After the War: A Southern Tour* (New York, 1866), 367.

15. For endorsements for M. J. Bulger see John J. Seibels to Abraham Lincoln, April 14, 1865; for D. C. Humphries see F. W. Sykes and James S. Clark to Andrew Johnson, May 21, 1865, David P. Lewis to Andrew Johnson, May 21, 1865; for D. H. Bingham see John A. Bingham to Andrew Johnson, May 29, 1865, A. G. Mackey to Andrew Johnson, June 16, 1865; for W. H. Smith see George E. Spencer et al. to Andrew Johnson, May 17, 1865, Alabama Citizens to Andrew Johnson, June 2, 1865; for L. E. Parsons see Petition to Andrew Johnson, June 6, 1865, James Q. Smith to Andrew Johnson, June 6, 1865, Huntsville Citizens to Andrew Johnson, June 6, 1865; for T. M. Peters see Alabama Citizens to Andrew Johnson, June 8, 1865, Lucius C. Miller to Andrew Johnson, June 10, 1865, J. F. Wood to Andrew Johnson, June 17, 1865, in Johnson Papers.

16. Jeremiah Clemens to Andrew Johnson, April 21, 1865, ibid.

17. John J. Seibels to Abraham Lincoln, April 14, 1865, Alabama Citizens to Andrew Johnson, May 8, 1865, Alabama Citizens to Frederick Steele, May 1, 1865, C. C. Andrews to Andrew Johnson, May 11, 1865, K. B. Sewall to W. H. Seward, June 2, 1865, Henry W. Hilliard to Andrew Johnson, June 13, 1865, ibid.

18. John J. Seibels to Abraham Lincoln, April 14, 1865, ibid.

19. September 12, 1865.

20. Jeremiah Clemens to Andrew Johnson, April 21, 1865, in Johnson Papers.

21. J. W. Lapsley to L. E. Parsons, July 3, 1865, Alexander McKinstry to L. E. Parsons, July 23, 1865, in Governor Parsons Papers. Many other letters from Unionists and old Democrats who praised this appointment are in Governor Parsons Papers.

22. Brewer, *Alabama,* 542–43; Montgomery Daily *Mail,* May 23, 1867; Montgomery Daily *Alabama State Journal,* March 27, 1873; Harvey M. Watterson to Andrew Johnson, September 26, 1865, in Johnson Papers.

23. Proclamation of Governor Lewis E. Parsons, July 20, 1865, in Lewis E. Parsons Papers, Alabama State Department of Archives and History, Montgomery.

24. Joseph C. Bradley to Andrew Johnson, September 8, 1865, in Johnson Papers; A. W. Dillard to J. J. Seibels, July 31, 1865, in Governor Parsons Papers. See also Huntsville *Advocate,* August 17, 1865.

25. Lewis E. Parsons to Andrew Johnson, August 24, 1865, in Johnson Papers.

26. Allen Johnson and Dumas Malone (eds.), *Dictionary of American Biography* (20 vols. and index, New York, 1928–1936), XVIII, 240–41.

27. Wager Swayne to O. O. Howard, August 21, 1865, in Reports of Swayne to Howard, RG 105.

28. Ibid., November n.d., 1865; Wager Swayne to J. S. Fullerton, June 13,

1866, in General Letters Sent, Headquarters Assistant Commissioner for Alabama, No. 5, RG 105; L. E. Parsons to Andrew Johnson, September 29, 1865, in Johnson Papers.

29. Harvey M. Watterson to Andrew Johnson, September 26, 1865, in Johnson Papers; Montgomery Daily *Mail,* May 23, 1867. For a critical view of Swayne see George R. Bentley, *A History of the Freedmen's Bureau* (Philadelphia, 1955), 196–97. William S. McFeely, *Yankee Stepfather: General O. O. Howard and the Freedmen* (New Haven, 1968), 77–78, reserves judgment of Swayne and notes the need for a thorough study of the bureau in Alabama.

30. Carl Schurz to Andrew Johnson, September 15, 1865, in Carl Schurz Papers, Division of Manuscripts, Library of Congress.

31. Montgomery Daily *Advertiser,* October 1, 1865; Elizabeth Studley Nathans, *Losing the Peace: Georgia Republicans and Reconstruction, 1865–1871* (Baton Rouge, 1968), 9; William C. Harris, *Presidential Reconstruction in Mississippi* (Baton Rouge, 1967), 50. For valuable studies of Georgia Reconstruction see also Alan Conway, *The Reconstruction of Georgia* (Minneapolis, 1966), and Olive Hall Shadgett, *The Republican Party in Georgia From Reconstruction through 1900* (Athens, 1964).

32. Wager Swayne to O. O. Howard, September 18, 1865, in Reports of Swayne to Howard, RG 105.

33. L. E. Parsons to Andrew Johnson, September 13, 23, 28, 1865, in Johnson Papers; *Journal of Proceedings of the Convention of the State of Alabama Held in the City of Montgomery on Tuesday September 12, 1865* (Montgomery, 1865), 49, 57–59, 76, 81; *The Constitution and Ordinances Adopted by the State Convention of Alabama Which Assembled at Montgomery on the Twelfth of September, A.D., 1865 . . .* (Montgomery, 1865), 45, 48, 53, 57–58; Malcolm Cook McMillan, *Constitutional Development in Alabama, 1798–1901: A Study in Politics, the Negro, and Sectionalism,* "The James Sprunt Studies in History and Political Science," Vol. XXXVII (Chapel Hill, 1955), 95–109.

34. Andrew Johnson to L. E. Parsons, October 3, 1865, in Johnson Papers.

35. A. B. Moore to Joseph C. Bradley, October 9, 1865, in Huntsville *Advocate,* November 9, 1865.

36. Fleming, *Civil War and Reconstruction in Alabama,* 372.

37. New York *Times,* May 8, 1867; Montgomery Daily *Mail,* May 23, 1867; R. M. Patton to Andrew Johnson, n.d., in Records of Adjutant General's Office, Record Group 94, National Archives.

38. Wager Swayne to O. O. Howard, November n.d., 1865, December 22, 1866, in Reports of Swayne to Howard, RG 105.

39. Joseph C. Bradley to Andrew Johnson, November 15, 1865, in Johnson Papers.

40. Alexander, "Persistent Whiggery in Alabama and the Lower South,

1860–1867,'' 35–52; Harris, *Presidential Reconstruction in Mississippi,* 119; Nathans, *Losing the Peace,* 13–14; W. C. Nunn, *Texas Under the Carpetbaggers* (Austin, 1962), 7.

41. November 30, 1866.

42. Montgomery Daily *Mail,* November 21, 1867; Mobile *Advertiser and Register,* January 1, 1867; New York *World,* January 2, 1867; L. E. Parsons to Andrew Johnson, January 17, 1867, Andrew Johnson to L. E. Parsons, January 17, 1867, in Edwin Stanton Papers, Division of Manuscripts, Library of Congress.

43. Alabama Testimony, VIII, 226–27.

44. Final Report of Generals Steedman and Fullerton on the Inspection of Operations of the Bureau, in New York *Times,* August 10, 1866; Alexander Forney to Wager Swayne, May 4, 1867, in BRFAL; New York *Tribune,* November 30, 1866; United States Senate *Executive Documents,* No. 6, ''Annual Report of the Assistant Commissioner for Alabama,'' 39th Cong., 2nd Sess., p. 20; Wager Swayne to J. S. Fullerton, June 13, 1866, in General Letters Sent. The most complete study of the bureau in Alabama is Elizabeth Bethel, ''The Freedmen's Bureau in Alabama,'' *Journal of Southern History,* XIV (February, 1948), 49–92. For a recent study of some aspects of the activities of the Freedmen's Bureau in Alabama see Loren Schweninger, ''The American Missionary Association and Northern Philanthropy in Reconstruction Alabama,'' *Alabama Historical Quarterly,* XXXII (Fall and Winter, 1970), 129–56.

45. Willard Warner to John Sherman, December 19, 1867, Wager Swayne to John Sherman, December 28, 1867, in John Sherman Papers, Division of Manuscripts, Library of Congress, hereafter cited as Sherman Papers, L. C.; Montgomery Daily *Advertiser,* July 23, 1865; Montgomery Daily *Mail,* June 29, 1866.

46. Wager Swayne to J. S. Fullerton, June 13, 1866, in General Letters Sent, RG 105. For further elaboration by Swayne of the value of the bureau in Alabama see United States House *Reports,* No. 30, ''Report of the Joint Committee on Reconstruction,'' 39th Cong., 1st Sess., Part III, pp. 138–41.

47. Jabez Curry to Lewis Parsons, September 29, 1865, in Letters Received, RG 105; A. B. Cooper to L. E. Parsons, February 3, 1866, in Applications for Collectors of Customs, Records of the Department of the Treasury, Record Group 56, National Archives; Report of the Joint Committee on Reconstruction, Part III, pp. 12, 30; Theodore B. Wilson, *The Black Codes of the South* (University, Ala., 1965), 76–77, and John Richard Dennett, *The South As It Is: 1865–1866,* introduction by Henry M. Christman (New York, 1965), 302. Important recent studies of the freedmen in postwar Alabama are Peter Kolchin, *First Freedom: The Responses of Alabama's Blacks to Emancipation and Reconstruction* (Westport, Conn., 1972); John B. Myers, ''Reaction and Adjustment: The Struggle of Alabama Freedmen in Post-Bellum Alabama, 1865–1867,'' *Alabama*

Historical Quarterly, XXXII (Spring and Summer, 1970), 5–22; "The Freedmen and the Labor Supply: The Economic Adjustments in Post-Bellum Alabama, 1865–1867," *Alabama Historical Quarterly,* XXXII (Fall and Winter, 1970), 157–66; "The Freedmen and the Law in Post-Bellum Alabama, 1865–1867," *Alabama Review,* XXIII (January, 1970), 56–69; Sylvia H. Krebs, "Will the Freedmen Work? White Alabamians Adjust to Free Black Labor," *Alabama Historical Quarterly,* XXXVI (Summer, 1974), 151–63; John B. Myers, "Black Human Capital: The Freedmen and the Reconstruction of Labor in Alabama, 1860–1880" (unpublished Ph.D. dissertation, Florida State University, 1974).

48. A. B. Moore, "Railroad Building in Alabama During the Reconstruction Period," *Journal of Southern History,* I (November, 1935), 422; William Elejius Martin, *Internal Improvements in Alabama,* "Johns Hopkins Studies in Historical and Political Science" (Baltimore, 1902), 76–79.

49. *Acts of the Session of 1866–7, of the General Assembly of Alabama, Held in the City of Montgomery, Commencing on the Second Monday in November, 1866* (Montgomery, 1867), 686–94.

50. Ethel Armes, *The Story of Coal and Iron in Alabama* (Birmingham, 1910), 107–08; United States House *Reports,* No. 34, "Affairs of the Southern Railroads," 39th Cong., 2nd Sess., p. 696; Bond, "Social and Economic Forces," 317, 318.

CHAPTER 2

1. Eric McKitrick, *Andrew Johnson and Reconstruction* (Chicago, 1960), 287–90, 314–16, 394–420; J. G. Randall and David Donald, *The Civil War and Reconstruction,* second edition (Lexington, Mass., 1969), 576–80; LaWanda and John H. Cox, *Politics, Principle, and Prejudice, 1865–1866: Dilemma of Reconstruction America* (New York, 1963), 105–06. For discussion of Alabama and the National Union movement see Marjorie Howell Cook, "Restoration and Innovation: Alabamians Adjust to Defeat, 1865–1867" (unpublished Ph.D. dissertation, University of Alabama, 1968), 192–96, and Earlene W. Collier, "Response of Southern Editors and Political Leaders to the National Union Convention Movement of 1866" (unpublished master's thesis, University of Alabama, 1963), 3–6, 88–92. Collier's thesis contains a list of Southern delegates to the convention, 93–96.

2. McKitrick, *Andrew Johnson,* 428–47; Randall and Donald, *Civil War and Reconstruction,* 589–91.

3. _____ to Dear Sir, October 8, 1866, in Robert Jemison Papers, University of Alabama Library, Tuscaloosa. For discussion of attitudes in other Southern states see Trelease, *Reconstruction,* 46–47.

4. Montgomery Daily *Advertiser,* April 4, 1866.

5. Ibid., April–October, 1866.

6. Livingston *Journal,* January 5, February 2, 1867; New York *Times,* April 19, 1867; Montgomery Daily *Mail,* April 19, 1867.

7. Wager Swayne to Salmon P. Chase, June 28, 1867, in Salmon P. Chase Papers, Division of Manuscripts, Library of Congress; David P. Lewis to Wager Swayne, July 5, 1867, John H. Hundley to Wager Swayne, August 1, 1867, Francis M. Dansby to John Pope, August 9, 1867, in BRFAL. Michael L. Benedict, *A Compromise of Principle: Congressional Republicans and Reconstruction, 1863–1869* (New York, 1974), 210–43, argues persuasively that the Reconstruction Acts of 1867 reflected more the ideas of moderate Republicans than those of Radical Republicans.

8. Mobile *Nationalist,* March 4, 1867; Montgomery Daily *Mail,* March 15, 19, April 19, 1867; Moulton *Advertiser,* March 16, 1867.

9. Montgomery Daily *Advertiser,* March 12, May 19, 1867; Mobile *Nationalist,* March 4, 1867; Athens Weekly *Post,* May 16, 1867; Moulton *Advertiser,* May 18, 1867.

10. Montgomery Daily *Mail,* March 13, 27, 1867; Montgomery Daily *Advertiser,* March 27, 1867; Moulton *Advertiser,* April 27, 1867.

11. Walter L. Fleming, "The Formation of the Union League in Alabama," *Gulf States Historical Magazine,* II (September, 1903), 76; Fleming, *Civil War and Reconstruction in Alabama,* 554–58; Alabama Testimony, VIII, 305, 487; IX, 894; Bond, "Social and Economic Forces," 327.

12. J. H. Davis to W. H. Smith, May 1, 1867, A. Bingham to W. H. Smith, April 11, 1867, Albert Griffin to John C. Keffer, April 11, 1867, W. E. Connelly to Wager Swayne, April 15, 1867, S. Palmer to Wager Swayne, April 15, 1867, Thomas M. Peters to Wager Swayne, April 20, 1867, Albert Griffin to Wager Swayne, April 22, 1867, in BRFAL.

13. Montgomery Daily *Mail,* April 9, 17, 1867.

14. Joseph C. Bradley to Wager Swayne, April 6, 12, 1867, in BRFAL.

15. Livingston *Journal,* May 11, 1867.

16. Montgomery Daily *State Sentinel,* June 4, 1867; Montgomery Daily *Mail,* June 5, 1867.

17. June 10, 1867.

18. Montgomery Daily *Mail,* June 5, 1867; Montgomery Daily *Advertiser,* June 5, 1867.

19. Montgomery Daily *Mail,* June 5, 1867.

20. The committee was composed of these men in addition to D. C. Humphries: first district, John Hardy (Southerner) and Ovid Gregory (black); second district, Wager Swayne (Northerner) and L. J. Williams (black); third district, J. J. Martin (Southerner) and William V. Turner (black); fourth district, J. H. Speed (Southerner) and Isaac Burt (black); fifth district, J. W. Burke (Northerner) and Alfred McClonley (black); sixth district, Thomas M. Peters (Southerner) and James T. Rapier (black). Ibid.

21. Montgomery Daily *Advertiser,* June 6, 1867; Moulton *Advertiser,* June 15, 1867.

22. For differing reactions of conservatives see Nathans, *Losing the Peace,* 45–57; Thomas B. Alexander, *Political Reconstruction in Tennessee* (Nashville, 1950), 141–42; Joe M. Richardson, *The Negro in the Reconstruction of Florida, 1865–1877* (Tallahassee, 1965), 150–52; Francis Butler Simkins and Robert H. Woody, *South Carolina During Reconstruction* (Chapel Hill, 1932), 83–89.

23. Montgomery Daily *Advertiser,* July 23, August 18, 21, 23, 31, September 1, 3, 1867.

24. Ibid., September 4, 5, 1867. Counties represented were Autauga, Bullock, Chambers, Conecuh, Dallas, Elmore, Greene, Lee, Lowndes, Macon, Montgomery, Russell, Tallapoosa.

25. Joseph Hodgson to Robert McKee, August 1, 1867, in Robert McKee Papers, Alabama State Department of Archives and History, Montgomery. For discussion of a similar situation in Mississippi see Pereyra, *James L. Alcorn,* 93–96.

26. Montgomery Daily *Advertiser,* September 6, 15, 1867.

27. Thomas Haughey to Wager Swayne, April 15, 1867, in BRFAL.

28. Joseph C. Bradley to John C. Keffer, April 17, 1867, ibid.

29. Montgomery Daily *State Sentinel,* May 25, 1867.

30. William M. Cash, ''Alabama Republicans During Reconstruction: Personal Characteristics, Motivations, and Political Activity of Party Activists, 1867–1880'' (unpublished Ph.D. dissertation, University of Alabama, 1973), 86.

31. September 30, 1867.

32. Montgomery Daily *State Sentinel,* September 14, 1867.

33. October 30, 1867.

34. November 29, 1867; Montgomery Daily *State Sentinel,* October 17, 1867. Four Republicans cannot be identified. There is considerable variation in the identification of the origins of the members of the convention. See Fleming, *Civil War and Reconstruction in Alabama,* 517–18; McMillan, *Constitutional Development,* 114–22; James D. Thomas, ''Alabama Constitutional Convention of 1867'' (unpublished master's thesis, Alabama Polytechnic Institute, 1947); Kolchin, *First Freedom,* 178; Richard L. Hume, ''The 'Black and Tan' Conventions of 1867–1869 In Ten Former Confederate States: A Study of Their Membership'' (unpublished Ph.D. dissertation, University of Washington, 1969), 11, 13, 657, 659, 675; Montgomery Daily *Alabama State Journal,* November 13, 1875. See Appendix for identification of convention members.

35. New York *Herald,* November 29, 1867.

36. Brewer, *Alabama,* 560–61; Alabama Testimony, VIII, liii; Montgomery Daily *State Sentinel,* September 25, November 16, 1867; New York *World,* November 11, 1867.

37. John W. Forney to L. E. Parsons, July 8, 1865, in Governor Parsons Papers.

38. Montgomery Daily *State Sentinel*, November 5, 1867; *Official Journal of the Constitutional Convention of the State of Alabama Held in the City of Montgomery, Commencing on Tuesday, November 5th, A.D. 1867* (Montgomery, 1868), 5–10, hereafter cited as *Journal of the 1867 Convention*.

39. New York *Herald*, November 29, 1867.

40. *Journal of the 1867 Convention*, 6–8. For Bingham's ideas for the state constitution see D. H. Bingham to Thaddeus Stevens, October 23, 1867, in Thaddeus Stevens Papers, Division of Manuscripts, Library of Congress.

41. *Journal of the 1867 Convention*, 8–10; Montgomery Daily *State Sentinel*, November 12, 1867.

42. Selma Daily *Messenger*, November 16, 1867. The work of this convention fits the estimate that the Reconstruction conventions of 1867 and 1868 embarked on programs of basic constitutional reform as studied for the South Atlantic states in Jack B. Scroggs, "Carpetbagger Constitutional Reform in the South Atlantic States, 1867–1868," *Journal of Southern History*, XXVII (November, 1961), 475–93. For details of the work of the Alabama convention see McMillan, *Constitutional Development*, 123–50.

43. *Journal of the 1867 Convention*, 30–37.

44. Ibid., 30–35; New York *Herald*, November 29, 1867.

45. Hume, "The 'Black and Tan' Conventions," 25–30.

46. New York *Herald*, November 29, 1867.

47. A list of the classes of officials thus affected clearly illustrates the thoroughness of the disabilities. The classes included the following: U.S. Senators, U.S. Marshals, Treasurer, U.S. Consuls, Commissioners of Revenue, Commissioners of Roads, School Commissioners, Mayors, Aldermen, County Surveyors, Harbor Masters, Attorney General, State Solicitors, Sheriffs, Clerks of Court, Tax Assessors, Constables, Notaries Public, Chancellors, Port Warden, Secretary of State, Comptroller, Foreign Ministers, Governor of the State, Members of Congress, Members of the Legislature, Judges of the U.S. Courts, U.S. District Attorneys, U.S. Revenue Officers, Military, Naval, and Civil Officers of the U.S., State Court Judges, Electors of President and Vice-President, Justices of the Peace, County Superintendents of Schools, Registers in Chancery, Clerks of Supreme Court, Common Councilmen, Marshal of Supreme Court, Intendants of Towns, Librarians of Supreme Court, Commissioners of Pilotage, Board of Engineers, and Warden of Penitentiary. Tuscaloosa *Independent Monitor*, October 20, 1868; William Byrd to George S. Boutwell, December 15, 1868, in Records of the Select Committee.

48. Wager Swayne to Salmon P. Chase, June 28, 1867, in Chase Papers.

49. David P. Lewis to J. J. Giers, November 26, 1870, in Records of the Select Committee.

50. D. L. Dalton to R. M. Patton, November 30, 1867, in Governor R. M. Patton Papers, Alabama State Department of Archives and History, Montgomery.

51. D. L. Dalton to R. M. Patton, December 1, 1867, ibid.

52. Samuel H. Dixon to R. M. Patton, December 1, 1867, ibid. This letter contains the first use in Alabama of the term *carpet bag gentry* to describe the Northern-born wing of the Alabama Republican party.

53. Montgomery Weekly *Alabama State Journal,* July 15, 1870; William H. Smith, *Message of Governor W. H. Smith to the Two Houses of the Alabama Legislature, April 14, 1868* (Montgomery, 1868); *Acts of the Sessions of July, September, and November, 1868, of the General Assembly . . .* (Montgomery, 1868), 27.

54. Approximately one hundred applications from Alabamians for removal of these disabilities are in the Records of the Committee on the Judiciary, Disabilities, Alabama, 42 Cong., Records of the U.S. House of Representatives, Record Group 233, National Archives.

55. Montgomery Daily *Mail,* November 21, 1867; Huntsville *Advocate,* July 10, 1868; Montgomery Daily *Alabama State Journal,* October 14, 1868; Selma *Southern Argus,* August 25, 1869.

56. See Appendix for list and identification of these men.

57. Neander H. Rice to R. M. Patton, August 22, 1867, in Governor Patton Papers.

58. *Journal of the 1867 Convention,* 224–25.

59. Jerrell H. Shofner, *Nor Is It Over Yet: Florida in the Era of Reconstruction* (Gainesville, Fla., 1974), 194.

CHAPTER 3

1. Montgomery Daily *Mail,* December 11, 1867.

2. Montgomery Daily *State Sentinel,* December 14, 1867.

3. Montgomery Daily *Advertiser,* December 15, 1867.

4. Huntsville *Independent,* January 11, 1868.

5. Samuel Dixon to R. M. Patton, December 1, 1867, in Governor Patton Papers.

6. A. W. Dillard to Andrew Johnson, January 24, 1868, in Johnson Papers.

7. Montgomery Daily *State Sentinel,* January 15, 1868; Montgomery Weekly *Mail,* January 8, 1868; L. E. Parsons to Andrew Johnson, January 16, 1868, in Johnson Papers.

8. J. Hayden to W. H. White, January 5, 1868, J. Hayden to Pierce Burton, January 15, 1868, J. Hayden to J. B. Healy, February 1, 1868, George Shockley to Samuel S. Gardner, February 3, 1868, J. Hayden to O. O. Howard, February 13, 1868, in General Letters Sent.

9. J. Hayden to O. O. Howard, January 27, 1868, ibid.

10. Joseph Hodgson to Robert McKee, January 2, 1868, in McKee Papers; Montgomery Daily *Advertiser,* January 7, 1868.

11. Alabama Testimony, VIII, 227; Montgomery Daily *Advertiser,* January 17, February 2, 1868; Montgomery Daily *State Sentinel,* January 18, 1868. For discussion of the Georgia boycott see Nathans, *Losing the Peace,* 45–50.

12. Huntsville *Advocate,* January 7, 1868.

13. Ibid., January 10, 1868; Huntsville *Independent*, January 11, 1868; Montgomery Daily *Advertiser,* January 18, 1868.

14. New York *Tribune,* February 15, 1868.

15. Original Manuscript Returns for Presidential, Congressional, and State Elections in Alabama, 1868, in Papers of the Secretary of State of Alabama, Alabama State Department of Archives and History, Montgomery, hereafter cited as Original Returns.

16. George Ely to E. B. Washburne, February 9, 1868, in Washburne Papers; Montgomery Daily *State Sentinel,* February 12, 13, 1868; Montgomery Daily *Advertiser,* February 11, 1868; United States House *Executive Documents,* No. 303, "Election in Alabama," 40th Cong., 2nd Sess., and House *Miscellaneous Documents,* No. 111, "Affidavits of Discharge from Employment in Alabama for Voting," 40th Cong., 2nd Sess.

17. Athens Weekly *Post,* February 20, 1868.

18. United States House *Executive Documents,* No. 238, "Report of General George Meade on Alabama Election, March 27, 1868," 40th Cong., 2nd Sess., p. 5.

19. F. L. Pennington to Thaddeus Stevens, March 22, 1868, in Stevens Papers. See also C. W. Buckley to Elihu Washburne, May 1, 1868, in Washburne Papers; B. W. Norris et al. to George Meade, March 17, 1868, in Records of the Select Committee.

20. *Congressional Globe,* 40th Cong., 2nd Sess., pp. 3466, 3484; J. W. Beck to Robert McKee, February 17, 27, March 12, 17, 18, 21, 30, 31, April 11, 23, May 9, 11, June 14, 16, July 21, 1868, in McKee Papers.

21. William H. Smith to Andrew Johnson, August 14, 1865, William H. Smith to Lewis E. Parsons, August 15, 1865, in Records of Adjutant General's Office; Register of Applications for Amnesty and Pardons, 1865, 2 vols., Alabama State Department of Archives and History, Montgomery, I, 123; United States House *Executive Documents,* No. 16, "Pardons by the President," 40th Cong., 2nd Sess., p. 35.

22. New York *Herald,* June 20, 1867.

23. Smith, *Message of Governor Smith, July 14, 1868*, 6–7.

24. W. H. Smith to T. M. Peters and Alexander White, July 9, 1870, in Montgomery Weekly *Alabama State Journal,* July 15, 1870.

25. Smith, *Message of Governor Smith, July 14, 1868*, 4–5.

26. Samuel F. Rice to W. H. Smith, August 4, 1868, John Gill Shorter to W. H. Smith, August 22, 1868, W. M. Byrd to W. H. Smith, August 29, 1868, in Governor William H. Smith Papers, Alabama State Department of Archives and History, Montgomery; Selma *Times and Messenger,* August 13, 1868; New York *Herald,* August 12, 13, 16, 17, 26, 1868; Montgomery Daily *Advertiser,* August 15, 1868; Montgomery Weekly *Alabama State Journal,* May 6, 1870; Huntsville *Advocate,* November 20, 1868.

27. Selma *Times and Messenger,* July 29, 1868.

28. Original Returns, 1868.

29. W. H. Smith to Andrew Johnson, July 16, 1868, in Letterbook of Governor William H. Smith, No. 11, in Letterbooks of Governors of Alabama, Alabama State Department of Archives and History, Montgomery.

30. Alabama Testimony, VIII, 34; Willard Warner to John Sherman, April 5, 1866, in Sherman Papers, L. C.

31. Sarah Van V. Woolfolk, "George E. Spencer: A Carpetbagger in Alabama," *Alabama Review,* XIX (January, 1966), 41–42.

32. Montgomery Daily *Mail,* January 14, 1868; George S. Malden to W. H. Smith, July 2, 1868, John Henderson to W. H. Smith, July 4, 1868, in Governor Smith Papers.

33. Original Returns, 1868. See Appendix for names and identification of these Republicans.

34. Allen W. Trelease, *White Terror: The Ku Klux Conspiracy and Southern Reconstruction* (New York, 1971), 81–88, 123–24; Montgomery Daily *Alabama State Journal,* September 23, October 2, 1868; Montgomery Daily *Advertiser,* March 19, 24, 26, September 22, 1868. For discussion of the militia in Southern Reconstruction see Otis A. Singletary, *Negro Militia and Reconstruction* (Austin, 1957).

35. Alabama Testimony, VIII, 93, 94.

36. Montgomery Daily *Alabama State Journal,* September 30, 1868; Montgomery Daily *Advertiser,* August 13, 20, September 16, October 11, 17, 20, 28, 30, 1868; James Holt Clanton to Robert McKee, August 18, 1868, in McKee Papers.

37. William H. Hargrove to A. C. Hargrove, August 14, 1868, in Jemison Papers; M. M. Cooke to Robert McKee, July 13, 1868, in McKee Papers. For activities of Louisiana Democrats see Joe Gray Taylor, *Louisiana Reconstructed, 1863–1877* (Baton Rouge, 1974), 165–67.

38. L. W. Duggar to A. C. Hargrove, August 2, 1868, in Jemison Papers; New York *Herald,* August 17, 1868. Alabama Democratic attitudes toward the black vote were similar to those of Georgia Democrats. See Nathans, *Losing the Peace,* 137–38.

39. George E. Spencer to E. B. Washburne, May 23, 1868, in Washburne Papers; Montgomery Daily *Alabama State Journal,* November 17, 1868;

Montgomery Daily *Advertiser,* August 4, 11, September 4, 16, October 2, 6, 7, 17, 28, 1868; New York *Herald,* August 12, October 7, 1868.

40. Montgomery Daily *Alabama State Journal,* November 11, 14, 1868. For an analysis of the 1868 election and the significance of U. S. Grant in Reconstruction politics see Martin E. Mantell, *Johnson, Grant, and the Politics of Reconstruction* (New York, 1973).

41. W. H. Smith to A. C. Ducat, December 11, 1868, in Governor Smith Letterbook 11.

42. Moore, "Railroad Building in Alabama," 423–24; John F. Stover, *The Railroads of the South, 1865–1900: A Study in Finance and Control* (Chapel Hill, 1955), 88–89.

43. John Ralph Scudder, Jr., "The Alabama and Chattanooga Railroad Company, 1868–1871" (unpublished master's thesis, University of Alabama, 1951), 6–17, provides details of Patton's maneuvers to unite the two roads.

44. Tuscaloosa *Independent Monitor,* October 13, 1868.

45. *Journal of the House of Representatives, Session of 1871–72, held in the City of Montgomery, Commencing on the Third Monday in November, 1871* (Montgomery, 1872), 305.

46. Scudder, "The A. & C. Railroad," 18, 19, 24.

47. Ibid., 28–38; Stover, *Railroads of the South,* 89–90; Bond, "Social and Economic Forces," 321, incorrectly names the Wills Valley and the Northeast and Northwest as the two roads that merged to make the Alabama and Chattanooga.

48. Hilary A. Herbert, *Why the Solid South? Or Reconstruction and Its Results* (Baltimore, 1890), 52; Moore, "Railroad Building in Alabama," 427; Scudder, "The A. & C. Railroad," 54; Alabama *vs.* Burr, 115 *U.S. Reports,* 418.

49. Alabama Testimony, VIII, 193–94; *Journal of the House of Representatives, 1871–72,* 309, 314–18; Herbert, *Why the Solid South?,* 52–53.

50. Herbert, *Why the Solid South?,* 52–53; Armes, *Story of Coal and Iron,* 216; Alabama Testimony, VIII, 232, X, 1411, 1417–18; Alabama *vs.* Burr, 115 *U.S. Reports,* 416.

51. *Journal of the House of Representatives, 1871–72,* 313.

52. Alabama *vs.* Burr, 115 *U.S. Reports,* 418–21; "Reports of Col. James L. Tait, Receiver of Lands, of the Alabama and Chattanooga R.R. to the Governor," *Alabama Public Documents, 1873,* No. 16 (Montgomery, 1873), 507.

53. Armes, *Story of Coal and Iron,* 218–23.

54. Montgomery Daily *Advertiser,* July 28, August 2, 6, 8, 9, 11, 12, 13, 1868; New York *Herald,* August 12, 17, 1868.

55. Montgomery Daily *Advertiser,* August 11, 13, 15, 25, 1868; New York *Herald,* August 12, 17, 1868; Willard Warner to W. H. Smith, July 28, 1868, M. J. Saffold to W. H. Smith, July 28, 1868, Samuel F. Rice to W. H. Smith,

August 14, 1868, J. W. Burke to W. H. Smith, August 16, 1868, D. C. Humphries to W. H. Smith, September 5, 1868, in Governor Smith Papers; Citizens of Montgomery County to Andrew Johnson, September 24, 1868, in Johnson Papers.

56. Montgomery Daily *Advertiser,* July 14, 17, 18, 24, 27, 30, 31, August 4, 5, 6, 13, 15, 1868.

57. A. W. Dillard to John Hardy, August 24, 1868, in Governor Smith Papers.

58. David P. Lewis to W. H. Smith, August 12, 1868, ibid.

59. William Bibb Figures to W. H. Smith, August 24, 1868, ibid.

60. J. W. Burke to W. H. Smith, August 16, 1868, ibid.

61. Joseph C. Bradley to W. H. Smith, August 29, September 3, 1868, ibid.

62. D. C. Humphries to W. H. Smith, September 5, 1868, ibid.

63. See Appendix for names and identification of these Republicans. Twenty-two Republicans remain unidentified in the 1868 house of representatives.

64. David P. Lewis to J. J. Giers, November 26, 1870, David P. Lewis to Benjamin F. Butler, June 23, 1870, William Byrd to George Boutwell, December 15, 1868, in Records of the Select Committee. A. W. Dillard to R. A. Moseley, June 12, 1875, in Applications for Appraisers of Customs, Records of the Department of Treasury, Record Group 56, National Archives.

65. *Biographical Directory of the American Congress, 1774–1927* (Washington, D.C., 1928), 1688; U.S. Bureau of the Census, *Eighth Census of the United States: 1860,* Schedules I and II, Dallas County, Schedule I, Talladega County, hereafter cited as 1860 Census.

66. Alexander White to George Boutwell, December 14, 1868, in Records of the Select Committee; Alexander White to W. H. Smith, December 14, 1868, in Governor Smith Papers.

67. Ibid. See also William Byrd to George Boutwell, December 15, 1868, in Records of the Select Committee.

68. Montgomery Daily *Alabama State Journal,* December 5, 1868; Opelika *East Alabama Monitor,* January 8, 1869.

69. Alexander White to W. H. Smith, December 20, 1868, in Governor Smith Papers.

70. Alexander White to W. H. Smith, January 2, 1869, ibid.

71. Selma *Times,* October 29, 1870.

72. Owen, *Alabama,* IV, 1435; Brewer, *Alabama,* 470–71; Samuel F. Rice to Andrew Johnson, n.d., in Records of Adjutant General's Office; 1860 Census, I, II, Montgomery County.

73. Camden *Wilcox News and Pacificator,* December 15, 1868.

74. Ibid., February 23, 1869; Opelika *Union Republican,* July 31, 1869.

75. Alexander White to L. W. Grant, November 18, 1868, in Talladega *Alabama Reporter,* December 2, 1868.

76. Alexander White to W. H. Smith, January 2, 1869, in Governor Smith Papers.

77. Alexander White to W. H. Smith, March 13, 1869, ibid.

78. Alexander White to W. H. Smith, July 16, 1869, ibid. See also recommendations for White in file of applications and recommendations for judgeship of First Judicial District of Alabama, ibid.

79. Speech of Alexander White, August 2, 1869, in Montgomery Weekly *Alabama State Journal,* August 14, 1869; Pereyra, *James L. Alcorn,* 98.

80. Brewer, *Alabama,* 542; Birmingham *Ledger,* January 14, 1917, in Lewis E. Parsons File, Library, Alabama State Department of Archives and History, Montgomery.

81. Talladega *Alabama Reporter,* March 17, 1869; Columbiana *Shelby County Guide,* March 18, April 1, 1869; Talladega *Sun,* July 1, 1869.

82. Montgomery Daily *Advertiser,* March 27, 1869; Columbiana *Shelby County Guide,* April 1, 1869.

83. W. H. Smith to D. L. Dalton, September 13, 1869, in Governor Smith Papers.

84. Alabama Testimony, VIII, 95, 99.

85. Brewer, *Alabama,* 368; Register of Applications for Amnesty and Pardons, II, 174; David P. Lewis to Andrew Johnson, August 11, 1865, Lewis E. Parsons to Andrew Johnson, August 25, 1865, in Records of Adjutant General's Office.

86. Moulton *Advertiser,* February 19, 1869.

87. Brewer, *Alabama,* 423–24; A. Pegues to ———, August 27, 1859, in Autograph Collection, Military Records Division, Alabama State Department of Archives and History, Montgomery.

88. Alexander McKinstry to Albert Griffin, July 15, 1869, in Mobile *Nationalist,* July 16, 1869.

89. The problem of determining motivations of scalawags is not unique to Alabama, and an interesting alternative approach to this question is explored in studies of roll call votes in the U.S. Congress to determine Republican interests and motivations in David Donald, *The Politics of Reconstruction, 1863–1867,* ''Walter Lynwood Fleming Lectures in Southern History'' (Baton Rouge, 1965).

90. December 8, 1868.

91. Montgomery Weekly *Alabama State Journal,* February 13, 1869.

92. Montgomery Daily *Advertiser,* August 29, 1869.

93. Mobile Daily *Register,* January 28, 1869.

94. Greensboro *Alabama Beacon,* March 13, 1869; Selma *Southern Argus,* March 17, 1870.

CHAPTER 4

1. Mobile Daily *Register,* May 16, 1869; Montgomery Weekly *Alabama State Journal,* April 10, May 22, 1869.

2. Talladega *Sun,* June 17, July 22, 1869; Montgomery Daily *Advertiser,* July 10, 1869; Selma *Southern Argus,* July 14, 1869. See Trelease, *White Terror,* 246–52, 261–63 for details of Klan activity.

3. Selma *Southern Argus,* July 28, 1869; Montgomery Daily *Advertiser,* June 25, July 14, 1869; Montgomery Weekly *Alabama State Journal,* July 10, 1869.

4. Selma *Southern Argus,* July 14, 1869; Montgomery Daily *Advertiser,* August 8, 1869; Mobile *Nationalist,* September 27, 1869; *Biographical Directory,* 1074; Charles A. Beckert to W. H. Smith, August 7, 1869, James Haughey to W. H. Smith, August 8, 1869, in Governor Smith Papers.

5. Montgomery Daily *Advertiser,* August 8, 1869; Jerome J. Hinds *vs.* William Sherrod, Records of Legislative Proceedings, Committee on Elections, Disputed Elections, 41 Cong., Records of the U.S. House of Representatives, Record Group 233, National Archives.

6. *Biographical Directory,* 1553; Montgomery Daily *State Sentinel,* October 25, 1867.

7. Selma *Times,* October 29, 1870; Selma *Southern Argus,* October 7, 1870.

8. Alexander White to W. H. Smith, February 27, 1870, Charles Turner to W. H. Smith, March 9, 1870, in Governor Smith Papers.

9. W. H. Smith to U.S. Grant, March 13, 1869, ibid.

10. W. H. Smith to D. L. Dalton, April 11, 1869, ibid.

11. J. J. Giers to D. L. Dalton, March 1, 1869, ibid.

12. Wager Swayne to F. G. Bromberg, November 30, 1869, Frederick G. Bromberg Papers, Division of Manuscripts, Library of Congress.

13. Montgomery Weekly *Alabama State Journal,* July 15, 1870.

14. *Congressional Globe,* 41st Cong., 2nd Sess., Part III, pp. 2019, 2020.

15. Ibid., Part IV, p. 3668.

16. Selma *Southern Argus,* October 7, 1870; Montgomery Daily *Alabama State Journal,* July 8, 1870.

17. W. H. Smith to Charles Hays, June 20, 1870, in Governor Smith Letterbook 13; Montgomery Daily *Alabama State Journal,* July 15, 1870; Montgomery Daily *Advertiser,* July 17, 21, 1870.

18. D. L. Dalton to George W. Houston, August 1, 1869, D. L. Dalton to Charles Hays, August 12, 1869, in Governor Smith Letterbook 12; W. H. Smith to George P. Charlton, December 26, 1868, in Governor Smith Letterbook 11.

19. D. L. Dalton to J. L. Pegues, June 17, 24, 1869, D. L. Dalton to Sheriff of Marshall County, February 13, 1869, in Governor Smith Letterbook 11; D. L. Dalton to Ignatius Yew, August 18, 1869, D. L. Dalton to W. J. Haralson and G. W. Malone, August 26, 1869, in Governor Smith Letterbook 12; W. H. Smith to

H. H. Thomas, April 11, 1870, W. H. Smith to J. F. Moulton, May 10, 1870, in Governor Smith Letterbook 13; Trelease, *White Terror,* 263–65, believes Smith was too limited in his conception of what he could do to maintain order.

20. See Trelease, *White Terror,* 28–46, 149–225, for an excellent account of Klan activities and the suppression of violence in Tennessee, Arkansas, and North Carolina.

21. New York *Tribune,* June 30, 1870; Samuel F. Rice to the People of Alabama, July 30, 1870, in Talladega *Sun,* August 9, 1870.

22. Thomas M. Peters and Alexander White to W. H. Smith, July 6, 1870, in Governor Smith Papers.

23. *Congressional Globe,* 41st Cong., 2nd Sess., Part III, pp. 2811–12, Part IV, p. 3493; Willard Warner to Charles Sumner, December 6, 1869, in Autograph Collection.

24. *Congressional Globe,* 41st Cong., 2nd Sess., Part IV, p. 3669; Montgomery Daily *Alabama State Journal,* July 9, 1870; Willard Warner to John Sherman, August 23, 1870, in Sherman Papers, L.C.

25. Albert Elmore to John W. A. Sanford, June 8, 1870, in John W. A. Sanford Papers, Alabama State Department of Archives and History, Montgomery. Newspapers favoring use of the black vote included the Montgomery *Advertiser,* Selma *Southern Argus,* Huntsville *Independent,* Tuskegee *News,* Opelika *Recorder,* Tuscumbia *Times,* Wilcox *Vindicator,* Eutaw *Whig and Observer.* Those opposed included the Montgomery *Mail,* Tuscaloosa *Independent Monitor,* Huntsville *Democrat,* Mobile *Tribune.*

26. Montgomery Daily *Advertiser,* January 11, 18, 23, 25, 29, February 2, 5, 19, 22, 24, 27, March 4, 31, April 3, 9, 1870; Montgomery Daily *Mail,* June 11, 1870.

27. Montgomery Daily *Mail,* February 10, 17, 25, 26, May 7, 21, August 24, 1870; Tuscaloosa *Independent Monitor,* March 8, 15, April 5, 1870.

28. W. W. B. Howard to Robert McKee, October 17, 1870, in McKee Papers.

29. Montgomery Daily *Advertiser,* July 8, 1870; Montgomery Daily *Mail,* May 17, 1870.

30. Albert Elmore to John W. A. Sanford, June 13, 1870, in Sanford Papers.

31. Brewer, *Alabama,* 190; Garrett, *Reminiscences,* 732; Montgomery Daily *Mail,* September 8, 1870; James Holt Clanton to Robert McKee, March 22, 1870, in McKee Papers; Montgomery Daily *Advertiser,* September 3, 7, 1870.

32. Alabama Testimony, VIII, 183–84.

33. Montgomery Weekly *Alabama State Journal,* August 26, 1870.

34. Ibid., September 1, 1870.

35. Willard Warner to John Sherman, August 23, 1870, in Sherman Papers, L.C.; Willard Warner to W. E. Chandler, September 20, 1870, in William E. Chandler Papers, Division of Manuscripts, Library of Congress, hereafter cited as Chandler Papers.

36. Original Returns, 1870; Montgomery Weekly *Alabama State Journal,* May 6, September 2, 1870. See Appendix for committee members.

37. George E. Spencer to W. E. Chandler, September 9, October 8, 1870, in Chandler Papers. See also George E. Spencer to the Public, September 17, 1870, in Montgomery Weekly *Alabama State Journal,* October 7, 1870.

38. Loren Schweninger, "John H. Rapier, Sr.: A Slave and Freedman in the Antebellum South," *Civil War History,* XX (March, 1974), 23–34, and "James Rapier and the Negro Labor Movement, 1869–1872," *Alabama Review,* XXVIII (July, 1975), 185–201; *Biographical Directory,* 1631, 1719; Bond, *Negro Education in Alabama,* 66. The best study of James T. Rapier is Loren Schweninger, "James Rapier and Reconstruction" (unpublished Ph.D. dissertation, University of Chicago, 1971).

39. Montgomery Daily *Alabama State Journal,* September 1, 2, 1870.

40. Tuscaloosa *Independent Monitor,* September 13, 1870; Talladega *Watchtower,* September 21, 1870; Moulton *Advertiser,* September 23, 1870.

41. J. McCaleb Wiley to W. H. Smith, September 27, 1870, in Governor Smith Papers. See also Opelika Semi-Weekly *Locomotive,* September 3, 1870.

42. Albert Elmore to John W. A. Sanford, September 5, 1870, in Sanford Papers; Montgomery Weekly *Alabama State Journal,* September 9, 23, 1870; Hayneville *Examiner,* September 21, 1870; Tuscaloosa *Independent Monitor,* September 13, 1870.

43. Milton J. Saffold to W. J. Bibb, September 12, 1870, in Columbiana *Shelby Guide,* September 20, 1870; Milton J. Saffold, "Address to Native White Republicans" [October, 1870] undated pamphlet, in Parsons Papers.

44. Montgomery Weekly *Alabama State Journal,* September 30, 1870. For the Republican strategy in Georgia see Nathans, *Losing the Peace,* 90–92.

45. Selma *Southern Argus,* September 30, 1870.

46. Selma *Times and Messenger,* September 22, 30, 1870.

47. Montgomery Weekly *Mail,* November 2, 1870.

48. Huntsville *Advocate,* October 18, 1870.

49. Selma *Times,* October 29, 1870.

50. Tuscaloosa *Independent Monitor,* September 13, 1870.

51. W. H. Smith to W. B. Figures, October 13, 1870, in Selma *Southern Argus,* October 28, 1870.

52. George E. Spencer to W. E. Chandler, October 8, 1870, in Chandler Papers.

53. Alabama Testimony, VIII, 183.

54. Original Returns, 1870.

55. Selma *Times,* November 29, 30, December 2, 1870; Montgomery Daily *Advertiser,* November 27, 1870; *Journal of the Session of 1870–71 of the Senate of Alabama, Held in the City of Montgomery Commencing on the 21st November, 1870* (Montgomery, 1871), 13–16. Barr had been elected president of the senate after the death of Lieutenant Governor Andrew Applegate, August 21, 1870.

56. Ibid.

57. Montgomery Weekly *Alabama State Journal,* December 2, 1870.

58. Selma *Times,* December 2, 1870.

59. U. S. Grant to C. W. Buckley, November 21, 1870, in Willard Warner Papers, Tennessee State Archives, Nashville (microfilm copy at University of Alabama Library, Tuscaloosa); Montgomery Weekly *Alabama State Journal,* December 9, 1870; *Journal of the 1870–71 Senate of Alabama,* 34.

60. Counties classed as "black" are those containing over 50% black population. Counties classed as "white" are those with less than 25% black population.

61. New York *Tribune,* December 8, 10, 1870; Montgomery Weekly *Alabama State Journal,* December 16, 1870.

62. J. A. Minnis to George H. Williams, July 3, 1874, in Source Chronological Files, Alabama, Records of the Department of Justice, Record Group 60, National Archives, hereafter cited as Source Chronological Files.

63. Original Returns, 1868, 1870; Alabama Testimony, X, 1822. For a detailed study of Klan activities prior to the 1870 election see Trelease, *White Terror,* 246–73. General violence of the Reconstruction period is analyzed in Ray Granade, "Violence: An Instrument of Policy in Reconstruction Alabama," *Alabama Historical Quarterly,* XXX (Fall and Winter, 1968), 181–202, while the Klan's impact on the elections of 1870 and 1872 are considered in John Z. Sloan, "The Ku Klux Klan and the Alabama Election of 1872," *Alabama Review,* XVIII (April, 1965), 113–23.

CHAPTER 5

1. Montgomery Daily *Alabama State Journal,* January 26, 1871.

2. Ibid., January 25, 1871; *Journal of the Session of 1870–71, of the Senate of Alabama, Held in the City of Montgomery, Commencing on the 21st November, 1870* (Montgomery, 1871), 153–55; *Journal of the House, 1870–71,* 234–44.

3. Montgomery Daily *Alabama State Journal,* January 14, 21, February 8, 1871.

4. *Journal of the House, 1871–72,* 310; John A. Winston to Robert McKee, May 12, 1871, in McKee Papers.

5. Montgomery Daily *Alabama State Journal,* April 12, 1871, November 24, 1872.

6. Robert B. Lindsay, "Message of Robert B. Lindsay, Governor of Alabama, to the General Assembly, Nov. 21, 1871," *Alabama State Documents, 1871* (Montgomery, 1871), 13–15; *Journal of the House, 1871–72,* 312–13.

7. *Journal of the House, 1871–72,* 304.

8. Armes, *Story of Coal and Iron,* 243–49; Montgomery Daily *Alabama State Journal,* May 19, 1871. Several months later when the L. and N. leaders had a disagreement with the incumbent president of the South and North, the man so instrumental in salvaging the South and North, James W. Sloss, became its new president.

9. "Report of John H. Gindrat, Receiver of the Alabama and Chattanooga Railroad, to the Governor," *Alabama State Documents, 1871* (Montgomery, 1871).

10. "Message of Robert B. Lindsay, November 21, 1871," 14–15; Allen J. Going, "A Shooting Affray in Knoxville with Interstate Repercussions: The Killing of James Holt Clanton by David M. Nelson, 1871," *The East Tennessee Historical Society Publications*, No. 27 (1955), 39–48, details the events surrounding Clanton's death.

11. *Journal of the House, 1871–72*, 303–19, 354. See also B. B. Lewis to Robert McKee, January 30, 1872, in McKee Papers.

12. "Message of Robert B. Lindsay, November 21, 1872," in Montgomery Daily *Advertiser*, November 24, 1872; Moore, "Railroad Building in Alabama," 434.

13. John A. Winston to Robert McKee, March 21, April 13, 1871, R. K. Boyd to Robert McKee, April 2, 1872, C. C. Langdon to Robert McKee, October 28, 1871, in McKee Papers.

14. Montgomery Weekly *Alabama State Journal*, January 6, 20, May 5, 19, June 23, July 21, 1871.

15. O. E. Babcock to G. E. Spencer, May 25, 1871, U. S. Grant Letterbook, vol. I, in U.S. Grant Papers, Division of Manuscripts, Library of Congress; Selma *Southern Argus*, May 28, June 16, 1871; Greensboro *Alabama Beacon*, June 3, 1871.

16. J. D. Cunningham to C. W. Buckley, May 22, 1871, in Source Chronological Files.

17. John A. Minnis to A. T. Ackerman, May 29, 1871, ibid. See also Republican Central Council of Mobile to U. S. Grant, November 27, 1871, in Applications for Appraisers of Customs.

18. Montgomery Daily *Alabama State Journal*, March 23, 1872; United States House *Reports*, No. 262, "Affairs in Alabama," 43rd Cong., 2nd Sess., p. 1249; hereafter cited as Affairs in Alabama.

19. George E. Spencer to Benjamin F. Butler, April 1, 17, 1871, Benjamin F. Butler to George Boutwell, May 17, 1871, B. S. Turner to George Boutwell, June 22, 1871, R. M. Reynolds to George Boutwell, July 31, 1871, in Customhouse Applications, Alabama, Records of the Department of the Treasury, Record Group 56, National Archives.

20. William Miller to George Boutwell, June 6, 1871, ibid.

21. Willard Warner to Carl Schurz, March 29, 1871, in Schurz Papers; Greensboro *Alabama Beacon*, August 26, 1871; Willard Warner to George Boutwell, August 4, 1871, in Customhouse Nominations, Alabama, Records of the Department of the Treasury, Record Group 56, National Archives.

22. George E. Spencer to U. S. Grant, July 6, 1871, in Mobile Daily *Register*, July 2, 1872.

23. George Spencer to George Putnam, August 12, 1871, in *Report of the Joint Committee of the General Assembly of Alabama in Regard to Alleged Election of George E. Spencer as United States Senator, together with Memorial and Evidence* (Montgomery, 1875), 16–17, hereafter cited as *Report on Spencer Election; Mobile Herald,* August 7, 12, 1871.

24. John A. Minnis to John Sherman, November 18, 1871, in Source Chronological Files; Mobile *Herald,* December 18, 1871, January 8, 30, 1872; Montgomery Daily *Alabama State Journal,* January 25, 27, 30, 1872; Mobile Daily *Register,* January 26, February 3, 1872; John Sherman to Willard Warner, May 20, 1871, May 24, 1872; J. D. Cox to Willard Warner, May 30, June 9, 1871, in Warner Papers.

25. Montgomery Daily *Alabama State Journal,* January 25, 1872.

26. Ibid., March 16, 1872.

27. Eufaula Daily *Times,* May 2, 1872.

28. Frederick G. Bromberg to Carl Schurz, April 12, 1906, in Schurz Papers; Paul Strobach to George E. Spencer, April 18, 1872, in Chandler Papers. For a survey of Bromberg's career see Margaret Davidson Sizemore, "Frederick G. Bromberg of Mobile: An Illustrious Character, 1837–1928," *Alabama Review,* XXIX (April, 1976), 104–12.

29. John L. Swearingen to Lyman Trumbull, April 15, 1872, in Lyman Trumbull Papers, Division of Manuscripts, Library of Congress; Nicholas Davis to F. P. Blair, April 17, 1872, in Schurz Papers.

30. R. W. Healy to W. E. Chandler, April 11, May 18, 1872, M. D. Brainard to W. E. Chandler, May 28, 1872, in Chandler Papers.

31. Charles S. Scott to Robert McKee, June 10, 1872, B. B. Lewis to Robert McKee, May 14, 1874, in McKee Papers.

32. Brewer, *Alabama,* 428–29; Sutton S. Scott, "Personal Recollections of Thomas Hord Herndon, with Remarks upon his Life and Character," *Transactions of the Alabama Historical Society, 1904,* Vol. V, reprint 37 (Montgomery, 1905), 267–68, 274, 276.

33. J. G. Harris to Robert McKee, July 9, 1872, in McKee Papers; Paul Strobach to W. E. Chandler, June 20, 1872, in Chandler Papers; Montgomery Daily *Alabama State Journal,* September 1, 1872; Mobile Daily *Register,* July 5, 1872.

34. Montgomery Daily *Advertiser,* June 22, 1872.

35. Montgomery Daily *Alabama State Journal,* July 21, 1872.

36. Willard Warner to Carl Schurz, July 22, 1872, in Schurz Papers.

37. Paul Strobach to W. E. Chandler, August 18, 1872; D. C. Whiting to W. E. Chandler, August 19, 1872, in Chandler Papers.

38. Original Returns, 1872. See Appendix for names and identification of these Republicans.

39. Montgomery Daily *Alabama State Journal,* August 21, 1872.

40. Ibid., August 16, 1872; James T. Rapier to W. E. Chandler, August 30, 1872, D. C. Whiting to W. E. Chandler, August 19, September 1, 1872, in Chandler Papers.

41. J. A. Minnis to George H. Williams, August 22, 1872, in Source Chronological Files.

42. D. C. Whiting to W. E. Chandler, September 1, 1872, in Chandler Papers.

43. New York *Times,* August 20, 1872; John H. Henry to E. D. Morgan, July 18, 1872, John G. Stokes to W. E. Chandler, October 12, 1872, in Chandler Papers.

44. D. P. Lewis to D. C. Whiting, August 23, 1872, in Montgomery Daily *Alabama State Journal,* August 29, 1872.

45. Montgomery Daily *Alabama State Journal,* July 21, 23, August 29, September 6, 11, October 1, 1872; Eufaula Daily *Times,* October 4, 1872; Montgomery Daily *Advertiser,* August 20, September 21, 1872.

46. D. C. Whiting to W. E. Chandler, September 2, 16, 24, October 13, 24, 1872, James T. Rapier to W. E. Chandler, September 19, 1872, J. J. McLaren to E. D. Morgan, September 24, 1872, George Spencer to W. E. Chandler, September 26, October 7, 17, 22, 25, 26, November 1, 20, 27, 1872, James A. Grace to W. E. Chandler, September 28, 1872, Lewis E. Parsons to Republican National Committee, October 11, 1872, C. W. Hatch to W. E. Chandler, October 14, 1872, J. J. Noah to W. E. Chandler, October 3, 1872, Paul Strobach to W. E. Chandler, November 22, 25, 1872, in Chandler Papers. For details of Spencer's financial maneuvers, see Woolfolk, "George E. Spencer," 41–52.

47. *Report on Spencer Election,* 19, lxxiii; George E. Spencer to W. E. Chandler, November 20, 1872, in Chandler Papers; Montgomery Daily *Alabama State Journal,* October 25, 30, 1872; Florence *Lauderdale Times,* October 29, 1872.

48. John G. Stokes to W. E. Chandler, October 22, 1872, in Chandler Papers; Original Returns, 1872.

49. Joseph F. Johnston to F. G. Bromberg, September 11, November 9, 1872, in Frederick G. Bromberg Papers, Southern Historical Collection, University of North Carolina, Chapel Hill; Montgomery Daily *Alabama State Journal,* October 31, 1872; Selma *Southern Argus,* November 15, 1872.

50. Original Returns, 1872.

51. Montgomery *Advance,* November 11, 1872.

52. *Report on the Spencer Election,* cxxiii. Fleming, *Civil War and Reconstruction in Alabama,* 755, credited Lewis E. Parsons with concocting this scheme. However, carpetbagger Mark D. Brainard was the true author of the plan.

53. David P. Lewis to U. S. Grant, November 30, 1872, George E. Spencer to

W. E. Chandler, November 29, 1872, a.m., George E. Spencer to W. E. Chandler, November 29, 1872, p.m., November 30, 1872, in Chandler Papers.

54. The delegation included scalawag W. H. Smith, former governor, and carpetbaggers B. W. Norris, former congressman, and R. M. Reynolds, former state auditor.

55. David P. Lewis to U. S. Grant, November 30, 1872, in Chandler Papers; Levi Lucky to William H. Smith et al., December 2, 1872, U. S. Grant Letterbook I, in Grant Papers; George H. Williams to David P. Lewis, December 11, 1872, George H. Williams to P. Hamilton, December 11, 1872, Letterbook I, in Papers of the Attorney General, Records of the Department of Justice, Record Group 60, National Archives.

56. Alexander McKinstry to George H. Williams, December 31, 1872, in Source Chronological Files.

57. *Report on Spencer Election,* 3–48, xcvi–xcvii, xxviii, ix; Montgomery Daily *Alabama State Journal,* January 26–February 6, 1873; Lewis E. Parsons to W. E. Chandler, January 9, 1873, in Chandler Papers. See Appendix for names and identification of Republican legislators.

58. Moore, "Railroad Building in Alabama," 434.

59. Montgomery Daily *Advertiser,* February 20, 21, 25, 1873; *Journal of the House of Representatives of the State of Alabama, Session 1872–73* (Montgomery, 1873), 122, 333–34.

60. Montgomery Daily *Advertiser,* February 26, 27, 28, March 1, 4, 12, 1873; *Journal of the House, 1872–73,* 341, 364, 370, 387, 399, 451–52.

61. Montgomery Daily *Advertiser,* March 7, 8, 13, 14, 15, 19, April 5, 6, 24, 1873; *Journal of the Senate of 1872–73 of the State of Alabama, Held in the City of Montgomery, Commencing on the 18th of November, 1872* (Montgomery, 1873), 190, 250–51, 522.

62. Montgomery Daily *Advertiser,* February 25, 26, March 27, 1873.

63. Ibid., February 25, March 1, 1873.

64. Ibid., February 27, 1873; Levi Lawler to A. Cunningham, March 7, 1873, in Levi Lawler Letterbooks, Vol. I (typescript of letterbooks in University of Alabama Library, Tuscaloosa, 2 vols.).

65. R. K. Boyd to Robert McKee, February 18, 1873, B. B. Lewis to Robert McKee, May 14, 1874, in McKee Papers; Selma *Southern Argus,* February 14, 1873.

66. E. W. Peck to D. P. Lewis, March 3, 1873, D. P. Lewis to R. C. Brickell, May 21, 1873, R. C. Brickell to D. P. Lewis, May 25, 1873, in Governor David P. Lewis Papers, Alabama State Department of Archives and History, Montgomery; Montgomery Daily *Alabama State Journal,* June 5, 7, 10, 1873; Union Springs *Herald and Times,* June 11, 1873.

67. C. T. Stearns et al. to John Douglas, April 14, 1873, Alabama Republican

Executive Committee to U. S. Grant, April 12, 1873, Charles Hays to J. W. Douglas, November 28, 1872, Charles Hays to Secretary of the Treasury, April 11, 1873, Charles Pelham to George Spencer, April 17, 1873, Alexander White to John W. Douglas, May 7, 1873, George Spencer to J. W. Douglas, May 3, 1873, in Applications for Collectors of Internal Revenue, Alabama, Records of the Department of the Treasury, Record Group 56, National Archives.

68. George E. Spencer to W. E. Chandler, April 21, 1873, in Chandler Papers; George E. Spencer et al. to U. S. Grant, June 13, 1874, in Applications for Collectors of Customs; Montgomery Daily *Alabama State Journal,* June 16, 1874. Goodloe had withstood considerable Confederate harassment during the Civil War, and in 1872 the Southern Claims Commission found him to be loyal and awarded him $7,446. See Frank W. Klingberg, *The Southern Claims Commission* (Berkeley, 1955), 107, 121. See George E. Spencer to C. W. Dustan, May 18, 1869, in C. W. Dustan Papers, Alabama State Department of Archives and History, Montgomery, for an earlier complaint of Spencer about Reynolds.

69. Montgomery Daily *Alabama State Journal,* February 1, 1874.

70. Ibid., March 11, 1874; Linden *Marengo News-Journal,* February 7, 1874; Phoenix City *Russell Recorder,* February 12, 1874; Selma *Southern Argus,* March 27, 1874. For information on Busteed's judicial behavior which led to impeachment efforts in 1867 and 1874 see Sarah Van V. Woolfolk, "Carpetbaggers in Alabama: Tradition Versus Truth," *Alabama Review,* XV (April, 1962), 135.

71. Mobile Daily *Tribune,* March 12, 1875.

CHAPTER 6

1. *Congressional Globe,* 43rd Cong., 1st Sess., Part I, pp. 10–12; Part IV, pp. 3053, 3451–57; Part V, p. 4176; Part VI, p. 5162.

2. Montgomery Daily *Alabama State Journal,* March 8, 1874; R. K. Boyd to Robert McKee, June 1, 1874, in McKee Papers.

3. Montgomery Daily *Alabama State Journal,* August 4, 1874.

4. Ibid., February 20, 1874.

5. Selma *Southern Argus,* July 10, 1874. See also Edward C. Williamson, "The Alabama Election of 1874," *Alabama Review,* XVII (July, 1964), 210–18, and Allen Johnston Going, *Bourbon Democracy in Alabama, 1874–1890* (University, Ala., 1951), 9–19.

6. B. B. Lewis to Robert McKee, May 14, 1874, in McKee Papers.

7. Mobile Daily *Register,* August 1, 1874.

8. Owen, *Alabama,* 848; Brewer, *Alabama,* 324; Willis Brewer to Robert McKee, May 10, 16, 1874, R. K. Boyd to Robert McKee, April 29, 1874, in McKee Papers.

9. George E. Spencer to William E. Chandler, July 21, 31, 1874, in Chandler Papers.

10. Tuscaloosa *Blade,* July 9, 1874; Selma *Southern Argus,* July 17, 1874; Montgomery Daily *Alabama State Journal,* June 26–28, 1874. See also complaints in the "Address of the Colored People of Alabama, In Convention Assembled, to the People of the United States," in Affairs in Alabama, 1116–17.

11. Livingston *Journal,* July 31, 1874; Talladega *Our Mountain Home,* July 29, 1874.

12. Montgomery Daily *Advertiser,* June 30, 1874.

13. Ibid., July 7, 1874. For example, 640 Republicans in the white counties of Covington, Washington, Geneva, Baker, Sanford had the same voice as 7,000 black voters in Dallas County; 1,200 Republicans in the white counties of Coffee, Fayette, Cherokee, Etowah, and Marion had the same number of delegates as 7,100 Republicans in Montgomery County. In white Jackson County 681 Republicans had the same vote as 3,658 Republicans in Hale. A few weeks after this committee work the chairman, carpetbagger D. C. Whiting, resigned because of ill health and was replaced by another carpetbagger, Charles Mayer. This change had no effect on the plans already made for the state convention. George E. Spencer to W. E. Chandler, July 21, 1874, in Chandler Papers. For discussion of the Florida situation see Shofner, *Nor Is It Over Yet,* 276.

14. George E. Spencer to W. E. Chandler, August 3, 1874, in Chandler Papers. See also Richard Busteed to D. S. Troy, August 29, 1874, in Livingston *Journal,* September 4, 1874.

15. Tuscaloosa *Blade,* September 10, 1874; Montgomery Daily *Alabama State Journal,* September 13, 1874.

16. Original Returns, 1874; Montgomery Daily *Advertiser,* August 4, 1874; George E. Spencer to William E. Chandler, September 17, 1874, in Chandler Papers. See Appendix for names and identification of these Republicans.

17. Tuskegee Weekly *News,* August 20, 1874; Tuscaloosa *Blade,* August 20, October 15, 1874; Montgomery Daily *Advertiser,* September 4, 5, 1874; Mobile Daily *Register,* August 15, 1874; Montgomery Daily *Alabama State Journal,* August 22, September 19, 1874.

18. Montgomery Daily *Alabama State Journal,* October 17, 1874; Mobile Daily *Register,* October 17, 1874. See Appendix for names and identification of these Republicans.

19. George E. Spencer to W. E. Chandler, September 8, 1874, in Chandler Papers.

20. Affairs in Alabama, ii, vi, vii. Nonviolent attacks on white Republicans in Alabama are discussed in Sarah Woolfolk Wiggins, "Ostracism of White Republicans in Alabama During Reconstruction," *Alabama Review,* XXVII (January, 1974), 52–65. See Pereyra, *James L. Alcorn,* 175–76, for discussion of the Mississippi Plan.

21. Affairs in Alabama, vi, xi, xiii, xvi.

22. J. G. Harris to Robert McKee, May 13, 1874, in McKee Papers.

23. Affairs in Alabama, i–xlvii; William Mills to Assistant Adjutant General Department of the South, September 22, 1874, and William P. Miller to "Sirs," September 28, 1874, in File 3579 AGO 1874, Records of the Adjutant General's Office, Record Group 94, National Archives (Roll 170, Microcopy 666, NA Publications).

24. Charles E. Mayer to George H. Williams, September 1, 1874, in Source Chronological Files.

25. Affairs in Alabama, 1285, 1288, 1290–92, 1294, 1296.

26. Selma *Southern Argus,* June 25, 1875.

27. Affairs in Alabama, 451, xxiii; Montgomery Daily *Alabama State Journal,* November 6, 8, 1874.

28. Montgomery Daily *Alabama State Journal,* November 5, 1874; F. B. Taylor to Assistant Adjutant General, November 4, 1874, in Roll 171, Microcopy 666.

29. Montgomery Daily *Alabama State Journal,* November 8, 1874; Affairs in Alabama, xxviii–xxix.

30. Affairs in Alabama, xix.

31. Montgomery Daily *Alabama State Journal,* November 22, 1874.

32. Affairs in Alabama, xvii–xix.

33. Original Returns, 1874.

34. Enclosure in E. D. Townsend to Irwin McDowell, September 23, 1874, in Roll 172, Microcopy 666.

35. George H. Williams to R. W. Healy, September 3, 1874, in Source Chronological Files.

36. F. B. Taylor to Assistant Adjutant General, November 4, 1874, in Roll 171, Microcopy 666.

37. Loomis L. Langdon to Assistant Adjutant General Department of the South, November 3, 5, 1874, in Roll 171, ibid.

38. A. S. Daggett to Assistant Adjutant General Department of the South, November 2, 1874, in Roll 173, ibid.

39. Chauncey McKeever to A. S. Daggett, November 3, 1874, in Roll 173, ibid.

40. A. S. Daggett to W. J. Turner, November 3, 1874, E. Schriver to the Adjutant General of the Army, December 22, 1874, in Roll 173, ibid.

41. E. Schriver to the Adjutant General of the Army, December 22, 1874, in Roll 173, ibid.

42. E. M. Keils to W. W. Belknap, December 1, 1874, in Roll 172, ibid.

43. E. R. Kellogg to the Assistant Adjutant General, Department of the South, November 4, 1874, in Roll 172, ibid.

44. Chauncey McKeever to E. R. Kellogg, November 16, 1874, in Roll 172, ibid.

45. Affairs in Alabama, xxxiv, xxxviii, lxiii. The situation in Alabama fits

substantially the view that the army did not play a major role in the South in Reconstruction as expressed in Franklin, *Reconstruction,* 36. James E. Sefton, *The United States Army and Reconstruction, 1865–1877* (Baton Rouge, 1967), disagrees with Franklin, feeling that generally troops were more significant than Franklin admits. However, in his one specific reference to the role of troops in Alabama elections, Sefton believes that they were not significant in carrying counties for Republicans in 1870.

46. Report of Secretary of War W. W. Belknap, January 5, 1875, in Affairs in Alabama, 1284; Sefton, *United States Army and Reconstruction,* 262, cites different figures. He states that there were 430 troops at eight stations in Alabama.

47. John A. Minnis to George H. Williams, n.d., 1874, John A. Minnis to George H. Williams, November 9, 1874, in Appointment Papers, Alabama, Records of the Department of Justice, Record Group 60, National Archives; Montgomery Daily *Alabama State Journal,* November 8, 25, 1874; Hilary A. Herbert, "Grandfather's Talks about His Life under Two Flags" (typescript of unpublished manuscript in Hilary A. Herbert Papers, Southern Historical Collection, University of North Carolina, Chapel Hill, 2 vols.), I, 278.

48. Selma *Southern Argus,* October 30, 1874.

49. George F. Harrington to D. D. Pratt, June 9, 1875, George Patrick to D. D. Pratt, June 14, 1875, in Applications for Collectors of Internal Revenue; H. Cochran to U. S. Grant, November 12, 1874, in Appointment Papers; A. W. Dillard to R. A. Moseley, June 12, 1875, in Applications for Appraisers of Customs; Montgomery Daily *Alabama State Journal,* November 19, 1874, October 6, 8, 9, 1875. For details of the work of the convention see McMillan, *Constitutional Development,* 189–210.

50. Montgomery Daily *Alabama State Journal,* November 19, 1874, June 16, 1875.

51. A. W. Dillard to R. A. Moseley, June 12, 1875, in Applications for Appraisers of Customs. See also C. F. Moulton to U. S. Grant, February 3, 1875, in Appointment Papers.

52. Affairs in Alabama, xxxix–xl.

53. Ibid., 1113–18; Montgomery Daily *Alabama State Journal,* November 13, 14, 1874; Mobile Daily *Register,* January 12, 1875.

54. Tuskegee Weekly *News,* April 1, 1875; Montgomery Daily *Alabama State Journal,* January 20, 24, 26, February 27, March 9, 1875; Lou H. Mayer to Adam C. Felder, June 23, 1875, in Adam C. Felder Papers, Alabama State Department of Archives and History, Montgomery; Affairs in Alabama, xli; United States Senate *Reports,* No. 704, "Elections of 1874, 1875, and 1876," 44th Cong., 2nd Sess., pp. 104–07, 225.

55. Montgomery Daily *Alabama State Journal,* November 29, December 5, 1874, January 31, March 9, 12, April 15, 1875, March 21, 30, April 6, 11–13,

23, 1876; Elections of 1874, 1875, and 1876, p. 154; *Report on Spencer Election;* Mobile Daily *Register,* February 4, 1875. For the details of Spencer's reelection efforts see Woolfolk, "George E. Spencer," 41–52.

56. Affairs in Alabama, i–lxxii.

57. Linden *Marengo News-Journal,* March 25, 1875; Montgomery Daily *Alabama State Journal,* February 18, 1875; Mobile Daily *Register,* June 18, 1875; *Congressional Record,* 43rd Cong., 2nd Sess., Part III, Appendix, pp. 15–24. See also C. F. Moulton to U. S. Grant, February 3, 1875, in Appointment Papers.

58. Montgomery Daily *Alabama State Journal,* February 7, 10, 1875.

59. Bond, "Social and Economic Forces," 338–42; Going, *Bourbon Democracy,* 61–78. The commission's work and the legislature's action are detailed in the letterbooks of one of the commissioners, Levi W. Lawler. See Levi W. Lawler to P. Hamilton, December 10, 1874, through Levi Lawler to F. Butterfield and Co., December 26, 1876, in Lawler Letterbooks, vol. II. The major Democratic critic of the commission's program of adjustment was Robert McKee, editor of the Selma *Southern Argus.* See L. W. Lawler to Robert McKee, July 3, 1875, C. C. Langdon to Robert McKee, August 30, 1875, Charles W. Raisler to Robert McKee, March 21, 1876, Joseph Hardie to Robert McKee, March 25, 1876, Willis Brewer to Robert McKee, April 5, 1876, Levi W. Lawler to Robert McKee, April 8, 1876, in McKee Papers.

60. Willis Brewer to Robert McKee, February 13, 1875, in McKee Papers.

61. Mobile Daily *Tribune,* June 18, 1875.

62. Montgomery Daily *Alabama State Journal,* June 27, 1875.

63. Livingston *Journal,* July 9, 1875.

64. Montgomery Daily *Alabama State Journal,* June 27, July 25, August 1, 1875.

65. Mobile Daily *Register,* August 12, 1875; McMillan, *Constitutional Development,* 210.

66. *Journal of the Constitutional Convention of the State of Alabama Assembled in the City of Montgomery December 6th, 1875* (Montgomery, 1875), 198–201.

67. Montgomery Daily *Alabama State Journal,* October 12, 28, November 3, 10–12, 1875; Montgomery Daily *Advertiser,* November 10–12, 1875.

68. Montgomery Daily *Advertiser,* October 23, 24, November 2, 1875.

69. Montgomery Daily *Alabama State Journal,* October 9, 1875.

70. Ibid., October 12, November 18, 1875.

CHAPTER 7

1. Mobile Daily *Register,* May 9, 1875.

2. Montgomery Daily *Alabama State Journal,* December 10, 1875, January 1, 1876.

3. Ibid., January 1, 1876; Talladega *Our Mountain Home,* February 16, 1876; L. C. Coulson to E. D. Morgan, March 6, 1876, in Chandler Papers.

4. Montgomery Daily *Alabama State Journal,* December 31, 1875, January 12, 1876.

5. Talladega *Our Mountain Home,* February 16, 1876.

6. Ibid.

7. New York *Sun,* February 10, 1876, in Selma *Southern Argus,* February 18, 1876; New York *Herald,* February 16, 1876, in Selma *Southern Argus,* February 25, 1876; Montgomery Daily *Advertiser,* July 18, 1876.

8. Mobile Daily *Register,* March 18, 1876; Talladega *Our Mountain Home,* March 22, 1876; Tuskegee Weekly *News,* March 23, 1876.

9. Montgomery Daily *Alabama State Journal,* March 22, 25, April 25, 26, 29, 1876.

10. Eutaw *Whig and Observer,* May 4, 1876.

11. W. H. Smith to Willard Warner, April 28, 1876, in Schurz Papers; Mobile Daily *Tribune,* May 7, 1876.

12. Joseph H. Sloss to C. C. Langdon, May 8, 1876, C. C. Langdon to Joseph H. Sloss, May 20, 1876, in C. C. Langdon Papers, Alabama State Department of Archives and History, Montgomery.

13. Willard Warner to Carl Schurz, May 1, 1876, in Schurz Papers; *Proceedings of the Republican National Convention Held at Cincinnati, Ohio, June 14, 15, 16, 1876* (Concord, N.H., 1876, microfilm copy at University of Georgia Library, Athens), 39–55.

14. Mobile Daily *Register,* May 9, 1876; Livingston *Journal,* May 19, 1876; Montgomery Daily *Alabama State Journal,* May 14, 16, 1876.

15. Montgomery Daily *Alabama State Journal,* May 17, 1876. See Appendix for names and identification of these Republicans.

16. Ibid.

17. Ibid., May 25, 1876.

18. Ibid., June 4, 1876.

19. Ibid., June 1, 1876.

20. Mobile Daily *Tribune,* June 17, 1876.

21. Montgomery Daily *Advertiser,* July 14, 1876; Mobile Daily *Register,* June 20, 1876; Willard Warner to Carl Schurz, July 4, 1876, in Schurz Papers.

22. Montgomery Daily *Alabama State Journal,* June 22, 1876.

23. Montgomery Daily *Advertiser,* July 23, 28, 1876.

24. Montgomery Daily *Alabama State Journal,* June 29, 1876.

25. Ibid., July 11, 1876; Mobile Daily *Tribune,* July 14, 1876.

26. Montgomery Daily *Advertiser,* July 23, 25, 1876.

27. Mobile Daily *Register,* July 19, 1876; Greensboro *Alabama Beacon,* July 22, 1876. See Appendix for names and identification of these Republicans.

28. H. R. Hood to Robert McKee, July 29, 1876, in McKee Papers; Original

Returns, 1876. See also J. W. Burke to R. B. Hayes, June 13, 1877, in Rutherford B. Hayes Papers, Rutherford B. Hayes Library, Fremont, Ohio. See Appendix for names and identification of these Republicans.

29. Montgomery Daily *Alabama State Journal,* July 29, 1876.

30. Selma *Southern Argus,* June 9, 1876.

31. Original Returns, 1876; Montgomery Daily *Advertiser,* August 18, 1876; Mobile Daily *Register,* August 23, 1876; Lou H. Mayer to George E. Spencer, August 10, 1876, in Grant Papers; J. W. Burke to R. B. Hayes, June 18, 1877, in Hayes Papers; Greensboro *Alabama Beacon,* February 10, 1877.

32. See Appendix for names and identification of these Republicans.

33. Montgomery Daily *Advertiser,* October 14, 1876; Mobile Daily *Tribune,* October 11, 1876; Mobile Daily *Register,* October 14, 15, 1876; Frederick G. Bromberg to Edward McPherson, December 9, 1874, Frederick G. Bromberg *vs.* Jeremiah Haralson, Records of Legislative Proceedings, 43rd Cong.

34. Montgomery Daily *Alabama State Journal,* October 14, 1876.

35. Selma was now in the first district and Montgomery in the second.

36. Montgomery Daily *Alabama State Journal,* September 21, October 14, 1876; Selma *Southern Argus,* September 22, 1876.

37. See Appendix for names and identification of these Republicans.

38. Montgomery Daily *Alabama State Journal,* August 20, 1876.

39. Ibid., August 9, 11–13, 1876. See also Lou H. Mayer to George E. Spencer, August 10, 1876, in Grant Papers; Elections of 1874, 1875, and 1876, pp. viii–xiv, 204–06, 209–11.

40. Linden *Marengo News-Journal,* July 12, 1877.

41. Willard Warner to John Sherman, June 10, 1876, in Sherman Papers, L.C.

42. Isaac Heyman to Rutherford B. Hayes, May 28, 1877, in Hayes Papers.

43. H. L. Watlington to Rutherford B. Hayes, June 13, 1877, ibid.

44. D. B. Booth to E. A. O'Neal, September 25, 1877, in Edward A. O'Neal Papers, Southern Historical Collection, University of North Carolina, Chapel Hill.

45. George F. Harrington to D. D. Pratt, June 9, 1875, in Applications for Collectors of Internal Revenue.

46. J. D. Vandeventer to Rutherford B. Hayes, December 2, 1876, in Hayes Papers.

47. W. H. Smith to Rutherford B. Hayes, January 1, 1877, ibid.; C. F. Moulton to U. S. Grant, February 3, 1875, in Appointment Papers; L. D. Cabaniss to Luke Pryor, January 26, 1880, in Papers Pertaining to Presidential Nominations to Civil and Military Positions in the U.S. Government, Records of U.S. Senate, Record Group 46, hereafter cited as Presidential Nomination Papers; A. W. Dillard to R. A. Moseley, June 12, 1875, in Applications for Appraisers of Customs.

48. Benjamin Gardner to R. D. Locke, February 22, 1877, in Hayes Papers.

49. George H. Williams to R. W. Healy, September 3, 1874, George H. Williams to Z. E. Thomas, September 30, 1874, Z. E. Thomas to George H. Williams, October 20, November 1, 1874, James Rapier to George H. Williams, October 31, November 2, 1874, in Source Chronological Files; Thomas M. Peters to George H. Williams, September 18, 1874, in Presidential Nomination Papers; Alpheus Baker to U. S. Grant, October 30, 1874, L. H. Mayer to George E. Spencer, August 10, 1876, in Grant Papers.

50. Montgomery Daily *Advertiser*, July 7, 1878; Original Returns, 1874, 1876. See also Wiggins, "Ostracism of White Republicans," 52–65.

51. Original Returns, 1872, 1874.

52. Linden *Marengo News-Journal*, September 14, 1876; Mobile Daily *Register*, September 21, 1880.

53. Linden *Marengo News-Journal*, May 6, 1882.

54. Mobile Daily *Register*, October 28, 1876; *Biographical Directory*, 1999.

55. Joseph H. Speed to G. T. Harris, May 1, 1877, in Appointment Papers.

56. J. N. Tyner to J. M. Conly, December 23, 1876, in Hayes Papers. For a detailed report of the course of the congressional investigation of Spencer's election, see F. W. Sykes to E. A. O'Neal, February 4, 10, 21, 28, November 14, 1874, in O'Neal Papers.

57. Montgomery Daily *Advertiser*, March 3, 1868; Republicans of Alabama File, Alabama State Department of Archives and History, Montgomery; New York *Herald*, November 11, 1867; *Register of Officers and Agents, Civil, Military, and Naval, in the Service of the United States, 1811– . . .* (Washington, 1811– . . .), 1873, p. 127; 1875, p. 90, hereafter cited as *U. S. Official Register;* Montgomery Daily *Alabama State Journal*, June 16, 1874.

58. Levi Lucky to Hamilton Fish, March 29, 1873, R. M. Reynolds to U. S. Grant, August 14, 1874, R. M. Reynolds to W. W. Belknap, August 14, 1874, in Grant Papers; L. D. Mills to H. S. Vanderbilt, April 26, 1873, R. M. Reynolds to W. A. Richardson, April 26, 1873, R. M. Reynolds to B. H. Bristow, July 8, 1874, in Customhouse Nominations; George E. Spencer to W. E. Chandler, April 11, 21, 1873, in Chandler Papers; George E. Spencer to U. S. Grant, June 13, 1874, in Applications for Collectors of Customs; R. M. Reynolds to Adam Felder, August 5, 1875, in Felder Papers.

59. Paul Strobach to W. E. Chandler, August 10, 1880, in Chandler Papers.

60. George E. Spencer to S. W. Dorsey, February 19, 1877, in Hayes Papers; George E. Spencer to W. E. Chandler, March 7, April 7, 1881, in Chandler Papers.

61. W. H. Smith to Rutherford B. Hayes, December 15, 1877, in Hayes Papers; Mobile Daily *Register*, June 12, 1877.

62. Vincent P. DeSantis, "Republican Efforts to 'Crack' the Solid South," *Review of Politics*, XIV (April, 1952), 244–49, and "President Hayes's Southern

Policy," *Journal of Southern History,* XXI (November, 1955), 476–94; R. C. Brickell to R. B. Hayes, June 5, 1877, in Autograph Collection; R. K. Boyd to Robert McKee, December 15, 1877, in McKee Papers.

63. W. W. D. Turner et al. to Rutherford B. Hayes, May 18, 1877, Anderson Johnson to Rutherford B. Hayes, May 22, 1877, in Hayes Papers; John Sherman to Rutherford B. Hayes, May 31, 1877, in John Sherman Papers, Rutherford B. Hayes Library, Fremont, Ohio, hereafter cited as Sherman Papers, Hayes Library.

64. Willard Warner to John Sherman, April 21, May 25, 1877, in Sherman Papers, L.C.; Willard Warner to John Sherman, May 15, 1877, in Sherman Papers, Hayes Library; Willard Warner to Carl Schurz, May 19, 1877, in Schurz Papers.

65. Mobile Daily *Press,* June 16, 1877.

66. W. H. Smith to Rutherford B. Hayes, May 30, 1877, in Hayes Papers; Willard Warner to John Sherman, June 16, 1877, in Sherman Papers, L.C.; Tuskegee Weekly *News,* June 7, 1877.

67. Mobile Daily *Register,* June 12, 1877.

68. Montgomery Daily *Advertiser,* June 17, 1877; Samuel F. Rice to R. B. Hayes, June 11, 1877, in Source Chronological Files; Willard Warner to John Sherman, June 16, 1877, in Sherman Papers, L.C.; W. B. Woods to Charles Devans, June 18, 1877, R. T. Smith to S. G. Reid, August 16, 1877, in Appointment Papers; George Turner to George E. Spencer, February 24, 1878, in Presidential Nomination Papers.

69. Montgomery Daily *Advertiser,* August 23, September 2, 4, 1877; Lewis E. Parsons to Charles Devans, August 7, 1877, in Source Chronological Files.

70. Richard Busteed to Judiciary Committee of the U.S. Senate, October 31, 1877, L. J. Bryan to George F. Edmunds, December 14, 1877, and M. G. Candee to George F. Edmunds, January 10, 1878, in Presidential Nomination Papers.

71. Willard Warner to George F. Edmunds, November 22, 1877, ibid.

72. Marshall Jewell to Charles Devans, January 25, 1878, in Appointment Papers.

73. John Tyler Morgan to Rutherford B. Hayes, December 4, 1877, in Hayes Papers. See also John Bruce to George F. Edmunds, November 19, 1877, N. S. McAfee to George F. Edmunds, November 19, 1877, in Presidential Nomination Papers; W. H. Smith to Rutherford B. Hayes, December 15, 1877, J. T. Morgan to W. H. Smith, December 15, 1877, in Hayes Papers.

74. Montgomery Daily *Advertiser,* September 2, 4, 1877; Tuskegee Weekly *News,* November 22, 1877.

75. Montgomery Daily *Advertiser,* December 1, 1877, March 13, 31, 1878; Mobile Daily *Register,* March 26, 30, 1878; Linden *Marengo News-Journal,* March 28, April 4, 1878.

76. George Cottin to Rutherford B. Hayes, June 27, 1878, in Appointment

Papers; Montgomery Daily *Advertiser,* June 29, 1878; R. M. Reynolds to Rutherford B. Hayes, March 1, 1880, in Hayes Papers.

77. George E. Spencer to U. S. Grant, February n.d., 1871, October 16, 1871, George E. Spencer to J. W. Douglas, May 3, 1873, Charles Hays to D. D. Pratt, May 18, August 16, 1875, W. R. Chisholm to Jere Haralson, June 1, 1875, Jeremiah Haralson to D. D. Pratt, September 8, 1875, W. W. D. Turner to D. D. Pratt, September 16, 1875, George Patrick to P. B. Hunt, October 13, 1875, P. B. Hunt to D. D. Pratt, October 27, 1875, William H. Holley to Commissioner of Internal Revenue, May 26, 1877, Robert B. Jones to John Sherman, March 1, 1879, Charles Pelham to R. B. Hayes, June 15, 1880, R. M. Reynolds to John Sherman, July 12, 1880, W. H. Smith to John Sherman, June 17, 1880, M. D. Wickersham to Rutherford B. Hayes, July 23, 1880, Willard Warner to John Sherman, July 26, 1880, Louis H. Mayer to John Sherman, August 12, 1880, in Applications for Collectors of Internal Revenue; D. B. Booth to Rutherford B. Hayes, August 14, 1875, R. M. Reynolds to Rutherford B. Hayes, July 28, 1880, in Hayes Papers; Lou H. Mayer to Adam Felder, June 23, 1875, in Felder Papers.

78. Charles Pelham to John Sherman, May 15, 1878, in Applications for Collectors of Internal Revenue.

79. George E. Spencer to Commissioner of Internal Revenue, February 5, 1877, B. F. Saffold to Rutherford B. Hayes, May 20, 1878, C. W. Buckley and S. G. Reid to Jere Haralson, May 20, 1878, C. W. Buckley to R. M. Reynolds, May 20, 1878, Joseph C. Bradley et al. to Rutherford B. Hayes, May 21, 1878, Samuel F. Rice et al. to Rutherford B. Hayes, May 21, 1878, ibid.

80. R. B. Hayes to John Sherman, May 22, 1878, ibid.

81. Linden *Marengo News-Journal,* June 6, 1878.

82. W. M. Lowe to Rutherford B. Hayes, November 21, 1878, in Hayes Papers; J. D. Vandeventer to George F. Edmunds, January 25, 1879, James T. Rapier to George F. Edmunds, January 27, 1879, in Presidential Nomination Papers.

83. Linden *Marengo News-Journal,* June 13, 1878; Jacksonville *Republican,* June 22, 1878; Montgomery Daily *Advertiser,* June 18, July 7, 1878; Tuscumbia *North Alabamian,* July 12, 1878; *Proceedings of the Republican State Convention Held in Montgomery, Alabama on the Fourth Day of July, 1878* (Montgomery, 1878).

84. Montgomery Daily *Advertiser,* October 16, 17, 1878, May 1, 1879; Mobile Daily *Register,* April 3, 1879.

85. Montgomery *Republican Sentinel,* October 5, 1878.

86. Mobile Daily *Register,* November 18, 1879.

87. Tuskegee Weekly *News,* January 30, 1879; Montgomery Daily *Advertiser,* February 9, 1879; R. M. Reynolds to Rutherford B. Hayes, January 28, February 12, 13, March 4, 1879, Rutherford B. Hayes to Willard Warner, February 13, 1879, H. A. Herbert to Rutherford B. Hayes, February 27, 1879, in

Hayes Papers; *U.S. Official Register,* 1879, p. 151.

88. Louis H. Mayer to M. C. Osborn, May 8, 10, 1872, M. C. Osborn to L. H. Mayer, May 10, 1872, George Spencer to J. W. Douglas, May 18, 1872, in Applications for Collectors of Internal Revenue; W. H. Smith to Rutherford B. Hayes, February 14, 1880, in Appointment Papers; Willard Warner to R. M. Reynolds, March 1, 1880, R. M. Reynolds to Rutherford B. Hayes, March 1, 1880, Paul Strobach to Rutherford B. Hayes, June 13, 1880, in Hayes Papers; John Sherman to Rutherford B. Hayes, March 12, 1880, in Sherman Papers, Hayes Library; Willard Warner to George F. Edmunds, April 5, 1880, in Presidential Nomination Papers.

89. L. H. Mayer to George Turner, June 29, 1880, in Hayes Papers; Montgomery Daily *Advertiser,* May 21, 22, July 25, August 18, 1880; M. C. Osborn to L. H. Mayer, May 8, 1880, George Turner to L. H. Mayer, May 10, 1880, M. C. Osborn to L. H. Mayer, May 11, 1880, in Applications for Collectors of Internal Revenue.

90. Chicago *Times,* May 29, June 2, 1880; Tuskegee Weekly *News,* June 17, 1880; *Proceedings of the Republican National Convention Held at Chicago, Illinois, . . . June 2, 3, 4, 5, 6, 7* (Chicago, 1881, microfilm copy at University of Georgia Library, Athens), 83–93.

91. Paul Strobach to Rutherford B. Hayes, June 13, 1880, R. M. Reynolds to Rutherford B. Hayes, June 15, 1880, in Hayes Papers; Willard Warner to Carl Schurz, June 24, 1880, in Schurz Papers.

92. Linden *Marengo News-Journal,* July 8, 1880, March 3, 1881.

93. Joseph W. Burke to Rutherford B. Hayes, July 10, 1880, in Hayes Papers; Joseph W. Burke to W. E. Chandler, June 8, 1882, in Chandler Papers.

94. Montgomery Daily *Advertiser,* November 20, 1880; Original Returns, 1880.

95. W. B. Woods to Rutherford B. Hayes, December 16, 1880, C. J. L. Cunningham to Rutherford B. Hayes, December 16, 1880, Willard Warner to Rutherford B. Hayes, December 25, 1880, in Hayes Papers; Linden *Marengo News-Journal,* December 23, 1880.

96. George Turner to W. E. Chandler, June 4, 1881, George E. Spencer to W. E. Chandler, April 7, 1881, in Chandler Papers.

CHAPTER 8

1. Trelease, "Who Were the Scalawags?" 445–68.

2. The "gentleman" was Lewis Owen of Montgomery. 1860 Census, Schedule I, Montgomery County.

3. Pardons by the President; Register of Applications for Amnesty.

4. 1860 Census, Schedule I, Alabama.

5. Montgomery Daily *State Sentinel,* December 7, 1867.

6. See Appendix; John Witherspoon DuBose, *Alabama's Tragic Decade, Ten Years of Alabama, 1865–1874*, edited by James K. Greer (Birmingham, 1940), 249; Fleming, *Civil War and Reconstruction in Alabama*, Part IV. A scalawag is counted only once in each category of offices in which he served, regardless of the length of the appointment or the number of times he was reelected to that office.

7. See Appendix for names of these Republicans, their positions, and their identification as scalawags, carpetbaggers, or blacks.

8. Ibid.

9. Montgomery Daily *Alabama State Journal,* January 28, 1872.

10. September 7, 1877.

11. Charles Nordhoff, *The Cotton States in the Spring and Summer of 1875* (New York, 1876), 89.

12. Loren Schweninger, "Black Citizenship and the Republican Party in Alabama," *Alabama Review,* XXIX (April, 1976), 83–103; Olsen, "Reconsidering the Scalawags," 304–20.

13. William R. Brock, *An American Crisis: Congress and Reconstruction, 1865–1867* (London, 1963), 302.

APPENDIX

1. Original Returns, 1868, 1870, 1872, 1874, 1876; Mobile Daily *Register,* May 18, 1876; Montgomery Daily *Advertiser,* May 27, 1876.

2. Ibid., 1868, 1869, 1870, 1872, 1874, 1876, 1878, 1880.

3. *U.S. Official Register,* 1867, 1869, 1871, 1873, 1875, 1877, 1879, 1881.

4. Original Returns, 1868, 1872, 1876, 1880.

5. Montgomery Daily *Alabama State Journal,* June 20, 1867; Wetumpka *Elmore Standard,* October 25, 1867.

6. Mobile *Nationalist,* July 2, 1868.

7. Demopolis *Southern Republican,* June 8, 1870.

8. Ibid., September 14, 1870; Montgomery Weekly *Alabama State Journal,* September 2, 1870.

9. Montgomery Weekly *Alabama State Journal,* August 23, 1872.

10. Montgomery Daily *Alabama State Journal,* August 24, 1874.

11. Ibid., December 10, 1875.

12. Ibid., December 31, 1875.

13. *Proceedings of the Republican State Convention, July, 1878.*

14. *Proceedings of the Republican National Conventions,* 1868, 1872, 1876, 1880; Montgomery Daily *Advertiser,* May 22, 1880; Montgomery Daily *Alabama State Journal,* June 4, 1876.

15. Ibid.

16. Selma *Southern Argus,* December 2, 1870.

17. Ibid.

18. Montgomery Daily *Advertiser*, November 17, 1872; *Journal of the Senate, 1872–73*, 4.

19. Selma *Southern Argus*, December 4, 1874.

20. Montgomery Daily *Advertiser*, September 15, 1876.

21. Montgomery Daily *State Sentinel*, February 8, 20, 1868; Original Returns, 1868; *Journal of the House of Representatives During the Sessions Commencing in July, September, and November, 1868, Held in the City of Montgomery* (Montgomery, 1868, microfilm copy at University of Alabama Library, Tuscaloosa), 3–4. The composition of the 1868 house of representatives is a prime example of the disagreement on identification of Alabama Reconstruction Republicans. Fleming, *Civil War and Reconstruction in Alabama*, 738, found twenty-four. Unfortunately, since neither book lists members identified, no correlation can be made with this present list, which found twenty-seven blacks.

22. Selma *Southern Argus*, December 2, 1870; *Journal of the House, 1871–72*, 683–85; Garrett, *Reminiscences*, 741–69.

23. *Journal of the House, 1872–73*, 974–76; Montgomery Daily *Advertiser*, November 17, 1872.

24. Selma *Southern Argus*, December 4, 1874; *Journal of the House of Representatives of the State of Alabama Session of 1874–5, Held in the City of Montgomery, Commencing November 16, 1874* (Montgomery, 1875), 3–6.

25. Montgomery Daily *Advertiser*, September 15, 1876; *Journal of the House of Representatives, of the State of Alabama, Session of 1876–7 Held in the City of Montgomery, Commencing November 14, 1876* (Montgomery, 1877), 3–8.

26. Montgomery Daily *Advertiser*, August 24, 1878; *Journal of the House of Representatives of the State of Alabama, Session of 1878–9 Held in the City of Montgomery, Commencing November 12th, 1878* (Montgomery, 1879), 3–5.

27. Montgomery Daily *Advertiser*, November 9, 1880.

28. *Journal of the 1867 Convention*.

29. Original Returns, 1875.

30. Montgomery Daily *Alabama State Journal*, October 17, 1874.

31. *U.S. Official Register*, 1869, 1871, 1873, 1875, 1877, 1879, 1881.

BIBLIOGRAPHY

I. PRIMARY SOURCES

A. MANUSCRIPTS

Alabama State Department of Archives and History, Montgomery
  Autograph Collection.
  Papers of Bureau of Refugees, Freedmen, and Abandoned Lands.
  Confederate Military Records.
  John Witherspoon DuBose Papers.
  C. W. Dustan Papers.
  Adam C. Felder File.
  Adam C. Felder Papers.
  George S. Houston Papers.
  Index to Civil Registers of Appointments, Papers of the Secretary of State of Alabama.
  Robert McKee Papers.
  Charles C. Langdon Papers.
  Governor David P. Lewis Papers.
  Original Manuscript Returns for Presidential, Congressional, and State Elections in Alabama, Papers of the Secretary of State of Alabama.
  Wallace Parham Papers.
  Governor Lewis E. Parsons Papers.
  Lewis E. Parsons File.
  Lewis E. Parsons Papers.
  Governor R. M. Patton Papers.
  Register of Applications for Amnesty and Pardons, 1865, 2 vols.
  Republicans of Alabama File.
  John W. A. Sanford Papers.
  Papers of the Secretary of State of Alabama, Letters Received.
  Henry Churchill Semple File.
  Henry Churchill Semple Papers.
  Governor William H. Smith Letterbooks, No. 10–13.
  Governor William H. Smith Papers.
  Wager Swayne Papers.
  C. W. Tait Papers.
Rutherford B. Hayes Library, Fremont, Ohio
  Rutherford B. Hayes Papers.
  John Sherman Papers.
Howard University Library, Washington, D.C.
  James T. Rapier Papers.
Division of Manuscripts, Library of Congress, Washington, D.C.
  Frederick G. Bromberg Papers.

Salmon P. Chase Papers.
William E. Chandler Papers.
Zachariah Chandler Papers.
U. S. Grant Papers.
Andrew Johnson Papers.
Carl Schurz Papers.
John Sherman Papers.
Edwin Stanton Papers.
Thaddeus Stevens Papers.
Lyman Trumbull Papers.
Elihu B. Washburne Papers.

National Archives, Washington, D.C.

Applications for Appraisers of Customs, Records of the Department of the Treasury, Record Group 56.

Applications for Collectors of Customs, Alabama, Records of the Department of the Treasury, Record Group 56.

Applications for Collectors of Internal Revenue, Alabama, Records of the Department of the Treasury, Record Group 56.

Appointment Papers, Alabama, Records of the Department of Justice, Record Group 60.

Customhouse Applications, Alabama, Records of the Department of the Treasury, Record Group 56.

Customhouse Nominations, Alabama, Records of the Department of the Treasury, Record Group 56.

Letters Received, Letterbooks, Papers of the U.S. Attorney General, Record Group 60.

Papers of the Attorney General, Records of the Department of Justice, Record Group 60.

Papers Pertaining to Presidential Nominations to Civil and Military Positions in the U.S. Government, Records of the U.S. Senate, Record Group 56.

Records of Adjutant General's Office, Record Group 94.

Records of Adjutant General's Office, Record Group 94, Rolls 169–173, Microcopy 666, NA Publications.

Records of the Bureau of Refugees, Freedmen, and Abandoned Lands, Record Group 105.

Records of Legislative Proceedings, Committee on Elections, 41, 42, 43 Cong., Records of the U.S. House of Representatives, Record Group 233.

Records of the Committee on the Judiciary, 42 Cong., Disabilities, Alabama, Records of the U.S. House of Representatives, Record Group 233.

Records of the Select Committee on Reconstruction, 40 and 41 Cong., Records of the U.S. House of Representatives, Record Group 233.

Source Chronological Files, Alabama, Records of the Department of Justice,

Record Group 60.

Southern Historical Collection, University of North Carolina, Chapel Hill
Frederick G. Bromberg Papers.
Hilary A. Herbert Papers.
Edward A. O'Neal Papers.

University of Alabama Library, Tuscaloosa
Robert Jemison Papers.
Levi W. Lawler Letterbooks, 2 vols. Typescript, originals in Lawler-Whiting home near Talladega.
Willard Warner Papers. Microfilm, originals in Tennessee State Archives, Nashville.

B. UNITED STATES GOVERNMENT PUBLICATIONS

Alabama *vs.* Burr, 115 *U.S. Reports.*
Biographical Directory of the American Congress, 1774–1927. Washington, D.C., 1928.
Congressional Globe, 40, 41 Congress.
Congressional Record, 43, 44 Congress.
List of Southern Union Loyalists, 1861–1865. Washington, D.C., 1873.
Register of Officers and Agents, Civil, Military, and Naval, in the Service of the United States on the Thirtieth of September, 1865, 1867, 1869, 1871, 1873, 1875, 1877, 1879, 1881. Washington, D.C., 1866–1882.
U.S. Bureau of the Census. *Eighth Census of the United States: 1860,* Schedules I, II, Alabama.
————. *Ninth Census of the United States: 1870,* Alabama.
U.S. Congress, House. *Executive Documents,* No. 303, "Election in Alabama," 40th Cong., 2nd Sess.
————. *Executive Documents,* No. 16, "Pardons by the President," 40th Cong., 2nd Sess.
————. *Executive Documents,* No. 238, "Report of General George Meade on Alabama Election, March 27, 1868," 40th Cong., 2nd Sess.
————. *Miscellaneous Documents,* No. 111, "Affidavits of Discharge from Employment in Alabama for Voting," 40th Cong., 2nd Sess.
————. *Reports,* No. 262, "Affairs in Alabama," 43rd Cong., 2nd Sess.
————. *Reports,* No. 34, "Affairs of the Southern Railroads," 39th Cong., 2nd Sess.
————. *Reports,* No. 30, "Report of the Joint Committee on Reconstruction," 39th Cong., 1st Sess.
U.S. Congress, Senate. *Executive Documents,* No. 6. "Annual Report of Assistant Commissioner for Alabama," 39th Cong., 2nd Sess.
————. *Reports,* No. 22, "Alabama Testimony in Ku Klux Reports," 42nd Cong., 2nd Sess.

_____. *Reports*, No. 704, "Elections of 1874, 1875, and 1876," 44th Cong., 2nd Sess.

C. OFFICIAL ALABAMA DOCUMENTS

Acts of the Sessions of July, September, and November, 1868, of the General Assembly of Alabama. Montgomery, 1868.

Acts of the Session of 1866–7, of the General Assembly of Alabama, Held in the City of Montgomery, Commencing on the Second Monday in November, 1866. Montgomery, 1867.

The Constitution and Ordinances Adopted by the State Convention of Alabama Which Assembled at Montgomery on the Twelfth of September, A.D., 1865 . . . Montgomery, 1865.

Journal of the Constitutional Convention of the State of Alabama Assembled in the City of Montgomery December 6th, 1875. Montgomery, 1875.

Journal of the House of Representatives During the Sessions Commencing in July, September, and November, 1868, Held in the City of Montgomery. Montgomery, 1868, microfilm copy in University of Alabama Library, Tuscaloosa.

Journal of the Session of 1870–71 of the House of Representatives of the State of Alabama, Held in the City of Montgomery, Commencing on 21st November, 1870. Montgomery, 1871.

Journal of the House of Representatives, Session of 1871–72, Held in the City of Montgomery, Commencing on the Third Monday in November, 1871. Montgomery, 1872.

Journal of the House of Representatives of the State of Alabama, Session 1872–73. Montgomery, 1873.

Journal of the House of Representatives, of the State of Alabama, Session of 1874–5, Held in the City of Montgomery, Commencing November 16, 1874. Montgomery, 1875.

Journal of the House of Representatives, of the State of Alabama, Session of 1876–7, Held in the City of Montgomery, Commencing November 14, 1876. Montgomery, 1877.

Journal of the House of Representatives of the State of Alabama, Session of 1878–9, Held in the City of Montgomery, Commencing November 12th, 1878. Montgomery, 1879.

Journal of Proceedings of the Convention of the State of Alabama, Held in the City of Montgomery on Tuesday September 12, 1865. Montgomery, 1865.

Journal of the Session of 1870–71 of the Senate of Alabama, Held in the City of Montgomery, Commencing on the 21st November, 1870. Montgomery, 1871.

Journal of the Senate of 1872–73 of the State of Alabama, Held in the City of Montgomery, Commencing on the 18th of November, 1872. Montgomery, 1873.

Lewis, David P. "Message of David P. Lewis, Governor of Alabama, to the General Assembly, November 17, 1873," in *Public Documents, 1873.* Montgomery, 1873.

Lindsay, Robert B. "Message of Robert B. Lindsay, Governor of Alabama, to the General Assembly, Nov. 21, 1871," in *Alabama State Documents, 1871.* Montgomery, 1871.

Official Journal of the Constitutional Convention of the State of Alabama, Held in the City of Montgomery, Commencing on Tuesday, November 5th, A.D., 1867. Montgomery, 1868.

"Report of John H. Gindrat, Receiver of the Alabama and Chattanooga Railroad, to the Governor," in *Alabama State Documents, 1871.* Montgomery, 1871.

"Reports of Col. James L. Tait, Receiver of Lands, of the Alabama and Chattanooga R.R. to the Governor," in *Alabama Public Documents, 1873,* no. 16. Montgomery, 1873.

Report of the Joint Committee of the General Assembly of Alabama in Regard to Alleged Election of George E. Spencer as United States Senator, together with Memorial and Evidence. Montgomery, 1875.

Smith, William H. "Message of William H. Smith Governor of Alabama to the General Assembly, November 15, 1869," in *State Documents, 1869–1870.* Montgomery, 1870.

————. *Message of Governor W. H. Smith to the Two Houses of the Alabama Legislature on July 14, 1868.* Montgomery, 1868.

D. NEWSPAPERS

Athens Weekly *Post,* 1867–1869, 1871–1874.

Birmingham *Ledger,* 1917.

Birmingham *News,* 1962.

Camden *Wilcox News and Pacificator,* 1868–1869.

Chicago *Times,* 1880.

Columbiana *Shelby County Guide,* 1868–1870.

Columbiana *Shelby Guide,* 1870–1874.

Demopolis *Southern Republican,* 1869–1871.

Eufaula Daily *Times,* 1872–1873.

Eutaw *Whig and Observer,* 1870, 1872–1877.

Florence *Lauderdale Times,* 1871–1872.

Greensboro *Alabama Beacon,* 1869–1879.

Hayneville *Examiner,* 1870, 1872.

Huntsville *Advocate,* 1865, 1866, 1868–1872.

Huntsville *Independent,* 1868.

Jacksonville *Republican,* 1866–1883.

Linden *Marengo News-Journal,* 1873–1882.

Livingston *Journal,* 1865–1877.

Mobile *Advertiser and Register*, 1865–1868.
Mobile *Herald*, 1871–1872.
Mobile *Nationalist*, 1865–1869.
Mobile Daily *Press*, 1877.
Mobile Daily *Register*, 1868–1880.
Mobile Daily *Tribune*, 1874–1876.
Montgomery *Advance*, 1871–1872.
Montgomery Daily *Advertiser*, 1865–1885.
Montgomery Daily *Alabama State Journal*, 1868–1876.
Montgomery Weekly *Alabama State Journal*, 1869–1872.
Montgomery Daily *Mail*, 1865–1868.
Montgomery *Republican Sentinel*, 1872, 1878.
Montgomery Daily *State Sentinel*, 1867–1868.
Moulton *Advertiser*, 1867, 1868–1874.
New York *Herald*, 1866–1869.
New York *Times*, 1866–1867, 1872–1874.
New York *Tribune*, 1866–1870.
New York *World*, 1867, 1870–1878.
Opelika *East Alabama Monitor*, 1868, 1869.
Opelika Semi-Weekly *Locomotive*, 1869, 1870.
Opelika *Union Republican*, 1869.
Phoenix City *Russell Recorder*, 1873–1874.
Selma *Alabama State Sentinel*, 1860.
Selma *Southern Argus*, 1869–1878.
Selma Daily *Messenger*, 1865–1868.
Selma *Times*, 1870, 1871, 1873.
Selma *Times and Messenger*, 1868–1870.
Talladega *Alabama Reporter*, 1866–1872.
Talladega *Our Mountain Home*, 1872–1878.
Talladega *Sun*, 1869–1871.
Talladega *Watchtower*, 1871–1873.
Tuscaloosa *Blade*, 1872–1875.
Tuscaloosa *Independent Monitor*, 1868–1871.
Tuscaloosa *Reconstructionist*, 1867, 1868.
Tuscumbia *North Alabamian*, 1875–1879.
Tuskegee Weekly *News*, 1873–1882.
Union Springs *Herald and Times*, 1873.
Wetumpka *Elmore Standard*, 1867–1868.

E. CONTEMPORARY SPEECHES, BOOKS, ARTICLES, PAMPHLETS
Dennett, John Richard. *The South As It Is: 1865–1866*. New York, 1965.
Johnston, Joseph F. *Frederick G. Bromberg vs. Jeremiah Haralson, Contest for*

Seat in 44th Congress from First Congressional District of Alabama. n.p., n.d.

King, Edward. *The Great South: A Record of Journeys* . . . Hartford, Connecticut, 1875.

Nordhoff, Charles. *The Cotton States in the Spring and Summer of 1875.* New York, 1876.

Proceedings of the Republican National Conventions, 1868–1880. 1868–1880, microfilm copy at University of Georgia Library, Athens.

Proceedings of the Republican State Convention, Held in Montgomery, Alabama, on the Fourth of July, 1878. Montgomery, 1878.

Reid, Whitelaw. *After the War: A Southern Tour.* New York, 1866.

Saffold, Milton J. *Address to Native White Republicans, October, 1870.* n.p., n.d.

Somers, Robert. *The Southern States Since the War, 1870–71.* University, Alabama, 1965.

Trowbridge, John T. *The South, A Tour of Its Battlefields and Ruined Cities, A Journey Through the Desolated States* . . . Hartford, Connecticut, 1868.

II. SECONDARY SOURCES

A. STATE HISTORIES AND GENERAL WORKS

Brewer, Willis. *Alabama: Her History, Resources, War Record, and Public Men from 1540 to 1872.* Montgomery, 1872.

Garrett, William. *Reminiscences of Public Men in Alabama for Thirty Years.* Atlanta, 1872.

Johnson, Allen, and Malone, Dumas, eds. *Dictionary of American Biography.* 20 vols. New York, 1928–1936.

Moore, A. B. *History of Alabama.* Tuscaloosa, 1951.

Owen, Thomas McAdory. *History of Alabama and Dictionary of Alabama Biography.* 4 vols. Chicago, 1921.

B. MONOGRAPHS, BIOGRAPHIES, AND SPECIAL STUDIES

Alexander, Thomas B. *Political Reconstruction in Tennessee.* Nashville, 1950.

Armes, Ethel. *The Story of Coal and Iron in Alabama.* Birmingham, 1910.

Benedict, Michael L. *A Compromise of Principle: Congressional Republicans and Reconstruction, 1863–1869.* New York, 1974.

Bentley, George R. *A History of the Freedmen's Bureau.* Philadelphia, 1955.

Bond, Horace Mann. *Negro Education in Alabama: A Study in Cotton and Steel.* Washington, D.C., 1939.

Brock, William R. *An American Crisis: Congress and Reconstruction, 1865–1867.* London, 1963.

––––––. *Conflict and Transformation: The United States, 1844–1877.* Middlesex, England, 1973.

Cash, William M. "Alabama Republicans During Reconstruction: Personal Characteristics, Motivations, and Political Activity of Party Activists, 1867–1880," unpublished Ph.D. dissertation. University of Alabama, 1973.

Collier, Earlene W. "Response of Southern Editors and Political Leaders to the National Union Convention Movement of 1866," unpublished master's thesis. University of Alabama, 1963.

Conway, Alan. *The Reconstruction of Georgia*. Minneapolis, 1966.

Cook, Marjorie Howell. "Restoration and Innovation: Alabamians Adjust to Defeat, 1865–1867," unpublished Ph.D. dissertation. University of Alabama, 1968.

Coulter, E. Merton. *William G. Brownlow, Fighting Parson of the Southern Highlands*. Chapel Hill, 1937.

Cox, LaWanda, and Cox, John H. *Politics, Principle, and Prejudice, 1865–1866: Dilemma of Reconstruction America*. New York, 1963.

Degler, Carl N. *The Other South: Southern Dissenters in the Nineteenth Century*. New York, 1974.

Donald, David. *The Politics of Reconstruction 1863–1867*, "Walter Lynwood Fleming Lectures in Southern History." Baton Rouge, 1965.

DuBose, John Witherspoon. *Alabama's Tragic Decade, Ten Years of Alabama 1865–1874*, edited by James K. Greer. Birmingham, 1940.

Fleming, Walter Lynwood. *Civil War and Reconstruction in Alabama*. New York, 1905.

Franklin, John Hope. *Reconstruction: After the Civil War*, Chicago History of American Civilization. Chicago, 1961.

Gilmour, Robert Arthur. "The Other Emancipation: Studies in the Society and Economy of Alabama Whites During Reconstruction," unpublished Ph.D. dissertation. The Johns Hopkins University, 1972.

Going, Allen Johnston. *Bourbon Democracy in Alabama, 1874–1890*. University, Alabama, 1951.

Harris, William C. *Presidential Reconstruction in Mississippi*. Baton Rouge, 1967.

Herbert, Hilary A. *Why the Solid South? Or Reconstruction and Its Results*. Baltimore, 1890.

Hoole, W. S. *Alabama Tories, The First Alabama Cavalry, U.S.A., 1862–1865*. Tuscaloosa, 1960.

Hume, Richard L. "The 'Black and Tan' Conventions of 1867–1869 in Ten Former Confederate States: A Study of Their Membership," unpublished Ph.D. dissertation. University of Washington, 1969.

Kibler, Lillian Adele. *Benjamin F. Perry, South Carolina Unionist*. Durham, 1946.

Klingberg, Frank W. *The Southern Claims Commission*. Berkeley, 1955.

Kolchin, Peter. *First Freedom: The Responses of Alabama's Blacks to Emanci-*

pation and Reconstruction. Westport, Connecticut, 1972.

McFeely, William S. *Yankee Stepfather: General O. O. Howard and the Freed-men.* New Haven, 1968.

McKitrick, Eric. *Andrew Johnson and Reconstruction.* Chicago, 1960.

McMillan, Malcolm C[ook]. *Alabama Confederate Reader.* University, Alabama, 1963.

_____. *Constitutional Development in Alabama, 1798–1901: A Study in Poli-tics, the Negro, and Sectionalism,* "The James Sprunt Studies in History and Political Science," Vol. XXXVII. Chapel Hill, 1955.

Mantell, Martin E. *Johnson, Grant, and the Politics of Reconstruction.* New York, 1973.

Martin, William Elejius. *Internal Improvements in Alabama,* "Johns Hopkins Studies in Historical and Political Science." Baltimore, 1902.

Myers, John B. "Black Human Capital: The Freedmen and the Reconstruction of Labor in Alabama, 1860–1880," unpublished Ph.D. dissertation. Florida State University, 1974.

Nathans, Elizabeth Studley. *Losing the Peace: Georgia Republicans and Recon-struction, 1865–1871.* Baton Rouge, 1968.

Nunn, W. C. *Texas Under the Carpetbaggers.* Austin, 1962.

Patrick, Rembert. *The Reconstruction of the Nation.* New York, 1967.

Pereyra, Lillian A. *James Lusk Alcorn: Persistent Whig.* Baton Rouge, 1966.

Randall, J. G., and Donald, David. *The Civil War and Reconstruction.* 2nd ed. Lexington, Massachusetts, 1969.

Richardson, Joe M. *The Negro in the Reconstruction of Florida, 1865–1877.* Tallahassee, 1965.

Sanger, Donald Bridgman. *James Longstreet: Soldier, Politician, Officeholder, and Writer.* Gloucester, Massachusetts, 1968.

Schweninger, Loren. "James Rapier and Reconstruction," unpublished Ph.D. dissertation. University of Chicago, 1971.

Scott, Sutton S. "Personal Recollections of Thomas Hord Herndon, with Re-marks upon his Life and Character," *Transactions of the Alabama Historical Society, 1904,* Vol. V, reprint 37. Montgomery, 1905.

Scudder, John Ralph, Jr. "The Alabama and Chattanooga Railroad Company, 1868–1871," unpublished master's thesis. University of Alabama, 1951.

Sefton, James E. *The United States Army and Reconstruction, 1865–1877.* Baton Rouge, 1967.

Shadgett, Olive Hall. *The Republican Party in Georgia From Reconstruction through 1900.* Athens, 1964.

Shofner, Jerrell H. *Nor Is It Over Yet: Florida in the Era of Reconstruction.* Gainesville, Florida, 1974.

Simkins, Francis Butler, and Woody, Robert H. *South Carolina During Recon-struction.* Chapel Hill, 1932.

Singletary, Otis A. *Negro Militia and Reconstruction*. Austin, 1957.

Stampp, Kenneth M. *The Era of Reconstruction, 1865–1877*. New York, 1965.

Stover, John F. *The Railroads of the South, 1865–1900, A Study in Finance and Control*. Chapel Hill, 1955.

Taylor, Joe Gray. *Louisiana Reconstructed, 1863–1877*. Baton Rouge, 1974.

Thomas, James D. "Alabama Constitutional Convention of 1867," unpublished master's thesis. Alabama Polytechnic Institute, 1947.

Thornton, Jonathan Mills, III. "Politics and Power in a Slave Society: Alabama, 1806–1860," unpublished Ph.D. dissertation. Yale University, 1974.

Trelease, Allen W. *Reconstruction: The Great Experiment*. New York, 1971.

————. *White Terror: The Ku Klux Conspiracy and Southern Reconstruction*. New York, 1971.

Wilson, Theodore B. *The Black Codes of the South*. University, Alabama, 1965.

C. PERIODICALS

Alexander, Thomas B. "Persistent Whiggery in Alabama and the Lower South, 1860–1867," *Alabama Review*, XII (January, 1959), 35–52.

————. "Persistent Whiggery in the Confederate South, 1860–1877," *Journal of Southern History*, XXVII (August, 1961), 305–29.

Bethel, Elizabeth. "The Freedmen's Bureau in Alabama," *Journal of Southern History*, XIV (February, 1948), 49–92.

Bond, Horace Mann. "Social and Economic Forces in Alabama Reconstruction," *Journal of Negro History*, XXIII (July, 1938), 290–348.

Curry, Richard O. "The Civil War and Reconstruction, 1861–1877: A Critical Overview of Recent Trends and Interpretations," *Civil War History*, XX (September, 1974), 215–38.

DeSantis, Vincent P. "President Hayes's Southern Policy," *Journal of Southern History*, XXI (November, 1955), 476–94.

————. "Republican Efforts to 'Crack' the Solid South," *Review of Politics*, XIV (April, 1952), 244–64.

Donald, David. "The Scalawag in Mississippi Reconstruction," *Journal of Southern History*, X (November, 1944), 447–60.

Ellem, Warren A. "Who Were the Mississippi Scalawags?" *Journal of Southern History*, XXXVIII (May, 1972), 217–40.

Fleming, Walter L. "The Formation of the Union League in Alabama," *Gulf States Historical Magazine*, II (September, 1903), 73–89.

Going, Allen J. "A Shooting Affray in Knoxville with Interstate Repercussions: The Killing of James Holt Clanton by David M. Nelson, 1871," *The East Tennessee Historical Society Publications*, No. 27 (1955), 39–48.

Granade, Ray. "Violence: An Instrument of Policy in Reconstruction Alabama," *Alabama Historical Quarterly*, XXX (Fall and Winter, 1968), 181–202.

Harris, William C. "A Reconsideration of the Mississippi Scalawag," *Journal of Mississippi History,* XXXII (February, 1970), 3–42.

Kincaid, Larry. "Victims of Circumstance: An Interpretation of Changing Attitudes Toward Republican Policy Makers and Reconstruction," *Journal of American History,* LVII (June, 1970), 48–66.

Krebs, Sylvia H. "Will the Freedmen Work: White Alabamians Adjust to Free Black Labor," *Alabama Historical Quarterly,* XXXVI (Summer, 1974), 151–63.

Moore, A. B. "Railroad Building in Alabama During the Reconstruction Period," *Journal of Southern History,* I (November, 1935), 421–41.

Myers, John B. "The Freedman and the Law in Post-Bellum Alabama, 1865–1867," *Alabama Review,* XXIII (January, 1970), 56–69.

_____. "The Freedmen and the Labor Supply: The Economic Adjustment in Post-Bellum Alabama, 1865–1867," *Alabama Historical Quarterly,* XXXII (Fall and Winter, 1970), 157–66.

_____. "Reaction and Adjustment: The Struggle of Alabama Freedmen in Post-Bellum Alabama, 1865–1867," *Alabama Historical Quarterly,* XXXII (Spring and Summer, 1970), 5–22.

Olsen, Otto H. "Reconsidering the Scalawags," *Civil War History,* XII (December, 1966), 304–20.

Reid, Robert. "Changing Interpretations of the Reconstruction Period in Alabama," *Alabama Review,* XXVII (October, 1974), 263–81.

Schweninger, Loren. "The American Missionary Association and Northern Philanthropy in Reconstruction Alabama," *Alabama Historical Quarterly,* XXXII (Fall and Winter, 1970), 129–56.

_____. "Black Citizenship and the Republican Party in Alabama," *Alabama Review,* XXIX (April, 1976), 83–103.

_____. "James Rapier and the Negro Labor Movement, 1869–1872," *Alabama Review,* XXVIII (July, 1975), 185–201.

_____. "John H. Rapier, Sr.: A Slave and Freedman in the Antebellum South," *Civil War History,* XX (March, 1974), 23–34.

Scroggs, Jack B. "Carpetbagger Constitutional Reform in the South Atlantic States, 1867–1868," *Journal of Southern History,* XXVII (November, 1961), 475–93.

_____. "Southern Reconstruction: A Radical View," *Journal of Southern History,* XXIV (November, 1958), 407–29.

Sizemore, Margaret Davidson. "Frederick G. Bromberg of Mobile: An Illustrious Character, 1837–1928," *Alabama Review,* XXIX (April, 1976), 104–12.

Sloan, John Z. "The Ku Klux Klan and the Alabama Election of 1872," *Alabama Review,* XVIII (April, 1965), 113–23.

Trelease, Allen W. "Who Were the Scalawags?" *Journal of Southern History,* XXIX (November, 1963), 445–68.

Weisberger, Bernard A. "The Dark and Bloody Ground of Reconstruction Historiography," *Journal of Southern History,* XXV (November, 1959), 427–47.

Wiggins, Sarah Woolfolk. "Ostracism of White Republicans in Alabama During Reconstruction," *Alabama Review,* XXVII (January, 1974), 52–65.

———— . "What Is A *Scalawag?" Alabama Review,* XXV (January, 1972), 56–61.

Williamson, Edward C. "The Alabama Election of 1874," *Alabama Review,* XVII (July, 1964), 210–18.

Woolfolk, Sarah Van V. "Carpetbaggers in Alabama: Tradition Versus Truth," *Alabama Review,* XV (April, 1962), 133–44.

———— . "Five Men Called Scalawags," *Alabama Review,* XVII (January, 1964), 45–55.

———— . "George E. Spencer: A Carpetbagger in Alabama," *Alabama Review,* XIX (January, 1966), 41–52.

———— . "The Political Cartoons of the Tuskaloosa *Independent Monitor* and Tuskaloosa *Blade,* 1867–1873," *Alabama Historical* Quarterly, XXVII (Fall and Winter, 1965), 140–65.

INDEX

Page numbers 136–153 refer to listing in the Appendix, "Republican Nominations and Appointments, Alabama 1868–1881."